HISTORICAL DICTIONARIES OF RELIGIONS, PHILOSOPHIES, AND MOVEMENTS
Edited by Jon Woronoff

1. *Buddhism,* by Charles S. Prebish, 1993
2. *Mormonism,* by Davis Bitton, 1994
3. *Ecumenical Christianity,* by Ans Joachim van der Bent, 1994
4. *Terrorism,* by Sean Anderson and Stephen Sloan, 1995
5. *Sikhism,* by W. H. McLeod, 1995
6. *Feminism,* by Janet K. Boles and Diane Long Hoeveler, 1995
7. *Olympic Movement,* by Ian Buchanan and Bill Mallon, 1995
8. *Methodism,* by Charles Yrigoyen Jr. and Susan E. Warrick, 1996
9. *Orthodox Church,* by Michael Prokurat, Alexander Golitzin, and Michael D. Peterson, 1996
10. *Organized Labor,* by James C. Docherty, 1996
11. *Civil Rights Movement,* by Ralph E. Luker, 1997
12. *Catholicism,* by William J. Collinge, 1997
13. *Hinduism,* by Bruce M. Sullivan, 1997
14. *North American Environmentalism,* by Edward R. Wells and Alan M. Schwartz, 1997
15. *Welfare State,* by Bent Greve, 1998
16. *Socialism,* by James C. Docherty, 1997
17. *Bahá'í Faith,* by Hugh C. Adamson and Philip Hainsworth, 1998
18. *Taoism,* by Julian F. Pas in cooperation with Man Kam Leung, 1998
19. *Judaism,* by Norman Solomon, 1998
20. *Green Movement,* by Elim Papadakis, 1998
21. *Nietzscheanism,* by Carol Diethe, 1999
22. *Gay Liberation Movement,* by Ronald J. Hunt, 1999

Historical Dictionary of the Green Movement

Elim Papadakis

*Historical Dictionaries of Religions,
Philosophies, and Movements, No. 20*

The Scarecrow Press, Inc.
Lanham, Maryland, & London
1998

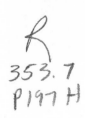

353.7
P197 H

SCARECROW PRESS, INC.

Published in the United States of America
by Scarecrow Press, Inc.
4720 Boston Way
Lanham, Maryland 20706

4 Pleydell Gardens, Folkestone
Kent CT20 2DN, England

British Library Cataloguing in Publication Information Available

Library of Congress Cataloging-in-Publication Data

Papadakis, Elim.
    Historical dictionary of the green movement / Elim Papadakis.
      p. cm. — (Historical dictionaries of religions,
  philosophies, and movements ; no. 20)
    Includes bibliographical references (p.   ) and index.
    ISBN 0-8108-3502-9 (alk. paper)
    1. Green movement—Dictionaries. 2. Green movement—History—
  Dictionaries. I. Title. II. Series.
  GE195.P36   1998
  353.7'052—dc21   98-7912
                                                    CIP

Contents

Editor's Foreword

Many movements have come and gone without leaving an enduring mark on the political landscape. One significant exception, probably the most important in recent decades, has been the environmental movement that has generated numerous political parties. Collectively known as the greens, these parties often differ notably from one another while retaining certain common features. Also, while sometimes regarded as one-issue parties, they have actually absorbed a large number of issues and are joining with, and sometimes even edging out, more conventional parties. Although green parties are not yet present in all countries, their numbers are growing; they are a strong presence in most advanced and many developing nations.

This *Historical Dictionary of the Green Movement* deals with these parties as well as their predecessors, whether part of the environmental movement or related to the antinuclear, feminist, or broader economic and social movements. In addition to considering them in their own right, it shows how they fit into the broader political scene of many countries. Entries also present early thinkers and pioneers and current advocates and leaders. Those on key concepts and issues are particularly useful. A chronology traces the green movement's evolution, while the introduction sums up its progress thus far. Those wishing to know more should consult the extensive bibliography.

This book has grown out of many earlier contributions on the subject. Along with numerous articles, Elim Papadakis is the author of a broad study of the field (*Environmental Politics and Institutional Change*) and two country studies (*The Green Movement in West Germany* and *Politics and the Environment: The Australian Experience*). Dr. Papadakis was previously professor of sociology and head of department at the University of New England in Armidale, New South Wales, Australia. He is presently professor of European studies at the Australian National University. The result of this experience is a broad study of a crucial twentieth-century political movement.

Jon Woronoff
Series Editor

vii

Abbreviations

ALÖ	Alternative Liste Österreichs
ALP	Australian Labor Party
CFCs	Chlorofluorocarbons
CND	Campaign for Nuclear Disarmament
DDT	Dichlorodiphenyltrichloroethane
GNP	Gross National Product
GPS	Grüne Partei der Schweiz
INFOTERRA	International Referral System
IUCN	International Union for the Conservation of Nature and Natural Resources
MPE	Mouvement populaire pour l'environnement
NATO	North Atlantic Treaty Organization
NDP	Nuclear Disarmament Party
OPEC	Organization of Petroleum Exporting Countries
RAC	Resource Assessment Commission
SAM	Sahabat Alam Malaysia
UNCED	United Nations Conference on the Environment and Development
UNCHE	United Nations Conference on the Human Environment
UNCLOS	United Nations Conference on the Law of the Sea
UNEP	United Nations Environment Programme
UNESCO	United Nations Educational, Scientific, and Cultural Organization
UTG	United Tasmania Group
VGÖ	Vereinte Grüne Österreichs
WWF	World Wide Fund for Nature (World Wildlife Fund)

Chronology

1908   Conference of Governors on Conservation held at the White House, Washington, D.C.
1909   Foundation of the Wildlife Preservation Society in Australia; creation of the Swiss League for the Protection of Nature; formation of the Swedish Society for the Protection of Nature; North American Conservation Congress held in Washington, D.C.; International Congress for the Protection of Nature convened in Paris
1913   Formation of the Consultative Committee for the International Protection of Nature in Switzerland; foundation of the British Ecological Society
1914   Establishment of the Swiss National Park; formation of the Mountain Trails Club in Australia
1919   Foundation of the National Parks and Conservation Association in the United States
1922   Foundation of the International Committee for Bird Protection (later named International Council for Bird Preservation)
1926   Foundation of the Council for the Protection of Rural England
1930   Creation of the U.S. Food and Drug Administration
1933   International Conference for the Protection of Fauna and Flora held in London
1934   Creation of the International Office for the Protection of Nature
1936   Foundation of the National Wildlife Federation in the United States
1942   Completion of the first atomic reactor at the University of Chicago
1945   The United States drops atomic bombs on Hiroshima and Nagasaki in Japan
1946   Formation of the International Whaling Commission
1948   Formation of the International Union for the Conservation of Nature and Natural Resources (now known as The World Conservation Union)
1949   Publication of *A Sand County Almanac*, by Aldo Leopold; UN Scientific Conference on the Conservation and Utilization of Resources, Lake Success, New York
1951   The United States begins testing nuclear weapons
1952   Britain begins testing nuclear weapons
1953   The Soviet Union begins testing nuclear weapons
1954   The United States conducts a hydrogen bomb test on Bikini Atoll and radioactive dust falls on the population of the Marshall Islands
1956   Enactment of the Clean Air Act in Britain
1957   Creation of the National Council for the Abolition of Nuclear Weapons Tests and of the Emergency Committee for Direct Ac-

tion Against Nuclear War in Britain in response to the conduct of nuclear tests on Christmas Island; publication of an article by J. B. Priestley entitled "Britain and the Nuclear Bombs" in the *New Statesman*; foundation of the International Atomic Energy Agency

1958   Formation of a committee to launch the Campaign for Nuclear Disarmament (CND); the first of a series of marches organized by the CND between Aldermaston and London

1959   Signing of the Antarctic Treaty with a view to using the territory for peaceful purposes only

1960   Formation of the Organization of Petroleum Exporting Countries (OPEC)

1961   Around 150,000 people assemble in Trafalgar Square at the end of a CND march from Aldermaston to London; foundation of the World Wildlife Fund; Arusha Conference on Nature Conservation in Africa; first compensation payments to victims of mercury poisoning at Minamata, Japan

1962   Publication of *Silent Spring* by Rachel Carson; first World Conference on National Parks held in Seattle, Washington

1963   Signing of the Partial Nuclear Test Ban Treaty

1967   Collision of the oil tanker *Torrey Canyon* with rocks off the southwestern coast of England leads to oil pollution on the shores of Cornwall and of Brittany; foundation of the Environmental Defense Fund in the United States

1968   African Convention on the Conservation of Nature and Natural Resources signed by 33 African states that were members of the Organization of African Unity; convention of the Biosphere Conference in Paris to discuss the impact of human beings on the environment; creation of the Club of Rome to examine the interrelationships between factors like economic growth, the environment, population, resources, and industrialization; publication of *The Population Bomb* by Paul Ehrlich and of the *Tragedy of the Commons* by Garrett Hardin

1969   David Brower leaves the Sierra Club to form Friends of the Earth; formation of the Don't Make a Wave Committee in Vancouver, Canada, as a precursor to the foundation of Greenpeace; foundation of the Union of Concerned Scientists

1970   Establishment of Friends of the Earth in London and Paris; first Earth Day attracts around 20 million people to protests held around the United States; creation of the Environmental Protection Agency in the United States

1971   Creation of Save the Whales; founding of the Gaucha Association for the Protection of the Natural Environment and the emergence of a green social movement in Brazil; publication of *The*

Closing Circle: Nature, Man and Technology by Barry Commoner; creation of the Greenpeace Foundation following protests against nuclear tests off the coast of Alaska by the U.S. government; establishment of the Department of the Environment, Canada

1972   Publication by *The Ecologist* magazine of *A Blueprint for Survival* by Edward Goldsmith and his collaborators and of *The Limits to Growth* by Donella H. Meadows, Dennis L. Meadows, Jorgen Randers, and William W. Behrens III; protests by Greenpeace against nuclear weapons tests by the French government in the Mururoa Atoll; UN Conference on the Human Environment, convened in Stockholm; formation of the UN Environment Programme, the first UN agency with headquarters located in a developing country; signing in Paris of the Convention concerning the Protection of the World Cultural and Natural Heritage; ratification in London of the Convention on the Prevention of Marine Pollution by Dumping of Waste and Other Matter (London Dumping Convention); foundation of Negative Population Growth; ban on DDT in the United States; citizens of Neuchâtel in Switzerland oppose the building of a new highway, contest the communal elections, and win eight of the 41 seats in the local parliament; formation of the United Tasmania Group in response to the destruction of Lake Pedder in Tasmania in order to promote a hydroelectric system; foundation of a Citizens' Initiative umbrella organization, Bundesverband Bürgerinitiativen Umweltschutz, in the Federal Republic of Germany; formation of the Values Party in Wellington, New Zealand, the first party to be established at the national level that champions both environmental protection and participatory democracy

1973   The Organization of Petroleum Exporting Countries (OPEC) initiates a steep increase in the price of oil, which leads Western countries to consider rapid expansion in the construction of nuclear power plants; the declaration by the electricity industry that it would build a nuclear power station near the village of Brokdorf in Schleswig-Holstein, Federal Republic of Germany, signals the beginning of a dispute that was crucial in the development of Antinuclear Protests in Europe; the emergence of the Chipko Andalan protest movement involving mainly women in Indian villages; Convention on International Trade in Endangered Species of Wild Flora and Fauna; formation of Écologie et Survie, which went on to contest elections to the National Assembly in Alsace, France; foundation of the party called People in Britain, which later became the Green Party; publication of *Small Is Beautiful: Economics as If People Mattered* by E. F. Schu-

macher; enactment of Endangered Species Act in the United
States; foundation of The Cousteau Society

1974   René Dumont, as the representative of environmental groups,
contests the French presidential elections on an environmental
platform; death of Karen Silkwood, a worker at the Kerr-McGee
plutonium plant, Oklahoma, in mysterious circumstances; foundation of the Environmental Policy Institute in the United States;
F. Sherwood Rowland and Mario Molina present the argument
that the release of CFCs into the atmosphere destroys the ozone
layer

1975   Mass protests against the proposal to construct a nuclear power
station at Kaiseraugst, Switzerland; publication of the *Monkey
Wrench Gang* by Edward Abbey; foundation of the Worldwatch
Institute

1976   Mass protests against the proposals to construct nuclear power
stations at Brokdorf and at Wyhl, Federal Republic of Germany;
formation of the Swedish Miljöverbund

1977   Mass protests against proposals to develop nuclear power installations at Grohnde, Kalkar, and Brokdorf in the Federal Republic
of Germany and at Creys-Malville in France; publication of *Soft
Energy Paths: Towards a Durable Peace* by Amory Lovins; formation of the Groupement pour la Protection de l'Environnement in Switzerland; foundation of Sea Shepherd Conservation
Society; emergence of the Green Belt Movement in Kenya; discovery of contamination by chemicals of Love Canal in Niagara
Falls, New York; *Amoco Cadiz* oil spill off the French coast

1978   U.S. ban on the use of CFCs in nearly all aerosols; formation of
the Grüne Partei Zürich in Switzerland; mass protests against
the nuclear power reprocessing plant at Gorleben, Federal Republic of Germany; foundation of Sahabat Alam Malaysia
(Friends of the Earth in Malaysia)

1979   In protests against government policies on nuclear energy
around 100,000 people assemble in Hanover and around 150,000
in Bonn, Federal Republic of Germany, and discussions are held
in Offenbach over the possibility of establishing a new political
organization; in Switzerland, election of the first green parliamentarian to a national legislature; a green list (political party)
in Bremen is successful in gaining the first seats ever won by a
green party in a state parliament in Germany; green parties or
lists participate in the first elections to the European Parliament;
accident at the Three Mile Island nuclear power plant in Harrisburg, Pennsylvania; Convention on Long Range Transboundary
Air Pollution is signed by 33 countries including Britain, Germany, and the United States; in Luxembourg green groups form

an umbrella organization, the Alternative Leescht: Wiert Ich, to compete at elections; formation of the Citizens' Committee in the United States; around 75,000 people gather in Washington, D.C., to take part in a demonstration against nuclear power; publication of *Gaia: A New Look at Life on Earth* by James Lovelock; beginning of the campaign against the construction of the Franklin Dam in Tasmania; signing in Bonn of the Convention of the Conservation of Migratory Species of Wild Animals

1980   Formation of Die Grünen in the Federal Republic of Germany, of Ecolo in Belgium, and of the Citizens Party in the United States; around 80,000 people participate in an Antinuclear Protest rally at Trafalgar Square in London; Canada and the United States sign a Memorandum of Intent Concerning Transboundary Air Pollution; publication of the *Global 2000 Report* to the president by the U.S. Council on Environmental Quality; publication and widespread dissemination of the World Conservation Strategy: Living Resource for Sustainable Development; creation of the Earth First! radical environmental group in the United States

1981   Brice Lalonde contests the French presidential elections on a green platform; formation of the Swedish Green Party, Miljöpartiet de Gröna, and of the Ecology Party of Ireland

1982   In Belgium Agalev detaches itself from Anders gaan leven and formally becomes a political party; formation of the Vereinte Grüne Österreichs in Austria; signing of the UN Convention of the Law of the Sea

1983   Die Grünen in Germany gains 28 seats in the federal parliament; formation of Dei Greng Alternativ in Luxembourg, De Grønne in Denmark, Comhaontas Glas in Ireland, and De Groenen in the Netherlands; formation, following a resolution by the UN General Assembly, of the World Commission on Environment and Development

1984   Inaugural meeting of the World Commission on Environment and Development; accidental release of poison gas from the Union Carbide pesticide plant in Bhopal, India; congress of European green parties at Liège in Belgium advocates a "Europe of the regions"; founding of Les Verts in France; green parties acquire 12 seats in the European Parliament and call themselves the Green-Alternative European Link; publication of *Fighting for Hope* by Petra Kelly and of *Seeing Green: The Politics of Ecology Explained* by Jonathan Porritt; formation of the Thirty Percent Club to tackle long-range transboundary air pollution; formation of Committees of Correspondence in the United States

1985   Scientists at the Villach Conference draw attention to the in-
        crease in the average temperature across the world over the past
        century (the greenhouse effect); endorsement of the Convention
        on the Protection of the Ozone Layer in Vienna; release of pesti-
        cides into the Rhine River following a fire in a Basel chemical
        storage facility destroys living things on a vast scale; death of a
        member of Greenpeace following the bombing by the French
        intelligence service of the *Rainbow Warrior* while it was moored
        at Auckland harbor in New Zealand; Die Grünen becomes mem-
        ber of a coalition government with the Social Democratic Party
        in Hesse between 1985 and 1987; Rudolf Bahro quits Die Grü-
        nen over the issue of animal rights; the British Ecology Party
        becomes the Green Party

1986   A federation of green groups form a national Swiss Green Party
        (Grüne Partei der Schweiz), and in Italy green groups form a
        Federation of Green Lists, Federazione delle Liste Verdi; explo-
        sion at the Chernobyl nuclear power plant near Kiev in the So-
        viet Union

1987   Die Grünen gains 42 seats in elections to the federal parliament;
        in elections to the national parliament green groups in Italy re-
        ceive around one million votes (2.5 percent) and gain 13 seats in
        the lower house and two in the Senate; Agalev gains 7.3 percent
        of the vote and six seats in the lower house in Flanders; signing
        of the Montreal Protocol on Substances that Deplete the Ozone
        Layer; publication of *Our Common Future* by the World Com-
        mission on Environment and Development

1988   Miljöpartiet de Gröna becomes the first new party in 70 years to
        gain representation in the Swedish parliament; Antoine Waechter
        contests the French presidential elections on behalf of environ-
        mental groups; several candidates of the Green Party in Brazil
        gain seats in municipal elections in large cities; formation by
        intellectuals, scientists, and artists of the Ruse Committee in
        Bulgaria; scientists and policymakers at the Toronto Conference
        call for a 20 percent reduction in carbon dioxide emissions by
        the year 2000; murder of the Brazilian environmental activist
        Chico Mendes

1989   Award to the victims of Bhopal of $470 million in compensation;
        formation of Brontosaurus in Czechoslovakia and later, of a
        Green Party; *Exxon Valdez* oil tanker runs aground in Prince
        William Sound, Alaska; green independent candidates gain 17
        percent of the vote in Tasmania, gain 5 out of 36 seats in the
        state parliament and form an accord with a government led by
        the Australian Labor Party; green parties achieve their best-ever
        results in elections to the European Parliament, gaining 32 seats;

dissolution of the Green-Alternative European Link and formation of the Green Group in the European Parliament; the Green Association is formed in Finland, though this subsequently divided into two separate strands, Vihreat (the Greens) and Vihreä Liitoo (the Green Association); formation of the Independent Union Ekoglasnost in Bulgaria; formation of the Ecologists-Alternatives Party and of the Federation of Ecological Organizations in Greece; publication of *Blueprint for a Green Economy* by David Pearce and his collaborators; ban on ivory trade by the Convention on International Trade in Endangered Species of Wild Fauna and Flora

1990 Die Grünen fails to gain seats in the federal parliament, though a new group from East Germany, Bündnis 90, does gain eight seats; formation of Groen Links (Green Left) in the Netherlands and of the Green Party in Prague, Czechoslovakia; formation of Génération Écologie under the leadership of Brice Lalonde as a competing party to Les Verts in France; signatories to the Montreal Protocol meet in London (London Conference of the Parties to the Montreal Protocol), and 80 countries now agree to phasing out, by the year 2000, of CFCs and other chemicals that contribute to the depletion of the ozone layer

1991 Die Grünen becomes member of a coalition government with the Social Democratic Party (as senior partner) in Hesse; green groups in Italy win 16 seats in the lower house and four in the Senate; formation of the Green Party USA; signing of an Environmental Protocol to the Antarctic Treaty (the Madrid Protocol) by 39 nations agreeing to a moratorium on mining in Antarctica; severe pollution of the Gulf region in the wake of the Gulf War due largely to oil well fires and oil spillage

1992 UN Conference on Environment and Development (the Earth Summit) held in Rio de Janeiro leads to signing of the Framework Convention on Climate Change by 153 nations and by the European Union; most nations attending the conference also support the Convention on Biological Diversity, the Declaration on Environment and Development, and the enactment of Forest Principles; formation of the UN Commission on Sustainable Development; signing of the Basel Convention by 20 countries in order to prevent the illegal dumping or transportation of waste; 93 nations that signed the 1987 Montreal Protocol on Substances that Deplete the Ozone Layer agree to meet their targets by 1996 rather than 2000, the date set in the original agreement; Petra Kelly and Gerd Bastian are found dead in their home

1993 European Federation of Green Parties agrees on a set of guiding principles at a conference held in Masala, Finland; the Green Party in the United Kingdom fields 566 candidates in local elections, who gain, on average, 5.7 percent of the vote; membership of the Sierra Club numbers over 550,000; signing of the North American Agreement on Environmental Cooperation; signing of an agreement to safeguard the Black Sea by six European nations; World Bank permits public inspection of any authorizations linked to environmental assessment of intended projects

1994   Die Grünen, in coalition with Bündnis 90, gains 7.3 percent of the vote and 49 seats in the federal parliament and displaces the Liberal Free Democrats as the third largest party; in elections to the European Parliament the number of seats won by green parties drops to 22; Die Grüne Alternative in Austria secures 7 percent of the vote in national elections and 13 seats; Miljöpartiet obtains 5 percent of the vote and 18 seats in the Swedish Parliament; green candidates poll over a million votes in local elections in the United States; the Constitution of the Federal Republic of Germany is amended to include a specific commitment to environmental protection; UN Conference on Population and Development held in Cairo, Egypt; declaration by the International Whaling Commission of Antarctica as a permanent sanctuary for whales

1995   In Sweden Miljöpartiet de Gröna gains four seats in elections to the European Parliament; Vihreä Liitoo secures 6.5 percent of the vote and nine seats in the Finnish parliament; Agalev secures 4.4 percent of the vote in national elections; Die Grüne Alternative obtains 4.8 percent of the vote in Austrian national elections and 6.8 percent in elections to the European Parliament; Die Grünen becomes member of coalition governments with the Social Democratic Party in Hesse and in North Rhine Westphalia; first Conference of the Parties to the Framework Convention on Climate Change held in Berlin, Federal Republic of Germany; membership of the World Wildlife Fund numbers well over five million; plan by the World Bank and international conservation groups to protect marine biological diversity in 155 Marine Protection Areas; ratification by over 100 countries of a UN Global Fishing Pact to curb the decrease in fish reserves

1996   Formation of the Australian Greens and election of Bob Brown to the Senate in federal elections; green independent candidates gain 11 percent of the vote and four seats in Tasmania; Vihreä Liitoo attracts 7.6 percent of the vote and gains a seat in the European Parliament; first presidential convention of the U.S. Green Party; second Conference of the Parties to the Framework Convention on Climate Change held in Geneva

1997   Les Verts in France gains seven seats in elections to the National

Assembly; membership of the European Federation of Green Parties consists of 28 political organizations from 24 countries, and seven other political associations comprise a group of applicants to join the federation; UN Convention on Climate Change held in Kyoto sets new targets for greenhouse emissions

Introduction

Human beings have been concerned about nature and their place in it for millennia. The endurance of ancient societies has been based partly on their success in living in alignment with nature. Although the relationship between aboriginal inhabitants of different regions and the natural environment has sometimes erroneously been portrayed as entirely harmonious, this romantic view is not without foundation. For instance, in Australia there was a vast difference between Aboriginals and Europeans in the nineteenth century in terms of their impact on the environment and of the technologies they used to exploit it. This has led some political activists to argue that Aboriginals waged "the longest and most successful conservation campaign" in history because they chose "to become part of the environment" rather than to destroy it in the name of progress (Burnam Burnam 1987).

While recognizing the distinctive approach by aboriginal communities in shaping their relationship to the environment, contemporary approaches to understanding how people construct their activities can be understood in a different way. If by a campaign we mean an organized attempt to change attitudes, values, and perceptions in order to challenge particular policies, then the notion may be less applicable to the actions by aboriginal communities than to the contemporary green movement. At any rate, the primary focus in the present context is on the emergence of campaigns and movements in both the nineteenth century (in the wake of the so-called great transformation that involved political upheavals as well as the rapid development of industrial capitalism and a free market economy) and the twentieth century (particularly the period since World War II that has seen both the further expansion of Western democratic free market economies and the questioning of some of the assumptions that underpin them). For current purposes the term green movement refers to organized attempts by modern associations to change attitudes, values, and perceptions about the relationship between human beings and nature. Although disquiet about the consequences of human action on the natural environment can be traced back to the ancient Greeks and Romans (McCormick 1995, xi), the emergence of interest groups, political parties, and mass social movements focusing primarily on environmental issues is a fairly recent phenomenon.

1

The origins of the green movement can be traced back to the nineteenth century. Yet it is most common to refer to events over the past few decades when considering the rise of this movement. For instance, there are close connections between the New Left of the 1960s (the student movements, the anti-Vietnam War protests, and civil rights movements) and new social movements concerned about environmental degradation and the development of nuclear energy. There is also some overlap between contemporary struggles and post-1960s women's movements. Many participants in the radical movements of the 1960s became involved in environmentalist groups in the 1970s. There has likewise been a degree of thematic continuity. One example is the connection between recent protests for peace and campaigns in the 1950s against nuclear weapons. Some questions, like the preoccupation with individual self-fulfillment and self-expression by many participants in the student protests of the 1960s, have developed into broader concerns like those of the women's movement—civil rights, equality of opportunity, and access to power.

These developments can be used to support one line of argument; namely, the green movement only emerged after World War II following the new prominence accorded to social movements in Western democracies. As a consequence of this argument proponents of environmentalism in contemporary society have often ignored the efforts of previous generations to address similar problems through organized campaigns. It is therefore helpful to place the green movement in the broader context of the emergence, in the nineteenth century, of campaigns to protect and preserve nature. There are, for instance, some remarkable historical continuities in organized campaigns for environmental protection. Among the most prominent groups concerned about environmental protection were the Commons, Open Spaces, and Footpaths Preservation Society founded in 1865 in Britain and the Sierra Club established in 1892 in the United States of America. These groups achieved notable successes, especially in influencing legislation for environmental protection, including the dedication of major national parks.

One of the major differences between the period since World War II and earlier experiences is the level of public support for environmental protection. It is only since World War II that action to protect the environment has been sustained by the readiness of significant sections of the population to take political action. This has entailed support for citizens' initiatives, regional, national, and international social movements, new political organizations, and the traditional political parties. The latter have, in recent years, been willing to assume a large portion of the agenda first promoted by the green movement. The eagerness of traditional political organizations to adopt many of the policies of the green movement is matched by a broadening of the social bases of support for environmental protection. Over the past three decades support for the green movement has been notable among certain social groups, including the young, the relatively affluent, and the well educated. Lately, however, public opinion has become much more aligned to some of the aims of green political organizations, and the social bases of the green movement have increasingly come to reflect those of the broader community.

In referring to the green movement there is an implicit assumption of similarities not only in the social bases for support of certain forms of political action and political agenda, but of equivalence in sources of inspiration for such action and of similar preoccupations. While this can be shown to be the case, it is also important to point out that there is great diversity in approaches to addressing environmental problems and in how people perceive the relationship between human beings and nature.

There is a further issue. The agenda of green political groups and organizations includes much that is not specifically green, even though these preoccupations or values can be accommodated by what Goodin (1992) refers to as a green theory or philosophy of value. Among these values are the focus on postmaterialism (*see* Inglehart 1990), the notion of nature as irreplaceable, the ideas of sustainability and sustainable development, the long-term consequences of our current actions, and the connection between environmental protection and ideas of the emancipation of oppressed groups (for instance, minorities, the poor, and women). Goodin describes these values as corollaries to a green theory of value. More problematic, in his view, is the association between various personal lifestyles, especially those that focus on a holistic approach (be it to medicine, diet, or religion), and the green agenda for changes in policies. At any rate, the following account will be framed by three sets of considerations: the philosophies underpinning the diversity of values that influence the actions of participants in the green movement; the political organizations, including social movements, political parties, and interest groups that attempt to articulate the concerns of the green movement; and the issues raised by the green movement.

Conceptual Bases for the Green Movement

Commitment to environmentalism manifests itself with different levels of intensity and in a variety of ways. Persons who are regarded as being radical or fundamentalist in their outlook may espouse a nonanthropocentric philosophy. In other words, they may take the viewpoint that nonhuman forms of life are valuable irrespective of their importance to human beings. They may also engage in militant opposition to established political institutions. This is not necessarily the norm. Many members and supporters of green political associations may prefer to work through traditional channels of the political system (like major political parties and interest groups), even though they share certain broad objectives (like the preservation of the environment) with the radical activists.

Influential Writers

One way of accounting for or understanding the ways of thinking that predominate in the green movement is to consider the views of influential writers. The success of social movements has always depended on the capacity of intellectuals, scientists, and writers to develop new concepts that might change perceptions and then influence behavior. Among the most dramatic and successful efforts to bring about a transformation of that kind was the publication in 1962 of *Silent Spring* by Rachel Carson. This work became a source of inspiration to millions of people. The term "silent spring" was used to characterize the devastating consequences of the continued use of chemical insecticides and pesticides like DDT on wildlife and its habitat. The book provoked strong opposition from the chemical industry, which tried unsuccessfully to have it banned. The extraordinary popularity of the work contributed to the establishment by President Kennedy of a special panel of the Science Advisory Committee, which supported the arguments presented by Carson about the hazards of pesticides.

Another highly influential treatise was, a decade later, *A Blueprint for Survival*, published by the editorial board of *The Ecologist* magazine. Like *The Limits to Growth*, published by the Club of Rome in the same year, *A Blueprint for Survival* advocated radical changes. Whereas *The Limits to Growth* urged governments to initiate drastic policies to reduce industrial and agricultural investment, reduce the birthrate, and transfer wealth from more developed to less developed countries, *A Blueprint for Survival* focused on radical changes in lifestyles in order to ensure the perpetuation of the planet. In particular, it advocated the formation of decentralized social structures as a way to ensure greater participation in decision making and encourage innovation. Anticipating the aims of the green political movements over the coming decade, the book argued for small, self-regulating communities in which people might achieve more fulfilling personal relationships. Like the authors of *The Limits to Growth* they advocated greater controls on population growth. An important distinction between the two books was the focus in *The Limits to Growth* on the role of elites in bringing about change and on scientific models for understanding the problems arising from economic growth, industrialization, and environmental degradation.

Arguments about "the limits to growth," particularly the focus on population growth, were of course anticipated in the late eighteenth century by the Reverend Thomas Malthus in *An Essay on the Principle of Population* and were echoed in the late 1960s in a book that received immense publicity, *The Population Bomb* by Paul Ehrlich. The issue of population growth is unresolved within the green movement. Some writers have argued for strong measures, including financial disincentives to procreation, as well as educational campaigns. In an essay on *The Tragedy of the Commons* Garrett Hardin argued that the principle of freedom in the use of common land had become anachronistic. Among the measures he proposed for restricting access to the commons and for preventing the overuse of scarce resources were constraints on the right to beget children.

Another important concept utilized by the green movement has been the notion of "small is beautiful," derived from the title and arguments of a book written by E. F. Schumacher. Schumacher developed an influential argument that questioned the appropriateness of large-scale ventures. This coincided with the interest among many activists in the green movement in forming decentralized and small-scale organizations that might facilitate participation and democratic decision making. Schumacher was also concerned about the impact of large-scale developments on the environment, again a very popular theme among supporters of the green movement.

Ways of Thinking about the Economy

The challenge issued by Schumacher impinged on prevailing ways of thinking about the economy. The questioning by the green movement of the dominant approaches to conceptualizing the economy has led to a number of reforms. Some governments have introduced carbon taxes with a view to reducing emissions that add to the warming of the earth's atmosphere, the so-called greenhouse effect. Others have, for decades, tried to enact the principle that requires the polluter to pay for the damage caused. The idea is that all the expenses, including the cost of trying to repair the damage to the environment, should be taken into consideration and that in the final instance the price for products will reflect entirely the environmental and social costs.

Another important tactic used by the green movement in applying pressure on governments not to proceed with a wide range of projects is to evoke the strict application of the so-called precautionary principle. In other words, the green movement has often ensured the stringent application of safety standards to new projects. In areas like the development of nuclear power this has meant that governments have decided not to proceed with a particular project.

The green movement has also challenged how we define economic benefits and several efforts have been undertaken to revisit how we measure the economic performance of a country. Traditionally the focus has been on the gross national product. However, in the wake of arguments about the limits to growth and the destruction wrought by industrial society, economists sympathetic to the green movement have attempted to devise new standards for measuring the performance of a nation, particularly in terms of the health of the population and other aspects of the quality of life. These efforts have the potential to enable citizens to influence government action and behavior since they question the basic premises of many policy decisions.

An important concept used to justify the reshaping of some policies and the perpetuation of some prevailing practices has been the notion of sustainable development. This concept has been widely used since the 1980s following the report by the World Commission on Environment and Development entitled *Our Common Future*. The report coincided with growing concern among Western nations about the dangers posed by environmental destruction and the enduring problems faced by less developed nations in meeting the basic needs of their populations. The term sustainable development was defined by the commission as meeting "the needs of the present without compromising the ability of future generations to meet their own needs." The commission attempted to show how a focus on economic growth would not necessarily damage the environment if it were guided by the principles of ecology. The idea of sustainable development has been used to forge close links between economic and environmental concerns by governments, businesses, and environmental groups. Governments have used the notion of sustainable development to try and shape debates about the environment and thereby diminish the electoral influence of some green political organizations. Although there has been much criticism of the concept by the latter, many supporters of the green movement have become involved in efforts to implement sustainable development.

Discussions about sustainable development have stimulated efforts to place a value on the environment. Among others, economists have tried to achieve this through the introduction of pollution charges and carbon taxes and, as indicated earlier, through questioning conventional ways of measuring economic costs and benefits. One initiative to bring about change in perceptions and policies was the publication by David Pearce and his associates of a *Blueprint for a Green Economy*, which mapped out measures for achieving sustainable development by placing values on the environment, including water and the atmosphere, that have had no price attached to them and have therefore been overexploited.

Another approach to reconceptualizing prevailing economic practices and beliefs has been the idea of green consumerism. In a book entitled

The Green Consumer Guide, John Elkington and Julia Hailes argue for the possibility of combining a comfortable lifestyle with environmental protection by buying products that do not destroy the environment. In certain respects this approach is in alignment with both the enactment of government policies and the aspirations of many supporters of the green movement. Still, some people are skeptical about the possibility of tackling serious environmental problems simply through the substitution of products. Rather than focus on the substitution of products, some green economists like Herman Daly have promoted the notion of a "steady-state" economy.

This implies support for a sustainable economy or for sustainable development. Daly argues for this from the perspective of the laws of thermodynamics: in other words, from the basis that in a closed system energy is neither produced nor consumed but only modified. Daly argues, among other things, that in our society the rate of modification of existing matter is greater than the rate of replacement by solar energy. In order to address this problem Daly has advocated the creation of a steady-state economy with defined limits to the size of population and the creation of wealth.

Like many supporters of the green movement, Daly has questioned the values that underpin the focus on economic growth and material prosperity. This could be read as a concern with issues like social justice. In revisiting how we measure economic performance the green movement has often raised the question of social justice. Many green political parties have advocated the introduction of a guaranteed minimum income in lieu of the existing system of social security and tax relief. While this scheme may have certain merits, the green movement has so far been unable to deal adequately with two major objections to the idea, namely the cost of implementing it and the disincentives it might create to people seeking employment.

Another dimension of the economic strategies proposed by the green movement has been the introduction of the idea of alternative energy as a framework for new policies. Green political organizations have drawn attention to the possibilities of using renewable energy sources like solar, wind, and air power. An influential example of this way of thinking is *Soft Energy Paths: Towards a Durable Peace* by Amory Lovins. Lovins's idea that the development of benign, or "soft," technologies could contribute to the formation of a less coercive and centralized social system than the prevailing one was well received by many in the green movement. These technologies would apparently allow for the evolution of a more participatory political culture. Without necessarily accepting these arguments, traditional political and industrial organizations have become willing to explore the possibilities for using solar, wind, water, or air power.

Fundamental Principles and Concepts

The focus by the green movement on economic considerations and social justice represents an important element in its agenda for change. Another significant aspect of the development of the green movement is a discussion about the fundamental principles that might shape a green society.

One of the distinctions frequently used to characterize different approaches within the green movement is that between "deep" and "shallow" ecologists. The term deep ecology was invented in 1972 by the Norwegian philosopher Arne Naess. Shallow ecologists are said to be interested primarily in preserving resources for the benefit of human beings in developed nations. By contrast, deep ecologists concentrate on the intrinsic value of the environment, hence on a nonanthropocentric focus, valuing nature for its own sake and resisting the notion that human beings can be understood as separate from their environment. Like the biocentrists, deep ecologists advocate unity with nature and the preservation of all forms of life. Among the most significant divisions within the green movement is the one between the proponents of an anthropocentric perspective and those who urge others to accept the intrinsic value of nature.

This conflict manifests itself, for instance, in the discussion of the rights of animals. Deep ecologists have argued that animals have moral rights. Hence supporters of groups like Earth First! concentrate as much on the defense of the earth and of all species of plant and animal life as on protecting individual human lives. The defense of the moral rights of animals is made in a book entitled *The Case for Animal Rights* by Tom Regan. Still, some of these efforts to argue for the basic moral rights of animals are often too intricate for most supporters of the green movement.

Other arguments are easier to follow: for instance, the concern about a loss of community. The idea of a loss of community is linked by many in the green movement to the rise of industrial society and the alienation of one person from another. This is a popular theme in writings by prominent intellectuals in the green movement. In *Socialism and Survival* Rudolf Bahro has argued that the interest of the human species should become the core point of reference for understanding the problems we confront and that social change could only be achieved if one went beyond the concept of class enunciated by Karl Marx. There is a parallel here with the arguments of deep ecologists who questioned an anthropocentric approach to nature.

In order to reverse the loss of community, leading figures in the green movement like Bahro have advocated a more spiritual approach and the development of communal lifestyles. Bahro was also willing to propose a fairly controversial means of embracing such a lifestyle: he championed a model based on the practices of the Benedictine order of monks.

Another vision for a green society, not too dissimilar to that espoused by Bahro, was articulated by Kirkpatrick Sale, who used the concept of a decentralized bioregional society. The idea is that people will live in accord with the rhythms of the land or the discrete territory defined by natural boundaries. The focus is not on reshaping nature but on adapting to it. The planned outcome would be a more balanced economic and social system that would enable people to enjoy more leisure, develop communal bonds, and live in proximity to nature.

Many of these ideas had been anticipated by earlier generations. For instance, in *A Sand County Almanac*, published in 1949, Aldo Leopold developed an ethic for the relationship between human beings and their environment that went beyond the predominant focus on economic relationships and posited the extension of the notion of community to include the soil, water, plants, and animals. Moreover, like Rachel Carson in *Silent Spring*, he presented a gloomy portrait of the damage being inflicted on the environment.

The notion of reversing trends toward industrialization and development has also been an important theme in the pronouncements by leading figures in the green movement. In a publication entitled *The Great U-Turn: De-Industrializing Society*, Edward Goldsmith argues against the construction of cities, factories, highways, and airports. In certain ways this represents a radical response to the claims about *The Limits to Growth*. A similar line of argument is pursued by writers who maintain that affluent lifestyles are unsustainable and that we need to redistribute resources from wealthy to poor countries and reverse trends in economic development.

The connection between ideas about biocentrism and the rise of social movements arises in various ways. Take the interest in ecology among some supporters of the feminist movement: this group has been often referred to as the ecofeminist wing of the green movement. Ecofeminists have suggested that women may be more inclined to support the aims of the green movement because they are inherently closer to nature than men. This has then been linked to arguments about patriarchy and the propensity of men, rather than women, to destroy the natural environment.

The focus by ecofeminists on the nonmaterial characteristics of the relationship between human beings and nature reflects an enduring interest among the progenitors of the green movement. Pioneers like John Muir in the United States and Myles Dunphy in Australia anticipated in their writings the contemporary interest in the spiritual qualities of nature. This theme is echoed by the recent interest in postmaterialism or postmaterial values as well as in deep ecology. Some writers have condemned industrial society on the grounds that it fragments life. They draw a sharp contrast between industrialization and a holistic approach that includes spirituality, particularly the aesthetic, caring, and loving aspects of existence. Still, the notion of spirituality does not feature in an explicit manner in the pronouncements of green political organizations and is often regarded with suspicion by them.

While the terms deep and shallow ecology have been used to differentiate between the approaches of green thinkers, activists, and sympathizers, the terms "fundamentalist" and "realist" have been utilized largely to refer to different factions within green political organizations. The terms were first used to describe groups that emerged in Die Grünen in Germany. The fundamentalists in the party were generally opposed to cooperation with traditional political parties, particularly to any notion of forming coalitions with them. The fundamentalists believed that they had a better understanding of the social movements that had given rise to the formation of green political parties than the realists. Whereas the realists appeared to accept that parliamentary politics involved compromise, the loss of the spontaneous character of the green movement, and an emphasis on professionalism, the fundamentalists argued for grassroots participation in the party, including the possibility of recall of delegates, rotating them out of office and achieving agreement through consensus rather than through majoritarian voting. In most green parties the outcome of protracted struggles for power between fundamentalists and realists has been a victory for the latter. At any rate, most supporters of green parties have been in favor of cooperation between green and traditional political parties in order to accomplish at least some of the goals of the green movement. Though bruised in the electoral arena, the fundamentalists, like the deep ecologists, reflect the vigor of the green movement.

This vigor is maintained by the infusion of new ways of thinking. Some ideas, like the Gaia hypothesis that was posited by James Lovelock in the 1970s, continue to provide inspiration to the green movement in questioning enduring ways of perceiving the environment. Though Lovelock has recognized that his belief in the existence of a complex system that can act as a "single living entity" (Mother Earth) cannot be tested scientifically, his argument continues to attract both supporters and detractors of the green movement, particularly since it implies that nature, if not the human species, has the capacity to survive the attack on it by human beings.

The tension between realism and fundamentalism also reflects persistent themes in socialist, or left-wing, politics. There has often been a close connection between the development of the green movement and left-wing politics. An important parallel has been the notion of social ecology. Whereas deep ecology is concerned about the exploitation of the environment, social ecology, as understood by anarchist-writer Murray Bookchin, represents the view that efforts to dominate nature originate in people's attempt to dominate their fellow human beings. The hope by Bookchin is that the green movement will seek to develop new social structures based on direct democracy rather than on the power of centralized and hierarchical bureaucracies. There is some overlap between these ideas and those of fundamentalists in green parties.

Another important theme in the development of the green movement has been that of peace and nonviolence. Many groups in the antinuclear protest movement that emerged in the 1970s presented nonviolence as one of the axioms guiding their activities, and this notion was adopted by Die Grünen as one of its four core principles. As with the Chipko Andalan movement in India, many other supporters of the green movement have been influenced, in this regard, by the writings and practices of Mahatma Gandhi and his followers in the campaigns against British rule in India. Still, green activists have not always agreed on precise forms of civil disobedience. These actions can range from noncompliance with tax regulations, to blocking the entrance to nuclear power installations to prevent the transportation of nuclear waste materials, to acts of sabotage as propounded by members of Earth First!

Despite these important and fundamental differences in approaches, the green movement has contributed to and been part of a huge shift in perceptions about how we relate to the environment. Detailed explanations for the rise of the green movement are too numerous to list here. Among those that have been widely used is the notion that postmaterialism explains changes in values. Though the distinction between material and postmaterial values can be traced to ancient times, recent empirical studies suggest that materialist and postmaterialist values were strongly associated with conflicts over environmental protection and economic development.

The notion of a shift in values is closely linked to the green movement's focus on the quality of life and on redefining what this means. This can entail rejecting economic growth and industrial development as the principal measures of the quality of life. Apart from a strong focus on environmental protection and preservation, the green movement has stimulated discussions on the quality of life in the workplace, in family relationships, and in local communities. This debate has had a significant impact on traditional political organizations, which have developed agendas that cover issues pertaining to immigrants, homosexuals, minorities, single parents, and women. In addition, the green movement has been influential in persuading governments to extend the notion of quality of life to include in an explicit manner the notion of the stewardship of nature.

Green Social Movements, Political Parties, and Interest Groups

For many political groups and movements environmental protection was at first only a small part of a broader agenda that included issues like the democratization of society, the defense of civil rights, and the pursuit of social justice. However, the issue of environmental protection has become a significant theme in many of these associations. The notion of protecting the environment has, of course, been used to broaden the appeal of these movements and served as a focal point for a heterogeneous constituency. More than any other issue, environmentalism has provided new social movements with opportunities for reshaping the political order, challenging assumptions about economic growth and industrial development, and drawing attention to different types of values.

Within new social movements, citizens' initiatives, and interest groups the focus on the environment has become the key theme. In addition, established organizations, notably political parties, have been selective in how they have adapted to the challenge by new social movements. They have primarily focused on the growing concern about the environment. They have also been reluctant to adopt aspects of environmentalism that may undermine economic imperatives and electoral considerations.

In terms of political action and political change, the most striking manifestation of a shift in perspective and a counter to prevailing trends has been the formation of social movements, interest groups, and political parties and the challenges posed by them. The impact of environmentalism on Western democracies is reflected in the great efforts by churches, trade unions, business and commercial interest groups, state bureaucracies, governments, and political parties to incorporate and respond to the demands of the green movement. The process of adaptation has become so widespread that one can now refer to the culture of environmentalism as one of the most significant elements in contemporary politics and society. This does not mean that the demands of environmentalists have been met or imply that traditional institutions have successfully defused the potential for conflict between environment and development.

The Rise of the Green Movement

The following account focuses primarily on the contribution to the green movement by social movements, political parties, and interest groups since World War II. An important stimulus to protest action was provided by campaigns conducted in the 1950s by associations like the Campaign for Nuclear Disarmament. This postwar movement against testing nuclear weapons anticipated social movements like the ones that protested the war in Vietnam and, from the 1970s, fought against the deployment of nuclear weapons. The latter contributed to a revival of the Campaign for Nuclear Disarmament in the 1970s, and it was no coincidence that the organization became affiliated with interest groups such as Friends of the Earth and Greenpeace and political associations like the Ecology Party.

The rise of the green movement, though most concentrated and visible in the formation of new political associations (as well as the revival of some old ones) in western Europe, was not confined to one continent. Reflecting the international character of the movement, political organizations and interest groups arose on most continents in the 1970s. In Latin America, the Gaucha Association for the Protection of the Natural Environment in Brazil emerged in 1971. From 1974 on, hundreds of green groups were formed throughout Brazil, and the first members of the green movement were elected to state assemblies in 1982. In Asia one of the most interesting initiatives to boost awareness about environmental problems was the creation in 1973 of the Chipko Andalan movement (involving mainly women in Indian villages). The protestors were principally concerned with preventing logging firms from destroying forests which were a vital source of fuel and food. To achieve their goals the protestors used the methods of nonviolent resistance advocated by Gandhi. The Chipko Andalan movement secured some important concessions from the government. Further significant initiatives were the movement to prevent logging in Malaysia led by Sahabat Alam Malaysia (the Friends of the Earth organization in Malaysia) and the Green Belt Movement for planting trees in Kenya. Other important environmental protests outside Europe include activities by campaigners in Australia, New Zealand, and the United States.

In Australia and New Zealand environmentalists have laid claim to being among the first to create green political parties, in substance if not in name. In the United States organizations like the Sierra Club have been campaigning for environmental protection for over a century, and in 1980 green groups formed the Citizens' Party to contest local and national elections.

Still, the greatest concentration of green political parties has emerged in western Europe. An important model for action by the green movement was the creation of citizens' initiatives in the 1960s. They arose at the local level and tended to deal with issues that had been neglected by traditional political parties and associations. A notable feature of these initiatives was the desire to involve people in decision making. The citizens' initiatives played a central role in the rise of protests against nuclear power projects from the 1970s on, and in the emphasis among green parties on grassroots democracy. Although divided over some issues, green political parties and other groups have usually taken a far stronger line than traditional political organizations and interest groups on issues like the humane treatment of animals, protection of wildlife, opposition to intensive animal husbandry and animal experimentation, the use of animal products, especially when it places an entire species under the threat of extinction, and opposition to hunting animals for recreational purposes.

An important factor in the development of green political movements and parties was the effort by Western governments to develop nuclear power. Protests were regularly initiated at a local level by small communities anxious about the impact of radiation on agricultural products. Though local in origin, these responses rapidly led to the defense of entire regions and their cultures against the plans of central governments. Protests in the Federal Republic of Germany became the most famous, as they spread from small rural communities to large cities with radical political groups. They also attracted supporters from other countries. These protests laid the basis for the formation of green lists and parties competing at local, regional, and then national elections. Again, the protests and organization of political groups were not unique to Europe. In May 1979 there was a huge gathering in Washington, D.C. In 1984 the Nuclear Disarmament Party was formed in Australia, attracting, at that time, an even higher proportion of votes than parties like Die Grünen in the Federal Republic of Germany.

The impact of the green movement on traditional political associations was so great that some of the leading figures in these organizations adopted significant elements of the green agenda. Among the many political leaders who were prepared to promote some of the ideas of the green movement were Prime Minister of Norway Gro Harlem Brundtland, who chaired the World Commission on Environment and Development from 1984 on; British Prime Minister Margaret Thatcher, who, in 1988, used an address to the Royal Society to express concern about issues like the greenhouse effect, the depletion of the ozone layer, and acid rain; and Australian Prime Minister Bob Hawke, who, from 1983 to 1990 placed the environment high on the political agenda and introduced many reforms.

However, prior to the efforts of established politicians to adopt much of the green agenda, leading figures in the green movement had already made important contributions. Even though these leading figures often found it hard to win the trust of the grassroots activists, the media ensured that they became famous. Petra Kelly was for a long time the most celebrated person in the green movement. Following her involvement in protests against the Vietnam War in the 1960s and in the German Social Democratic Party in the 1970s she became a founding member of Die Grünen. Kelly herself shared many of the misgivings among activists about involvement in parliamentary politics and dubbed Die Grünen an "antiparty" that should not form coalitions with traditional parties. Still, she became entangled in arguments about the professionalization of green politicians and found it hard to accept that the principle of rotation of delegates out of office would also be applied to her. Like Kelly, other green politicians had to grapple with the tension between the demands for the accountability or rotation of delegates and the requirements of professional politics. But unlike Kelly, other leading green politicians, like Joschka Fischer in the state of Hesse in the Federal Republic of Germany and Brice Lalonde in France, were prepared to make compromises in order to cooperate with traditional political organizations.

The creation and further development of green political parties reflected these deep tensions between the realists and the fundamentalists. However, there were also strong unifying elements, and it is remarkable how much green parties shared in terms of a common philosophical agenda across nations and continents even though circumstances varied from country to country.

The Distinctive Development of National Green Parties

There were several key factors that contributed to the distinctive development of particular green parties. First, there were some important differences in emphasis on particular issues. For instance, in Australia there was a much stronger focus than that in many European countries on the protection of wilderness areas; many of these tracts of land were eventually nominated for World Heritage listing. The issue of nuclear power played a much more crucial role in some countries, notably the Federal Republic of Germany, than in others in mobilizing opposition to established government policies.

Second, traditional patterns of political behavior and institutional practices that had evolved in different countries or regions had a significant impact on the fate of green political associations. For example, in countries like Britain the "winner-takes-all" electoral system has made it extremely difficult for new political parties or for small parties to gain representation in Parliament. In other countries, green parties have been able to benefit from the existence of electoral systems based on proportional representation. Another factor has been the capacity of traditional political organizations to engage in dialogue with or to co-opt new political movements.

The emergence of competent leaders who were able to innovate or seize on opportunities for change has been another important consideration. In some countries, certain individuals, expert communities, or intellectuals have played a crucial part in articulating concerns about the environment or the quality of life and in bringing together those who are disaffected with established political practices. In Belgium, for instance, the emergence of a green movement can be traced back to, among other factors, a Christian movement initiated by Luc Versteylen, a Jesuit priest and teacher. Among the key concerns of Versteylen and his associates was the meaning of the education offered to young people and of the values connected with a competitive, consumer society. These deliberations led to the formation of the Anders gaan leven movement, first in Antwerp and later in the provinces. This movement experimented with alternative lifestyles, attempted to achieve grassroots democracy, and engaged in campaigns to protect the environment. It also provided the basis for a new political organization, Agalev. Like Anders gaan leven, Agalev had as one of its primary aims getting young people to think about their problems and position in society. After competing in local and regional elections, Agalev participated in elections to the European Parliament in 1979. In 1982 Agalev separated itself from Anders gaan leven and formally became a political party.

The development of green political organizations in Belgium also shows how prevailing institutional practices and traditions shape such groups. In this case, cultural, religious, and ethnic differences intersect with green politics. Whereas Agalev represents the Flemish community, the other Belgian Green Party, Ecolo, represents the Walloon population.

France offers another illustration of the institutional factors that shape the development of green political parties. As in many other European countries, the origins of the green movement in France include a strong tradition of nature conservation groups, radical student groups that emerged in the 1960s, and citizen protests against the development of nuclear power. The French political system also presented both unique opportunities for and constraints on the development of green parties. In addition, several political leaders who had a decisive impact on the shape of these parties emerged. Although the green party Les Verts was formed in 1984, there were difficulties in uniting the green movement. There were clashes within the leadership, particularly over the questions of cooperating with traditional political organizations and of balancing two sets of considerations: the retention of many of the ideals of grassroots movements and the need to engage in pragmatic politics. In 1990 a second green party, Génération Écologie, was formed under the leadership of Brice Lalonde. In 1993 the parties presented a united front at the presidential elections.

It has not been unusual for more than one green party to emerge in a country. In Belgium this reflected religious and ethnic divisions. In other countries, divisions occurred along the lines of political ideology. As in France, two green parties have formed in the Netherlands. The first, De Groenen (The Greens), was founded in 1983 and has not been very successful in electoral terms. The second, Groen Links (Green Left), represented an electoral alliance of left-wing parties in 1989, before turning itself into a new political party in November 1990. One of the main differences between the two parties has been the extent to which they focus mainly on environmental issues or have a broader agenda for social change.

In some countries, green political issues were first promoted as a primary issue on the political agenda by radical reformist parties prior to the formation of a national green party. In Italy the agenda of the green movement had first been advanced by minor parties like the Radical Party and Worker Democracy. In Australia the platform of the Australian Democrats had long included environmental concerns as a fundamental issue.

When considering the development of green parties, Australia and New Zealand are interesting for a number of reasons. Green political organizations originated here earlier than in many European countries. These parties draw attention to the diversity of issues that can be used to launch campaigns for environmental protection. They also highlight the importance of political associations that did not bear the name "green party" even though they focused primarily on environmental issues. In both countries green political organizations were formed as early as 1972.

The United Tasmania Group was one of the first green political organizations ever to compete in state elections. Formed in the same year as the New Zealand Values Party, its purpose was to challenge government policies that led to flooding Lake Pedder in order to create a hydroelectric system. The manifesto of this political association was compatible with many of the broader aims of the green movement, including participatory democracy, more harmonious relationships between human beings and nature, and social justice. The New Zealand Values Party was one of the first endeavors by political activists to establish themselves at a national level on a platform that advocated both environmental protection and participatory democracy. Ideas from Europe and the United States about *The Limits to Growth* and *A Blueprint for Survival* permeated the manifesto of the new party. Its manifesto was called a *Blueprint for New Zealand.*

Although green parties now exist in most developed countries and in several less developed ones, their fortunes have been mixed or subject to rapid change. Institutional factors and the response of traditional political organizations have played an important part in these processes. In many countries green parties have made little impact in elections, either because of the rules and regulations that govern the process or because traditional political organizations have successfully adapted to the challenges issued by the green movement. In Sweden the greens simply took longer to effect a political impact than similar parties in other countries did. The Swedish Miljöpartiet de Gröna was founded in 1981. After seven years, in 1988, it made a significant breakthrough and became the first new party in seventy years to gain representation in the national parliament. Like other green parties it has had to struggle to retain its position. In 1991 it did not gain any seats. Yet, in 1994 this situation was reversed when it gained 18 seats. The reasons for the success of Miljöpartiet de Gröna include its capacity to develop a position on other issues (in this case opposition to membership in the European Union and the widespread mistrust of professional politicians) as well as, paradoxically, portray itself as a more traditional party with realistic policies and goals. In the 1995 European Parliament elections Miljöpartiet polled an impressive 17.2 percent and gained four seats.

This matched the notable performance of the British Green Party, which polled 15 percent of the vote in the 1989 European Parliament elections. However, because of the electoral system the Green Party received no seats. This situation again draws attention to the difficulties posed for minor parties by electoral systems. Despite strong support for the green movement in Britain, there is little prospect of a green party gaining electoral representation. Instead, green issues have increasingly been articulated by the traditional parties, and the primary sphere of influence of the Green Party has been in elections to local and district councils.

Die Grünen in the Federal Republic of Germany is one of the most successful parties in western Europe, and certainly the one receiving the most attention and publicity. This is partly due to the highly visible protests carried out by opponents of nuclear power in Germany. The program of Die Grünen became a model for other parties. Yet, the formation, development, and agenda of the party have also served to highlight many of the dilemmas confronting green parties in general. The party experienced conflicts over adherents' dual membership in Die Grünen and other political parties, the professionalization of the party and how it should treat its most prominent figures, the limits and possibilities of implementing direct or grassroots democracy and the imperative mandate, and the possibility of coalitions with other parties, notably the Social Democrats. Die Grünen gained in strength in elections throughout the 1980s. Like other green parties, however, Die Grünen has experienced mixed fortunes. Still, the party managed to recover very successfully from a disappointing performance in the 1990 federal elections; in alliance with Bündnis 90, their East German partners, they displaced the Liberal Free Democratic Party as the third largest party. However, Die Grünen's most significant successes have been achieved at the state level, where they have become the minor partner in coalition governments with the Social Democrats.

Another arena for parliamentary activities and influence by Die Grü-nen has been the European Parliament. When elections to the European Parliament were first held in 1979, the green movement throughout Europe had scarcely begun to organize itself to contest elections on either a regional or national level. In 1984 Die Grünen gained seven of the 12 seats that went to green parties in the European Parliament and joined their fellow greens in forming Green-Alternative European Link. In 1989 green parties gained 32 seats, though the number dropped to 22 in the 1994 elections. As a matter of policy, green parties have contested some of the trends toward European unity, arguing instead for a "Europe of the regions." This is consistent with their focus on decentralization and autonomy and their distrust of huge, centralized bureaucracies. While these issues have served to unite green parties, there have been disagreements among their delegates over the value of working in the institutions of the European Union; these disputes have reflected the tensions that emerged between realist and fundamentalist factions at the national level. In 1989, following disputes over how much green parties ought to focus on environmental issues as opposed to a broader agenda of social concerns, the majority of green parliamentarians formed the Green Group in the European Parliament. In an effort to achieve greater coherence in their agenda green parties have also formed the European Federation of Green Parties.

In the 1980s green parties emerged in most western European countries. Since the late 1980s the collapse of communist regimes has opened up new opportunities for the formation of green political organizations in eastern Europe. In 1996 the European Federation of Green Parties included political organizations from Austria, Belgium, Bulgaria, Denmark, Estonia, Finland, France, Georgia, Germany, Greece, Hungary, Ireland, Luxembourg, Malta, the Netherlands, Norway, Portugal, St. Petersburg in Russia, Slovakia, Scotland, Spain, Sweden, Switzerland, Ukraine, and the United Kingdom. Applications from green parties in Spain, Armenia, and Azerbaijan, as well as Latvia and Lithuania, were also being considered. The federation has attempted to provide more cohesion to the green movement, for example, in the articulation of goals through a series of conferences and formal declarations on issues like the environment, human rights, electoral reform, economic strategies, peace, and foreign policy.

In many former eastern European communist countries the green movement initially filled the vacuum created by the rush to stimulate economic growth and industrial development. In many cases green political action also arose during the struggle against the established governments. The formation of green parties was in many respects associated more with opposition to the communist regime than to initiatives emanating from these environmental organizations. This had at least one negative effect on green political associations: once the communist regimes had been overthrown, less attention was paid to environmental issues and more to economic development and social policies. This was the case in Czechoslovakia, prior to the division of the country into two autonomous nations, the Czech and the Slovak Republics. Among the environmental organizations formed in Czechoslovakia prior to the fall of the communist regime were Brontosaurus, the Czech Union of Nature Protectionists, and the Slovak Union of Protectionists of Nature and the Countryside. As in other east European countries, the agenda of greens became less relevant as the government struggled with the economic and social consequences of the fall of communism and the introduction of a free market system. The development of green (and other) political associations in Czechoslovakia was further complicated by the divisions between the Czechs and the Slovaks.

Still, green issues are likely to emerge again in eastern Europe in addressing the serious environmental problems that have arisen. At any rate, there are already several examples of vigorous green political campaigns, as in Ruse, Bulgaria, where there were strong protests against pollution from chlorine emissions at a factory in Giurgiu, a town across the Danube in Romania. Green political organizations like the Ruse Committee, the Independent Union Ekoglasnost, and the Bulgarian Green Party all contributed to the powerful articulation of environmental concerns.

In the 1990s attention in eastern Europe appears to be directed toward economic development and reconstruction, often along the lines of a free market system modeled on the United States. The United States embodies many other social experiments, however, and has also given rise to a powerful green movement. The U.S. electoral system presents a major hurdle to the participation of new political organizations in presidential campaigns and green associations have performed poorly in presidential contests. The creation of the Citizens Party in 1980 was the first major effort in that country to form a green political association to compete in local and national elections. The Citizens Party also contributed to the strengthening and organization of local and state environmental groups. Following the disintegration of the Citizens Party green activists formed Committees of Correspondence, which focused much more on local and regional political campaigns than on national ones. When the United States Green Party was formed in 1991 it drew on this experience and sought to strengthen a nationwide grassroots movement. It has consequently brought about many successes in gaining seats on local councils and education boards. The situation in the United States reflects the strength of the green movement not in attempting to challenge traditional political organizations in the electoral arena, but in promoting direct action and effectively lobbying for changes in policies.

Interest Groups Formed by Elites

As in the United States, eminent people, political activists, and sympathizers of the green movement in other countries have organized themselves into effective interest groups. Apart from the more popular image of a grassroots movement, the green movement on different continents therefore includes initiatives by small groups of prominent people. For instance, the Club of Rome, which commissioned the highly influential report *The Limits to Growth*, was begun by Aurelio Peccei, an entrepreneur who brought together industrialists, scientists, economists, politicians, and bureaucrats to debate the connection between environmental and economic issues and the political and social implications of changes in these areas. The Club of Rome, like the Business Council for Sustainable Development, formed in 1990, has exercised significant influence in the area of environmental and industrial policies.

Another example of the impact of a small but well-organized group of prominent people is the International Union for the Conservation of Nature and Natural Resources (formed by conservationists in 1948 and known, until 1956, as the International Union for the Protection of Nature). This organization has been instrumental in bringing about cooperation between government and nongovernmental organizations. In the 1970s it formulated a World Conservation Strategy and was active in developing the notion of sustainable development as well as in helping to convene the UN Conference on the Human Environment in 1972. The International Union for the Conservation of Nature also played a central role in the creation of the World Wildlife Fund (WWF) as well as in conservation initiatives in Africa. These initiatives included the African Convention on the Conservation of Nature and Natural Resources signed by 33 African states in 1968, and the African Special Project, which sought, with the assistance of African governments, to promote conservation and the economic, cultural, and scientific value of wildlife.

One of the most significant agencies coordinating the efforts of nongovernmental, as well as government, organizations to address environmental issues is the United Nations. Among the initiatives of this agency is the UN Educational, Scientific, and Cultural Organization's (UNESCO) work toward bringing experts together in order to establish a sound basis for gathering information on the state of the environment. This agency had a pivotal part in convening the Intergovernmental Conference of Experts on the Scientific Basis for Rational Use and Conservation of the Biosphere in 1968. This initiative also served to pave the way for the 1972 UN Conference on the Human Environment. Another UNESCO project was the 1971 Man and the Biosphere Program, which brought together experts from many countries to acquire more information on the condition of the environment and on the impact of human interventions.

The 1972 UN Conference on the Human Environment represented an important milestone in uniting government and nongovernmental organizations, with official delegates from 113 countries. This gathering highlighted both important differences between and opportunities for cooperation among developed and less developed nations. Apart from passing resolutions on a wide range of issues including whaling and the testing of nuclear weapons, the conference created the UN Environment Programme (UNEP). The aim of this program is to develop further the cooperation that had been achieved between government and nongovernmental organizations. It has focused on increasing knowledge about ecological systems, assisting in natural resource management, and providing expertise to less developed nations. UNEP has contributed to the design of international treaties, including the Framework Convention on Climate Change and the Convention on Biological Diversity that were signed at the 1992 United Nations Conference on the Environment and Development (UNCED).

This conference, held in Rio de Janeiro, represented a mammoth effort to bring together organizations from all arenas to address some of the most pressing issues on the political agenda. Despite the reservations expressed by many commentators about the capacity of such a gathering to bring about effective changes in policies, the conference drew considerable attention to questions of environmental protection and economic development. It also led to the signing of several agreements, including those on the implementation of sustainable development (Agenda 21), a Framework Convention on Climate Change (which outlined principles that would underlie efforts to deal with problems like global warming), the Convention on Biological Diversity, the Declaration on Environment and Development, and the enactment of Forest Principles.

Among the factors that determined these issues taken up by UNCED was the report *Our Common Future* produced by the World Commission on Environment and Development (1984–1987). This highly influential publication gave greater weight to the notion of sustainable development. It was used to guide responses to the challenges and political issues arising from the green movement. In the 1990s arguments for sustainable development made by governments and other traditional organizations provided an alternative to the difficulties of reconciling development with environmental protection.

Nongovernmental Interest Groups

Supporters of the green movement have responded in a variety of ways to debates about sustainable development. To a degree, the readiness of government and nongovernmental agencies to promote this concept reflects the influence of the green agenda on some aspects of policy making. However, many green groups, particularly the more radical ones that focus on direct action, remain highly skeptical of efforts to link a preoccupation with economic development to environmental protection. Among the most radical groups in the green movement are Greenpeace, founded in 1971, and Earth First!, formed in 1980. Both organizations promote direct action, which can involve breaking the law, though Greenpeace has been much more successful in gaining popular support for environmental causes.

Greenpeace reflects the close links between the protests of the 1960s and the green movement. It was formed by activists who, following their involvement in demonstrations against the Vietnam War, campaigned against the testing of nuclear weapons in the atmosphere around the Aleutian Islands. Greenpeace specialized in provocative actions designed to capture the attention of the media. Their protests were carried out by small groups of professional activists and involved risky actions like their 1973 attempt to penetrate the sites of nuclear tests. However, Greenpeace recently has become more willing to engage in conventional lobbying activities as well as in direct action that often breaks the law.

Greenpeace is unconventional in the context of the democratic participation espoused by many champions of the green movement. Although the organization has a vast number of supporters in many countries, it is run on strictly hierarchical lines with strong central control. In contrast to Greenpeace, Earth First! better fits the popular image of a green movement based on grassroots or direct democracy. However, Earth First! has distanced itself from the mainstream of the green movement through its commitment to the principles of biocentrism and deep ecology and its radical actions. It has sabotaged equipment used for development projects. This has at times provoked outrage, since actions like the insertion of metal spikes into trees in order to damage chain saws can cause serious injury to workers operating this equipment.

Whereas Earth First! epitomizes some of the more militant groups that have emerged over the past two decades, there is immense diversity in the methods used by green groups. The Sierra Club embodies the strong traditions of the green movement in the United States. It has focused on lobbying government to protect and preserve the environment, particularly to create national parks. In the early 1990s the club had well over half a million members and had considerably broadened its agenda to incorporate issues like the protection of endangered species, population growth, and the greenhouse effect. The Friends of the Earth, created in 1969 by David Brower, who had been forced to resign from the position of executive director of the Sierra Club, maintained the notions of democratic participation and grassroots involvement advocated by the student and other radical movements of the 1960s. Branches that emerged throughout the Western world were given considerable independence in how they organized themselves and in setting their own agenda. The WWF (also known as the World Wide Fund for Nature) is another highly influential lobbying group. Assisted by dignitaries like the Duke of Edinburgh, it has become one of the most successful organizations in raising funds for conservation projects and promoting dialogue between nongovernmental organizations and agencies of the United Nations. It has also shaped the conservation policies of many governments. In 1995 it had over five million supporters and national offices in 23 countries. The WWF supports numerous projects in these countries and has been extremely effective in disseminating information about conservation issues.

The Impact of Shifts in Values

Green political organizations and social movements are significant sources of political change because they reflect shifts in values and perceptions. Support for green groups rose steadily throughout the advanced, industrialized world of the 1980s, particularly among the young and those with higher education. The shift in values was accompanied by a loosening of the connection between political conflicts and divisions based on social class and the erosion of support for the major parties based on these divisions (Dalton 1996). Paradoxically, the emergence of new movements and political associations echoes the expectation that political institutions and organizations, notably those that evolved during the formation of the welfare state in the nineteenth century, remain heavily involved in regulating the actions of powerful groups in society and in shaping the social behavior of all individuals.

People still turn to traditional political organizations because the green movement does not appear to present a viable alternative form of government. In addition, there is the inertia of established institutional practices and traditions, particularly those associated with the electoral system, the media, and the connections between industry, bureaucracy, and government. Although the new green parties have been elected into parliaments all over the world, they remain minor players.

However, a transformation is occurring within the major parties, which have been receptive to some of the ideas of environmentalists. Although the efforts of the traditional parties have often been superficial, there has been a deeper action, one that acknowledges shifts in values and reflects a willingness to enact new policies, appoint supporters and leaders of new political movements to positions of influence, and, perhaps most importantly, focus attention on the principles underlying political decisions. All these responses have contributed to maintaining expectations that governments either can, or at least ought to, meet new challenges.

Green Political Issues

The focus on different issues, by the green movement as well as by the media, political parties, and interest groups, changes over time. In the 1980s a strong correspondence arose between some of the preoccupations of social movements and those of traditional political parties trying to address the green agenda. The prominence of some issues appears to follow a pattern of different "cycles of attention." To a degree, data seem to support this theory by Anthony Downs (1972) whereby interest in issues, including concern about the environment, moves through various stages, culminating in their displacement from the political agenda. In reality, the notion of an "issue-attention cycle" offers only a partially satisfactory account of interest in the green program since environmental issues have remained high on the political agenda over a long period of time. In Australia, for instance, reporting on topics like sustainable development reflects both cycles of attention and the widespread interest in this issue created by political and intellectual elites in recent years (Papadakis 1996).

Apart from the enduring character of green issues on national political agendas, one can also observe the emergence of a green program on a global scale. This phenomenon can be illustrated by the concern about the threat to African wildlife, particularly among groups like the WWF. Initiatives by such organizations represent a response to the consequences of the late nineteenth-century colonization of regions like East Africa by Britain and Germany. As far back as 1900 national governments like those of Britain, France, Germany, Italy, Portugal, and Belgium had signed the first ever international environmental accord, the Convention for the Preservation of Animals, Birds, and Fish in Africa.

Apart from governmental endeavors to deal with the global impact of environmental destruction, the media has, in recent times, contributed to raising awareness of issues that affect people across the boundaries defining nations or continents. Hence, media coverage of catastrophes that occur in distant locations has led to an understanding of the significance of the green movement and of the responsibilities of Western nations and multinational corporations. This is illustrated by reports on the death of thousands of people at Bhopal, India, in 1984 following the release of poison gas from the Union Carbide pesticide plant. Victims of the disaster had to wait five years before receiving any compensation from the multinational Union Carbide corporation based in the United States.

Other issues may paradoxically divide or unite the green movement. In 1985 Rudolf Bahro, a leading figure in Die Grünen, left the party in protest of the qualified support this political association gave for the invasive experimentation of animals if even one human life could be rescued. On the other hand, animal rights has been a significant feature of campaigns to change perceptions about the relationship between human beings and nature.

The question of nuclear power has not only united the green movement but provided a vital spur to the formation of green political organizations. Following the 1973 decision of the Organization of Petroleum Exporting Countries to increase the price of oil sharply, Western countries sought to substitute nuclear power for imported oil. This provoked strong opposition, and several powerful social movements followed the lead of the green antinuclear protest movement in the Federal Republic of Germany. The opposition was given an added impetus by a near disaster at the Three Mile Island nuclear power plant in 1979 and the 1986 catastrophe at the Chernobyl nuclear power plant near Kiev in the Soviet Union. The accident at Chernobyl highlighted the difficulty of dealing with the global consequences of human interventions into the environment at the national level as radioactive clouds spread across many European countries and induced governments to impose bans on the consumption of some foods.

Another issue that has come to symbolize the need and opportunity for international cooperation is the destruction of territory once occupied by a wide range of species and of these species themselves. The term biodiversity has been applied to describe efforts to stem the threats of extinction. An important contribution to addressing this issue has been the Convention on International Trade in Endangered Species of Wild Flora and Fauna signed in 1973 by a small number of countries, which has attracted many more government endorsements. Still, the question of how to deal with the threat of extinction of a vast number of plant and animal species remains an issue high on the agenda of the green movement as well as of government agencies and industrial interests. There is growing concern that the extinction of plant and animal species will lead to a loss of genetic resources that might have been used to cure illnesses as well as to resolve other problems.

The Limits to Growth

Among the issues that were first used to raise green awareness was the question of the "limits to economic growth." The publication in 1972 of *The Limits to Growth*, a study commissioned by the Club of

Rome, focused the attention of millions of people on the problems arising from economic growth, industrialization, environmental degradation, population change, and the depletion of natural resources. The study made use of computers and complex models to predict the pattern of economic change over the next century. The appeal of *The Limits to Growth* was also emotional and served as a point of reference for people who, since the 1960s, had either participated in or been sympathetic to the aims of environmental groups and social movements that arose on university campuses, especially against the war in Vietnam. Environmentalist opponents of the prevailing industrial system were interested in the study's prediction that, if the prevailing patterns of exponential economic growth were to continue, there would be a catastrophe by the end of the twentieth century arising from the rapid depletion of resources, pollution of the environment, shortages in food supply, and growth in world population. Although critics of the study pointed to its failure to take into account the possibilities of devising strategies to address these threats, the book became one of the most successful efforts to raise interest in and awareness of environmental problems.

Like *The Limits to Growth, The Global 2000 Report,* commissioned by the U.S. government and published in 1980, attempted to evaluate trends in environmental destruction, especially those that would occur if current practices were not replaced by more cooperation between nations. Though critical of the methods and assumptions of studies like *The Limits to Growth, The Global 2000 Report* also examined the connection between population growth, the state of the environment, and the depletion of natural resources and made predictions about disasters that would arise because of human interventions in the environment.

Above all, debates similar to the one over "the limits to growth" stimulated ideas on how to deal with threats such as the inefficient use of resources like oil and other fossil fuels, traffic congestion, and the greenhouse effect. In an effort to make polluters pay for the damage they inflict on the environment, some governments, particularly in the European Union, have introduced carbon taxes that have contributed to reducing emissions that pollute the atmosphere and contribute to global warming.

Acid Rain, the Greenhouse Effect, and the Depletion of the Ozone Layer

One of the three most salient environmental issues of recent times is the formation of acid rain. In many respects the question of acid rain is an abiding issue that has long been a source of tension among national governments. Lately, combined pressure from public opinion and national governments has led to significant initiatives to combat the problem. Acid rain is a form of pollution caused by emissions of sulphur dioxide gas and nitrogen oxide gases from industrial plants, coal-burning power stations, and cars. The Swedes have been the foremost campaigners against acid rain, and in the 1960s they applied pressure for governmental action across national boundaries. The 1979 Convention on Long Range Transboundary Air Pollution represents one important effort to deal with this problem. In 1984 the so-called Thirty Percent Club of nations committed themselves to reducing sulphur dioxide emissions by 30 percent over the period 1983 to 1993. Initiatives of this kind have resulted from the electoral success of green parties, particularly in countries like the Federal Republic of Germany where governments have made significant efforts to deal with this issue.

Another major question that has compelled traditional political organizations to take seriously many of the warnings issuing from the green movement is the warming of the earth's atmosphere due to the emission of gases (notably carbon dioxide) that prevent the escape of heat from the earth's surface. The consequences of this could be catastrophic. Damage wrought by extreme weather patterns could cause droughts and floods, and a possible rise in sea levels could displace millions of people living in coastal areas and obliterate some island nations. Evidence of global warming was widely disseminated by scientists and the media in the 1980s. At the 1992 UN Conference on Environment and Development, 153 nations and the European Union signed the Framework Convention on Climate Change with a view to reducing greenhouse gas emissions. It is still uncertain, however, whether all the signatories will comply sufficiently with this agreement to avoid the problems identified above.

The third major issue that has captured the attention of the public and propelled green issues high onto the political agenda has been the destruction of the ozone layer that surrounds the earth. Depletion of the ozone layer, which blocks ultraviolet radiation from the sun, could lead to a steep rise in incidences of skin cancer as well as damage the immune system of all species. Pressure by the green movement has led to fairly rapid responses by traditional political and industrial organizations. Chlorofluorocarbons, which damage the ozone layer, have been removed from many products. In 1987 most of the countries responsible for the production of chlorofluorocarbons signed an agreement, the Montreal Protocol on Substances that Deplete the Ozone Layer. The aim was to curtail the use of chlorofluorocarbons by 50 percent by the year 2000. Further scientific discoveries about the extent of ozone depletion have led to much more drastic measures in the United States and the European Union. The main difficulties now are to persuade less developed countries to ban these products and to provide them with alternative products at low cost.

There is also another category of green concerns that serve to shift public opinion. It consists of issues like nuclear testing and catastrophes that attract instant media attention. Intense coverage has been given to the crude oil spills by the *Torrey Canyon* in 1967 and the *Exxon Valdez* in 1989 when more than 10 million gallons spilled into Prince William Sound, Alaska.

* * *

Traditional organizations have been selective in their response to challenges by the green movement. They have been reluctant to adopt aspects of environmentalism that may undermine economic requirements and electoral considerations. However, strategies are being developed to counter these requirements. Some issues simply have to be addressed, and their implications transcend national boundaries. Problems like the depletion of the ozone layer and the emission of "greenhouse" gases mean that the green movement, though closely associated with the emergence of social movements in the West, cannot be confined to the politics of these countries. The mutual dependence of modern nations has been accentuated by the rapid expansion in trade over the last century and a half. In recent times, this has also been highlighted by the activities of international business corporations. For some time people have questioned the capacity of national governments to address the consequences of the economic interdependence between nations. This skepticism has extended to governments' capacity to combat environmental problems (*see* Jänicke 1990), though several initiatives to achieve greater cooperation between nation states have emerged (World Commission on Environment and Development 1990)

In Western countries exploitation of nature has been modified in a number of ways. People have become more aware of their capacity to destroy the basis for their material prosperity. They have come to appreciate much more the less tangible qualities of nature and the spiritual and moral implications of human intervention in the environment. Whether expressed in a radical or moderate way, environmentalism as a set of beliefs has been used, with some effect, to question certain basic values associated with industrial and political developments over the past two centuries, especially the belief in economic growth and material prosperity. There is nothing intrinsically new about the contemporary preoccupation with the spiritual and moral dimensions of the relationship between human beings and nature. The similarities between the past and the present are as striking as the discontinuities. The novelty lies in how these concerns have manifested themselves in recent times.

Opinion among writers on social movements and the New Politics is, at any rate, divided over the significance of environmentalism. Some have drawn attention to the novel character of green movements. Others have argued that the activities and implications of social movements are far from exceptional. Writers who have emphasized the unexceptional character of environmentalism have also argued that traditional institutions can incorporate this challenge. By contrast, those who have characterized environmentalism as something fundamentally new have posited that conflict between groups is likely to be high. In other words, the proponents of "economic" values may experience great difficulty in adapting to the demands of those who emphasize "environmental" values, including notions about the intrinsic value of nature and about a fundamental tension between material and spiritual values. These conflicting interpretations also represent the tension between materialist and idealist accounts of social change, between the focus on (material) interests and on values or ideas.

One is not obliged, however, to accept this dichotomous way of framing the issues. Explanations for the emergence of a culture of environmentalism include the tension between different values, the transformation of established beliefs and practices, and the conflicts between material interests (insofar as these can easily be attributed to particular social actors). The causal linkages between ideas and social change or between material interests and social conflict will vary from context to context. The linkages are also often difficult to identify with much precision. The culture of environmentalism may represent both the regular (ordinary) incorporation of environmental issues by traditional institutions and the irregular (extraordinary) transformation of these institutions. It may include elements drawn from both a dominant way of thinking oriented toward economic growth and an alternative environmental approach. The green movement implies a massive shift toward concern about the environment as well as a selective emphasis on principles from both approaches.

References

Burnam Burnam. "Aboriginal Australia and the Green Movement." In *Green Politics in Australia*, edited by Drew Hutton, 91–104. Sydney: Angus and Robertson, 1987.

Dalton, Russell. *Citizen Politics. Public Opinion and Political Parties in Advanced Industrial Democracies*. 2nd ed. Chatham, N.J.: Chatham House, 1996.

Downs, Anthony. "Up and Down with Ecology—The Issue-Attention Cycle." *The Public Interest* 28 (1972): 38–50.

Goodin, Robert E. *Green Political Theory*. Cambridge, England: Polity Press, 1992.

Inglehart, Ronald. *Culture Shift in Advanced Industrial Society.* Princeton, N.J.: Princeton University Press, 1990.

Jänicke, Martin. *State Failure. The Impotence of Politics in Industrial Society.* Cambridge, England: Polity Press, 1990.

McCormick, John. *The Global Environmental Movement.* 2nd ed. London: Wiley, 1995.

Papadakis, Elim. *Environmental Politics and Institutional Change.* Cambridge: Cambridge University Press, 1996.

World Commission on Environment and Development. *Our Common Future.* Melbourne: Oxford University Press, 1990.

The Dictionary

A

ACID RAIN (ACID POLLUTION). The question of how to combat acid rain has been a long-standing source of tension among national governments. This issue has also become a significant focal point of campaigns by environmental groups. Lately, the combined pressure from public opinion and governments has led to significant initiatives to address the problem.

Acid rain is a form of pollution caused by emissions of sulphur dioxide gas and nitrogen oxide gases from industrial plants, coal-burning power stations, and cars. Coal and oil are the sources of these gases. The term "acid rain" was coined by Robert Angus Smith, who, in 1872, associated the burning of coal with damage to plants in the Manchester area in England. His main finding was that acids from the coal-burning process were carried by the wind to the surrounding district.

Though primarily transported by rain, the acids also travel in snow, sleet, and fog. Pollution by acids has been noted for centuries in the British Isles. In 1880 smog in London brought about the deaths of 1,200 people. Similarly, in 1952 the deaths of over 4,000 people were attributed to smog over Greater London.

Since the 1880s Scandinavians have been concerned about acid pollution from Britain transported by the weather. Early in the twentieth century, damage to lakes and rivers and the loss of fish in Scandinavian countries have been ascribed to acid pollution from other regions. In 1948 the Swedish government created a network of observers to record levels of acid pollution across Europe. Concern about this issue was given further stimulus when, in the 1960s, Svante Oden, a Swedish soil scientist, exposed the connection between acid pollution and damage to thousands of lakes. Oden also suggested that the situation was getting progressively worse as a result of pollution generated as far away as Britain and central Europe. He used the term acid rain in describing these changes.

Pressure for international action to deal with the problem arose first in Scandinavia, notably in Sweden and Norway. The problem of acid rain induced the Swedes to bring their misgivings to the United Nations, resulting in the **UN Conference on the Human Environment (UNCHE)**, held in Stockholm in 1972.

The tensions between the Scandinavians and their neighbors were matched by the disquiet among Canadians about acid pollution from the United States. In Europe, Britain and West Germany resisted efforts by the Scandinavians to organize a convention with legally binding obligations to reduce air pollution that travelled across national borders. A weak version of these demands for curbing pollution was eventually signed by 33 countries in 1979 (Convention on Long Range Transboundary Air Pollution). Among the signatories were Britain, Germany, and the United States. Scandinavian countries, concerned about the ineffectiveness of this initiative, lobbied for a 30 percent reduction of sulphur dioxide emissions over the period 1983 to 1993. This led to the formation of the so-called Thirty Percent Club in 1984. By 1985 the club had 21 members, including many east European nations, all of whom committed themselves to lessening emissions by at least 30 percent.

In the early 1980s Scandinavian efforts for international agreements received a significant political boost when public opinion in West Germany was sensitized to the widespread destruction of native forests by acid rain. The success of **Die Grünen** in German elections contributed to a shift in direction among the political elites and Germans have since spent vast sums on remedying the problem. Even Britain, which first refused to join the Thirty Percent Club, committed itself to a policy of reducing emissions over a longer time frame. The issue of acid rain remains high on the agenda of national governments and green groups like **Friends of the Earth**, **Greenpeace**, and the **World Wide Fund for Nature** (WWF). There is still great difficulty, however, in reaching binding agreements between nations that are affected to varying degrees by acid rain.

In 1980 Canada and the United States signed a Memorandum of Intent Concerning Transboundary Air Pollution. This led to the creation of working groups to study the problem. Still, throughout the 1980s, neither country could agree on the implementation of an effective policy to deal with the acid rain falling on Canada, 50 percent of which came from the United States. Within the United States, there are significant problems with air pollution that travels across state boundaries. Efforts are currently underway to address these problems, including the 1990 Clean Air Act amendments that propose a vast reduction in nitrogen oxide and sulphur dioxide emissions by the year 2000.

AFRICAN CONVENTION ON THE CONSERVATION OF NATURE AND NATURAL RESOURCES. A convention signed in Algiers in September 1968 by 33 African states that were members of the Organization of African Unity. The convention came into force in 1969 and was largely the product of efforts by the **International Union for the Conservation of Nature and Natural Resources (IUCN)** to promote conservation and the well-being of the population. Like many other conventions, however, little or no provision was made for the administration or implementation of the recommendations.

AFRICAN SPECIAL PROJECT. An initiative by the **IUCN** to promote conservation and the economic, cultural, and scientific value of wildlife. The IUCN solicited the involvement of political elites in African states that had either gained independence or were about to do so. It organized the Pan-African Symposium on the Conservation of Nature and Natural Resources in Modern African States (held in Arusha, Tanganyika, in September 1961). The meeting was supported by the United Nations. The African Special Project provided a unique opportunity for African nations to articulate their views on the connection between conservation and their economic development. The African Special Project formed the basis for a dialogue that led to the signing of the **African Convention on the Conservation of Nature and Natural Resources** in 1968.

AFRICAN WILDLIFE. The threat to African wildlife has long been a concern of conservationists and was crucial in mobilizing support for groups like the **World Wide Fund for Nature.** Ever since the late nineteenth century, when Britain and Germany colonized East Africa, governments have been anxious about the destruction of wildlife by white settlers, professional hunters, and the indigenous population. Concern about preservation of game animals led to the signing, in 1900, of the first ever international environmental accord, the Convention for the Preservation of Animals, Birds, and Fish in Africa. The convention was signed by Britain, France, Germany, Italy, Portugal, and the Belgian Congo.

In 1903 the preservation of wildlife formed the rationale for the foundation of the first international environmental organization, the **Society for the Preservation of Wild Fauna of the Empire**, which focused on territories and colonies ruled by Britain. The plight of African wildlife was highlighted in several popular works by the German naturalist C. G. Schillings. These initiatives did not reverse the trend of mass destruction. In 1933 Britain organized an International Conference for the Protection of Fauna and Flora, seeking to protect the natural habitat for wildlife. Most colonial powers then signed a convention on the Preservation of Fauna and Flora, though it was not legally binding on the signatories and lacked any mechanism for implementation.

AGALEV. Reflecting the cultural and ethnic differences in Belgium, this political organization represents the Flemish community. By contrast, **Ecolo** has emerged as the voice of the Walloon population. The term Agalev derives from a movement called Anders gaan leven ("for an alternative way of life"). Agalev was founded in March 1982, though it originates in a Christian movement that began in 1970. The movement was initiated by Luc Versteylen, a Jesuit priest and teacher. His aim was to involve young people in reflection about their problems. Along with his collaborators, Versteylen questioned the value of the educational system and the competitive, consumer society. This formed the basis for the Anders gaan leven movement, which developed first in Antwerp and then in the provinces. The movement launched into grassroots action, including the promotion of alternative lifestyles and environmental protection. Later, a group from the movement, Agalev, contested local and regional elections.

In 1979 Agalev presented lists of candidates at the first elections to the European parliament and procured 2.3 percent of votes in Flanders. In 1981, with 3.9 percent of the votes, it gained two seats in the lower house of the Belgian parliament and a seat in the senate. Success in local elections created a new momentum. In March 1982 Agalev detached itself from Anders gaan leven and formally became a political party. In 1982 it attracted an average of 5.6 percent of the vote in 64 Flemish municipalities and won 44 seats. In elections to the European parliament in 1984, Agalev attracted 7.1 percent of the vote in Flanders and obtained a seat in the European parliament. In October 1985 Agalev attracted 6.2 percent of the vote in Flanders and gained four seats in national elections to the lower house, and in October 1987 the party did even better, with 7.3 percent of the vote and six seats. In 1988 Agalev secured 6.9 percent of the vote at local elections (and 108 seats). In the 1989 European elections it achieved its best result (12.2 percent), and in 1991 maintained its strong performance in national elections with 7.8 percent of the vote in Flanders and seven seats. In 1995 Agalev experienced its first setback in national elections. Its share of the total national vote dropped from 4.9 percent in 1991 to 4.4 percent in 1995. With the overall reduction in the number of seats available in the lower house from 212 to 150, Agalev lost two seats. These results led to internal debate within the party on the effectiveness of its strategies. Apparently much of the loss of votes for Agalev can be attributed to a switch in favor of the Socialist Party, which seemed to be under some threat because of various corruption scandals. Many green voters may have turned to the Socialist Party out of fear that its social welfare programs would be damaged if it were to suffer a serious electoral defeat. *See also* **GREEN PARTIES, BELGIUM.**

ALTERNATIVE ENERGY. The notion of sources of energy other than those that have been pivotal to the development of **industrial society** arises from concern about environmental damage caused by nuclear energy and by the depletion of natural resources like oil and coal. It also stems from concern about **the limits to growth** on this planet. Green political movements and parties have been quick to point to the possibilities of using renewable energy sources like solar, wind, and water power.

Writers like Amory Lovins, the author of *Soft Energy Paths*, have linked this preoccupation with alternative forms of energy to arguments about "soft" technologies (which are said to be sustainable, benign, flexible, and resilient) to the creation of a less coercive and centralized social system than the prevailing one. Alternative energy sources would be used to solve some of the economic and environmental problems arising within industrial societies, and the possibility of a more participatory culture, that might be associated with the use of technologies that require less centralized control, could be explored (*see A BLUEPRINT FOR SURVIVAL*).

At any rate, major corporations have been investigating the possibility of exploiting these technologies, and there is no necessary connection between the development of solar, wind, or water power and the development of more democratic political structures. Still, the notion of alternative energy remains a powerful one in the agenda of the green movement and has exercised some influence on traditional political organizations and on policymakers.

ALTERNATIVE LISTE ÖSTERREICHS (ALÖ). *See* **GREEN PARTIES, AUSTRIA.**

ANDERS GAAN LEVEN. *See* **AGALEV.**

ANIMAL RIGHTS. The question of the status of animals has both united and divided the green movement. In 1985 **Rudolf Bahro** quit **Die Grünen** in West Germany when the party qualified their support for animal rights by stating that invasive experimentation on animals was admissible if even one human life could be saved. Green political parties and groups have usually taken a far stronger line than traditional political organizations and interest groups on issues like the humane treatment of animals; protection of wildlife; opposition to intensive animal husbandry and animal experimentation; the use of animal products, especially when it places an entire species under the threat of extinction; and opposition to hunting animals for recreational purposes.

The principal division among supporters of the green movement has been between those who have, from an anthropocentric point of view, sought to protect animals and those who have argued that animals have moral rights. The latter have either described themselves or been described as **deep ecologists**. There are also parallels between this approach and the one adopted by radical environmental groups like **Earth First!** which place as much, if not more, emphasis on the defense of the earth and all species of plant and animal life than on saving individual human lives.

Tom Regan's *The Case for Animal Rights* is a seminal work in the defense of animal rights. Regan focuses on mammals aged one year or more which have developed perception, memory, desire, belief, self-consciousness, and a sense of the future before elaborating on why some animals have basic moral rights, which he distinguishes from "acquired" moral rights (in other words, rights that are procured by law, by voluntary action on the part of individuals, and by virtue of one's position in institutional arrangements). Although these efforts to argue for the basic moral rights of animals have been only partially understood or rejected by large parts of the green movement, the issue of animal rights has been a significant feature of campaigns to change perceptions about the relationship between human beings and nature.

ANTARCTICA. This vast area in the Southern Hemisphere has been a source of contention as different nations compete for the opportunity to exploit its natural resources. The freezing climate of this continent has rendered it inaccessible to humans and ensured the preservation of a pure environment. In 1959 a small number of countries signed the Antarctic Treaty with a view to using Antarctica only for peaceful purposes, mainly scientific research, and excluding attempts to undertake nuclear tests or the disposal of radioactive materials. The countries that first laid claim to the territory and signed the treaty (Argentina, Australia, Chile, France, New Zealand, Norway, and the United Kingdom) were joined in this agreement by Belgium, South Africa, Japan, the United States, and the former Soviet Union. Other countries have since signed the agreement. Subsequent demands by other nations to exploit the territory led, in 1991, to the signing of an Environmental Protocol to the Antarctic Treaty (the Madrid Protocol), which placed a fifty-year moratorium on mining in the region. The protocol was signed by 39 nations. Nongovernmental organizations have been fairly successful in campaigning for the preservation of Antarctica against efforts to exploit its natural resources (including oil) which could have a devastating effect on wildlife in the region. The Madrid Protocol reversed a 1988 decision by the signatories of the Antarctic Treaty (the Convention on the Regulation of Antarctic Mineral Resource Activities) to permit exploration for mineral resources.

ANTINUCLEAR PROTESTS. In 1973 the Organization of Petroleum Exporting Countries (OPEC) sharply increased the price of oil. Western countries responded by creating an International Energy Agency. Among other options, this agency devoted serious attention to increasing the supply of energy from nuclear power generators. In France, Belgium, and Germany, governments outlined plans for a vast increase in nuclear power plants. Although the highest percentage of nuclear-generated electricity produced in Europe was in France and Belgium, opposition was most fierce in West Germany.

The conflict over nuclear power in Western countries was a key factor in the advance of the green movement in the 1970s and the formation of green parties in the 1980s. Antinuclear protests normally involved small communities concerned about the effects of radiation on local produce. To some extent, this reflects the so-called NIMBY ("not-in-my-backyard") syndrome. In other words, people opposed a project only because it was going to be located in their vicinity. They were not committed to preventing the project if it was located elsewhere. However, this account of motivations tends to underestimate the capacity of people to link particular concerns about industrial development that affect their **quality of life** with a broader preoccupation about the impact of economic values on the environment. Moreover, protests against nuclear power in France and West Germany often became linked to regional issues and the defense of a particular culture against dominance by urban centers. In Britain there was a strong association between protests by the **Campaign for Nuclear Disarmament (CND)** against nuclear weapons in the 1950s and 1960s and the perceived danger of nuclear power generation for civilian purposes. Hence, there was rapid growth in the membership of the CND in the late 1970s and early 1980s.

In the Federal Republic of Germany the mobilization of the population in several small communities rapidly expanded into national and international protest movements. For instance, the 1975 protests in **Wyhl** by a community concerned about damage to the vineyards that were their livelihood escalated into widespread antagonism toward three things: the collusion between the state government of Baden-Württemberg and industrial interests, the deployment of the police to solve political problems, and the dominant political parties. Similar protests, on a much larger scale, happened in **Brokdorf**, Schleswig-Holstein (1976), Grohnde, Lower Saxony (1977), and Gorleben, Lower Saxony (1978).

Huge demonstrations also occurred at Kaiseraugst in Switzerland and at Creys-Malville in France (in July 1977). At some rallies many of the participants were from other countries, notably the Federal Republic of Germany. The largest gatherings were in that country. For instance, in March 1979 around 100,000 people participated in a protest rally against nuclear power in Hanover, the capital city of Lower Saxony, and in October 1979, around 150,000 people in Bonn staged the largest ever protest rally in the Federal Republic of Germany. During the same month, over 1,000 environmentalists met in Offenbach to discuss the possibility of establishing a new political organization that later became known as **Die Grünen**.

The connection between protests against nuclear power and new political movements and parties was evident throughout western Europe. In West Germany **citizens' initiatives** focused increasingly on this issue and were brought together under an umbrella organization called the Bundesverband Bürgerinitiativen Umweltschutz (Federal Association of Citizens' Initiatives for Environmental Protection), which was founded in 1972. The Organization for Information on Nuclear Power was formed in Denmark in 1974, the Initiative Against Nuclear Power Plants arose in the Netherlands in 1973, and Action Against Nuclear Power was founded in Austria in 1974. The Swedish Miljöverbund, formed in 1976, paved the way for the Miljöpartiet de Gröna, a green party founded in 1981.

Apart from mass protests across western Europe, public opinion about nuclear power was influenced by events and movements across the world. In Australia, a decision by the Australian Labor Party Conference in 1984 to allow the opening of a uranium mine led to the formation of the **Nuclear Disarmament Party (NDP)**. Within six months, the NDP had 8,000 members and attracted 643,000 (7 percent) first preference votes in elections to the Senate, thereby accumulating an even higher proportion of votes than did parties like Die Grünen in West Germany around the same time. In the United States, in May 1979 approximately 75,000 people gathered in Washington, D.C., to take part in the largest demonstration against nuclear power in that country.

Throughout the 1970s groups in the United States like the Clamshell Alliance had engaged in civil disobedience to prevent the construction of the Seabrook nuclear power plant in New Hampshire. Over 1,400 people were arrested at the site in October 1976. Another event that brought the issue of the safety of nuclear power to public attention was the death of Karen Silkwood in 1974. Silkwood died in a mysterious car accident while on her way to meet a newspaper reporter and a union official, to whom she was going to present evidence of serious safety infringements at the Kerr-McGee plutonium plant in Oklahoma. Her concerns appeared to be warranted following the closure of the plant. Another stimulus to worldwide protests against nuclear power was an accident, in March 1978, at the Three Mile Island plant in Harrisburg, Pennsylvania, which resulted in the emission of radioactive gases and the mass evacuation of the local population.

The accident coincided with the release of a Hollywood film called *The China Syndrome*, which presented a dramatic and plausible account of the serious difficulties that could arise in a nuclear power plant. The worst fears of opponents to nuclear power were realized less than a decade later. On 26 April 1986 there was an explosion at the **Chernobyl** nuclear power plant near Kiev in the Ukraine, then part of the Soviet Union. It is estimated that thirty people died very soon after the explosion, several hundred others had to be treated for the severe effects of radiation, and over 130,000 inhabitants had to be evacuated from the region.

Despite the protest and the accidents two contrasting trends are apparent. First, the main stumbling block to the development of nuclear power appears to be its economic viability. Second, the nuclear industry has derived some encouragement from concern about the **greenhouse effect** and the assertion that nuclear power may, in some respects, be a "cleaner" source of energy.

AUDUBON SOCIETY. Founded as a national organization in the United States in 1905, the Audubon Society was named after the naturalist John James Audubon. Audubon was the renowned author of *Birds of America*, completed in 1837. The Audubon Society was first formed in New York in 1886 with the aim of preventing poaching and hunting of birds and wildlife, and it gained public attention during a campaign to prevent the use of birds' feathers in hats. It has since grown into an organization with more than 500,000 members and has broadened its focus on questions of pollution of land, waterways, and oceans.

AUSTRALIA. Environmental policy in Australia has been shaped by factors like the strength of the green movement and by the introduction of innovative institutional mechanisms. Environmental issues reached the national political agenda in the early 1970s, particularly in **Tasmania** where the **United Tasmania Group (UTG)** contested state elections. In 1971 Australia established a Ministry of the Environment.

In response to the challenges raised by the green movement, traditional political parties like the ALP embraced issues, such as the environment, that traditionally lay outside of the economically dominated old politics agenda. In the 1980s the ALP began to concentrate to an unprecedented degree on environmental issues. Policy initiatives were largely driven by attempts to maintain a "progressive" image on environmental issues. To do this the ALP drew on its experience in creating consensus government and a corporatist state. The ALP dealt with conflicts over the **Franklin Dam**, the preservation of tropical rainforests (Daintree National Park), uranium mining (Kakadu National Park), and logging (the Lemonthyme and Southern forests in Tasmania).

Many of the ALP's efforts were directed toward "outflanking" green parties and movements by taking up green issues. Green groups like the **Wilderness Society** and the **Australian Conservation Foundation** began to gain direct access to the Ministry of the Environment in the early 1980s. Environmental groups secured an important advantage in influencing policies, particularly since mining, financial, and industrial groups tended to shun what they regarded as a weak ministry and focused their attention on the economic ministries, the prime minister, and the treasurer. The influence of environmental groups is reflected in the funding they received from the federal government. Following the election of the Hawke ALP government in 1983, there was a steady increase in grants to the Australian Conservation Foundation. In 1991 the federal government provided environmental groups with A$800,000 to enable them to participate in consultations over ecologically **sustainable development**.

By the end of the 1980s the government had abandoned a piecemeal approach to environmental problems in favor of shaping arguments about development and conservation and creating institutions to regulate and defuse the conflict between interest groups. In its attempt to set the political agenda, the government exploited the notion of sustainable development. Though this notion had been debated in the past, interest in it grew only after shifts in public concern about environmental issues and the report of the **Brundtland Commission**. Though the notion of ecologically sustainable development was interpreted by different social actors to suit their particular circumstances, the international debate over this issue provided the ALP government with an opportunity to move from a defensive posture to one of influencing arguments about the environment and the economy. The government also took on the role of arbiter between competing interests, calling for a "balance" between economic and environmental perspectives, especially over issues like mining and logging.

The most striking reforms, however, occurred in the 1980s as the ALP began to focus on the corporatist-style mediation of interests. Among the major initiatives of the ALP government were the establishment of a **Resource Assessment Commission**, preparation of a National Soil Conservation Strategy, and formulation of a Strategy for Ecologically Sustainable Development.

During the 1996 election campaign, which resulted in the election of a new government led by the Liberal Party in coalition with the National Party, many people were surprised at how the Liberal Party tried to change perceptions that the ALP was the most sympathetic of the major parties to environmental concerns. The Liberal and National parties committed themselves to spending A$1.15 billion on the environment by raising funds through the partial sale of the national telephone company. The sale was to be used to establish a A$1 billion Natural Heritage Trust of Australia. Initially (over a four- to five-year period), the coalition parties have undertaken to spend around A$700 million on a national vegetation plan, the rehabilitation of the Murray-Darling Basin, a national land and water resources audit, a national reserve system, and the reduction of pollution of the coast and seas. The money remaining in the trust fund will be used to support further initiatives. The present government also remains formally committed to the implementation of the Strategy for Ecologically Sustainable Development. *See also* **GREEN PARTIES, AUSTRALIA.**

AUSTRALIAN CONSERVATION FOUNDATION. Formed in 1965, the Australian Conservation Foundation was the first truly national environmental organization in Australia. Prominent politicians, administrators, and dignitaries (including the Duke of Edinburgh and the Chief Justice of the High Court, Sir Garfield Barwick) played a pivotal role in its formation. Efforts by these prominent figures to encourage changes in perceptions reflected the growing awareness, at least among conservation groups and sections of the political and administrative elites, of the dangers of environmental degradation. It initially lobbied for conservationists. However, it did not mobilize its support for militant direct action campaigns.

Like other voluntary organizations, the association received some support from the federal government. In 1964 it received A$1,000 from the Department of the Prime Minister. By 1990, under a Labor government, this figure had risen to A$175,631. During the campaigns to save Lake Pedder in **Tasmania** and to prevent the construction of the **Franklin Dam** the Australian Conservation Foundation became more militant. In 1983 it joined a coalition of 800 conservation groups to oppose the latter project.

From a modest 1,017 in 1967, membership in the association rose to 5,154 in 1971. In the 1980s there was a further rapid rise in membership—from 11,046 in 1982 to 21,400 in 1991. The group also had tens of thousands of supporters and in its 1990–91 *Annual Report* indicated that its total base of members and supporters had risen to 70,000. Since then, competition from other groups and an economic recession stopped the growth of the organization.

However, the Australian Conservation Foundation has long operated as a powerful lobby group, and it continued to exert influence on policymakers when, in 1991, it was invited to participate in consultations over ecologically sustainable development and received large amounts of financial support from the federal government in order to carry out the necessary research. Like other green groups, the association argued that the government was placing too much emphasis on economic values. Throughout the 1980s and early 1990s the association effectively lobbied the government for a wide range of issues, including specific concerns over the protection of forests and wilderness areas as well as broader policy issues like the **greenhouse effect** and **sustainable development**.

The Australian Conservation Foundation has played a pivotal role in gaining government recognition and support for action on preventing soil degradation, which is widely regarded as one of the most pressing problems facing Australia, especially in economic terms. The government supported a significant initiative by the Australian Conservation Foundation and the National Farmers Federation to integrate development and environmental protection. The government declared the 1990s the decade of Landcare and committed A$320 million to plant one billion trees over the decade. The unusual alliance between the farmers and the conservationists played an important part in enticing the government to address this problem.

Like the **Wilderness Society** the Australian Conservation Foundation has played an important part in endorsing candidates of green parties, as well as of the **Australian Democrats** and of the traditional political parties at federal and state elections.

AUSTRALIAN DEMOCRATS. The Australian Democrats were founded in May 1977 by Don Chipp, a former minister in the federal Liberal government. The primary justification for the formation of the Democrats was to keep the traditional parties "honest." The party soon developed a strong profile on green issues, focusing at first on the questions of uranium mining and the nuclear industry, always concentrating on protecting the environment as a fundamental objective. Its national constitution formulated, in 1978, as core objectives: "To accept the challenge of the predicament of mankind on the planet with its exponentially increasing population, disappearing finite resources, and accelerating deterioration of the environment" and "To seek the transition to a sustainable economy, in equilibrium with world resources and eco-systems, with a minimum of dislocation by planning the necessary changes in good time, and by increasing public awareness of the problem ahead." Like many green political organizations the Democrats have always emphasized participatory democracy (*see* **DIRECT DEMOCRACY**), including the involvement of party members in determining policy guidelines.

Like many green political associations the Democrats are consistently supported by those with tertiary education, younger rather than older persons, and women more than men. Supporters of environmental groups are more likely to vote for the Democrats than for any of the major parties, and in recent elections, most notably in 1990, the environment has been the most important consideration for people who voted for the Democrats. The Democrats' commitment to environmental protection is also mirrored by their policies.

In 1990 the Democrats achieved their best results in a federal election (12.6 percent of first preference votes in the elections to the Senate). This reflects the importance of environmental issues on the national political agenda in 1990. Interestingly enough, when the environment emerged as a less important issue than before, during the 1993 election, the Democrats scored their worst result, with 5.3 percent of first preference votes in the elections to the Senate.

The Democrats have also shown that they are in many respects in alignment with the values and policies of the green movement and are capable of adapting to changing perceptions and of exploring the possibilities of **sustainable development**. Their detailed policy proposals have contributed to efforts by all political parties to respond to the challenges posed by concern about the environment. Above all, they have led the way in focusing on problems that do not require immediate attention but are unlikely to be resolved without a fuller appreciation of their complexity and the need for a **precautionary** approach.

The Democrats were led by Senator Don Chipp between July 1978 and August 1986, Senator Janine Haines between August 1986 and March 1990, Senator Janet Powell between July 1990 and August 1991, Senator John Coulter between 19 August 1991 and April 1993, Senator Cheryl Kernot between April 1993 and October 1997, and Senator Meg Lees since November 1997. For most of the last decade the Democrats, either on their own or in conjunction with green independent senators, have held the balance of power in the Senate. Still, the party's strong commitment to environmental issues has not satisfied the aspiration among many green political activists to form a green party either with or without the Democrats. *See also* **GREEN PARTIES, AUSTRALIA.**

AUSTRIA. The emergence of the green movement in Austria is similar to developments in other countries as regards the connection with campaigns by social movements and by **citizens' initiatives.** An exceptional aspect of green politics in Austria is the formation of political organizations in an environment dominated, more than in most countries, by a corporatist style of policy making, a long and relatively successful partnership between labor and business groups and the government.

Initially, green political organizations like the Vereinte Grüne Österreichs (VGÖ) (United Greens of Austria) and the Alternative Liste Österreichs (ALÖ) (Alternative List of Austria) posed no threat to the political dominance of the two major (conservative and socialist) parties. However, along with recent electoral gains by Die Grüne Alternative (The Green Alternative), the green movement has prevailed in several campaigns to prevent projects to generate nuclear or hydroelectric power and to spur the major parties into adopting many pro-environment policies and governments into apportioning substantial amounts of money to environmental protection. *See also* **GREEN PARTIES, AUSTRIA.**

B

BAHRO, RUDOLF. Following his exile from East Germany, Rudolf Bahro, an intellectual and critic of the communist regime, became a leading figure in the formation of **Die Grünen** in West Germany. At first he espoused the possibility of combining socialism with environmental concerns. However, he rapidly became disillusioned first with socialism and then with the pragmatic reformers, or **realists**, in Die Grünen. Bahro increasingly articulated the position of **fundamentalists** within the party, before promoting **spirituality** and leaving Die Grünen in 1985 in protest at the compromises they were making over issues like animal experimentation (*see* **ANIMAL RIGHTS**).

Bahro was at first welcomed by the political establishment in the Federal Republic of Germany as an exile from the autocratic regime in East Germany. However, his criticism of the latter did not mean that he was an enthusiast for capitalism. Drawing on his marxist intellectual heritage, he expressed fears about the problem of alienation (rather than exploitation) arising from a capitalist economic system. In *Socialism and Survival* he referred to the loss of community associated with **industrial society** and to the alienation of one person from another. He also argued that the interest of the human species should become the core point of reference for understanding the problems we confront and that social change could only be achieved if one went beyond the concept of class enunciated by Karl Marx.

Bahro had shifted from being a fairly conventional marxist to aligning himself with utopian socialists and communists. Influenced by arguments about the limits to growth, he also began to abandon socialism and question attempts by environmentalists to reform the capitalist system. In *Building the Green Movement* he promoted the notion of drastically reducing consumption in Western societies. He also presented more fully his rejection of parliamentary politics and espousal of spirituality. Bahro agreed with the fundamentalists that the involvement by Die Grünen in parliamentary politics meant it was becoming just like any other traditional political party, losing touch with the grass roots, and abandoning many of the core principles of the green movement. Bahro was especially annoyed at the decision of Die Grünen not to oppose all experimentation on animals, and he left the party after it had agreed that "If even one human life can be saved, the torture of animals is permissible."

Bahro was aligning himself with **deep ecologists** and their rejection of anthropocentrism. He also elaborated on his own spiritual approach and how society might be transformed through the creation of communal lifestyles that resembled, in certain respects, the social organization of the Benedictine order of monks. Bahro argued that this communal form of social organization presented a cultural alternative to the prevailing focus on industrialism and capitalism. He also suggested that the new movement would differ from the original Benedictine order by rejecting a monotheistic idea of God (which had originated in despotic and hierarchical systems) and abandoning the separation of the sexes and sexual oppression. The retreat by the green movement into spirituality would, according to Bahro, eventually provide a much deeper and sounder basis for transforming social institutions and realizing the potential of the greens.

Although Bahro had identified some of the tensions and difficulties that arise when a new movement attempts to bring about social change, his withdrawal from contemporary politics and criticism of prevailing lifestyles were met with skepticism by many people within the green movement. Still, his involvement in the movement demonstrated the possibilities for dramatic shifts in perceptions of the relationship between different ideologies (including socialism, capitalism, and environmentalism) and the importance of notions of culture and spirituality in this process. There are parallels between Bahro's focus on these notions and the idea of a shift in values from materialism to **postmaterialism**. Bahro's strong stance on opposing technology and reducing consumption may simply reflect a more consistent and fundamentalist viewpoint than is acceptable to many in the green movement.

BANFF NATIONAL PARK. In 1885, Banff was the first national park to be dedicated in Canada, among the earliest to be established anywhere.

BELGIUM. A country in which the green movement has been relatively successful in influencing electoral politics, mobilizing popular support for environmental protection, and shaping policies. The formation of **Ecolo** and **Agalev** has left a lasting impact on the Belgian political system. Among the key environmental groups shaping the development of green politics is the **Friends of the Earth** formed in 1976 in Belgium. The origins of environmental groups in Belgium can also be traced to alternative lifestyle and countercultural groups that emerged in the 1970s in many west European nations.

Since the 1970s green political organizations have made a significant impact on voting patterns at local, regional, and national levels. These successes have, to a degree, been facilitated by a party system that contains an element of proportional representation (d'Hondt system). They are also linked to the deterioration of electoral support for regional parties and, as in other countries, to the tardy response by established parties to the advance of green issues on the political agenda.

An important consideration in explaining the success of green political organizations is the "pillarization" of Belgian politics, the connection between each of the major parties and either Catholicism, socialism, or liberalism. Each of these ideals, particularly Catholicism and socialism, has resulted in the formation of distinct social, political, and cultural networks. Consequently, traditional political organizations have found it difficult to absorb or adapt to new challenges like environmentalism. Still, the traditional political parties have endeavored, with varying degrees of success, to take up some green issues. *See also* **AGALEV; ECOLO; GREEN PARTIES, BELGIUM.**

BHOPAL. This city in India will be remembered as the setting for a catastrophe that began on 3 December 1984 following the release of poison gas from the Union Carbide pesticide plant. The gas, comprised mainly of methyl isocyanate, killed at least 2,500 people immediately, though some estimates put the death toll at four times that number. About 250,000 inhabitants of the slums around the factory suffered extreme discomfort (including temporary blindness and burning lungs). Many died from the effects of the poison gas in the following years. The rate of spontaneous abortions, stillbirths, and premature deaths among infants whose mothers were pregnant at the time has been estimated at about 25 percent. Around 100,000 people suffered disabilities, most of which were permanent and severe. After a lengthy court battle victims were awarded U.S.$470 million in compensation in February 1989, a figure well below original demands.

BIOCENTRISM. Biocentrism developed as a reaction to the concept of human conquest of nature associated with the industrial revolution and scientific progress. It entails a focus on oneness with nature and on the dangers of human distance from and interference with the natural environment. The biocentric view of the world was given a significant boost in the nineteenth century both by romantic poets and writers and by scientific studies like those of Darwin on the evolution of animal species. *See also* **BIOREGIONALISM.**

BIODIVERSITY. A term coined by Professor Edward O. Wilson, Harvard University, who in 1986 organized a conference in Washington, D.C., to address the problem of the reduction of biological diversity. Concern with the preservation of biological diversity originated in the nineteenth century. Formal attempts to address the problem can be detected in the recommendations by **UNCHE** (Stockholm, 1972), in the **World Conservation Strategy** launched by the **IUCN**, in the UN Educational, Scientific and Cultural Organization (UNESCO) **Man and the Biosphere Program**, and in the **Convention on International Trade in Endangered Species of Wild Flora and Fauna.** In the 1980s several groups of experts also raised the alarm about the threat to biological diversity.

The Global 2000 Report had previously estimated that by the end of this century, largely as a result of the destruction of tropical rainforests, hundreds of thousands of plant and animal species would become extinct. Estimates of the rate of destruction vary from 5,000 to 50,000 per annum. Concern by environmental groups and governments about this loss are derived from both aesthetic and utilitarian considerations. The cure for many illnesses may ultimately be found in plants that face the threat of extinction. There are also concerns about how the loss of genetic resources narrows the range of possibilities for dealing with problems, especially in agriculture, and about the destruction of forests without regard to the likely consequences on human life.

Major corporations and governments in more developed countries have a vested interest in preserving these resources as they are worth billions of dollars every year. Less developed countries have been concerned about exploitation of these genetic resources by corporations. The latter, it is argued, have profited immensely from the sale of products created from these assets without much financial benefit to the former. The seriousness of the problem has meant that environmental organizations have been fairly successful in persuading governments and corporations at least to sign the Convention on Biological Diversity.

BIOREGIONALISM. The vision of a decentralized society has been articulated in many different ways. The term bioregionalism is one such expression. It refers, in the words of Kirkpatrick Sale, to a society in which people live according to the rhythms of the land or the discrete territory defined by natural boundaries (flora, fauna, water, landforms, and climate soils). Rather than shape the land, humans would adapt to it. This, it is argued, would accelerate the formation of different cultures, different systems of government, and a more balanced or steady-state economic and social system. The perceived advantages of a bioregionalist society include an increase in leisure time, proximity to nature, the development of communal bonds, and the acceptance of the world "as it is" and of people "as they are" rather than a situation characterized by fragmentation, change, and violence. Contrary to the expectations of its proponents, the concept of bioregionalism has not been widely championed within the green movement. Still, some of the values that are said to be an integral part of bioregionalism have been significant in shaping aspects of the platforms, programs, and practices of the green movement. *See also* **BIOCENTRISM;** *A BLUEPRINT FOR SURVIVAL.*

BIOSPHERE CONFERENCE. Assembled in Paris between 1 and 13 September 1968, the Intergovernmental Conference of Experts on the Scientific Basis for Rational Use and Conservation of the Biosphere was an initiative by UNESCO to foster international debate among experts about the impact of human beings on the environment. The themes broached at this conference anticipated and provided a firmer basis for the **UN Conference on the Human Environment** (UNCHE) (Stockholm, 1972). The Biosphere Conference focused mainly on the potential contribution of natural scientists toward addressing issues like air and water pollution and the destruction of forests. UNCHE was to debate these issues in a broader socioeconomic and political context. The Biosphere Conference played an important part in voicing growing concerns about the scale of environmental destruction, focusing on the complex linkages between human activity and the environment, and raising awareness about the importance of collecting data on regional and international aspects of changes in the environment.

BLUEPRINT FOR SURVIVAL, A. In the early 1970s a number of parallel concepts drew attention to the threats posed by environmental destruction. *A Blueprint for Survival* was the title of an article published in 1972 by the editorial board of *The Ecologist* magazine led by Edward Goldsmith. Like *The Limits to Growth* published by the **Club of Rome**, *A Blueprint for Survival* was written to startle people into action. Sales of the book reached 750,000 copies. It called for radical changes in lifestyles in order to ensure the survival of the planet. The main proposal was the creation of a new, decentralized social system. This would supposedly facilitate more participation in decision making and cooperative attitudes than in a heterogeneous, centralized society and would lead to greater innovation both in agriculture and industry. Small, self-regulating communities might also be characterized by more fulfilling personal relationships, and there would consequently be less emphasis on consumption. Other possible benefits of decentralization would include self-sufficiency and a reduction in the use of expensive facilities like large-scale sewage treatment plants. The authors also prescribed policies of stable **population growth,** more efficient use of energy, and less reliance on pesticides and fertilizers.

BOOKCHIN, MURRAY. *See* **SOCIAL ECOLOGY.**

BROKDORF. The declaration in November 1973 by the electricity industry that it would build a nuclear power plant near the village of Brokdorf in Schleswig-Holstein, Federal Republic of Germany, signaled the beginning of a dispute that was crucial in the development of **antinuclear protests.** In August 1974 a local **citizens' initiative** collected over 30,000 signatures for a petition against the project. In October 1976, the electricity industry encircled the proposed site with barbed wire, triggering a series of demonstrations that led to bitter confrontations between the police and protestors. The conflict rapidly drew in militant groups from the city of Hamburg. The forceful reaction by the police also contributed to the escalation of violence.

The dispute attracted national and international attention to the possibilities of protest against the development of nuclear power. The successful campaign against further work on the site at Brokdorf contributed to a shift in public opinion against the construction of nuclear power plants, and the membership of radical environmental groups grew rapidly afterward. In addition, traditional political parties, like the Social Democratic Party in Hamburg and Schleswig-Holstein, began to reconsider their positions on the development of nuclear power at Brokdorf.

However, there were tensions within the labor movement, as many trade unionists perceived the campaign by green groups as a threat to the employment of workers. Campaigns like the one against the proposed nuclear power plants at Brokdorf and **Wyhl** were crucial to the advance of **Die Grünen** in Germany and the emergence of protest movements and green political organizations in other countries.

BROWER, DAVID. (1912–). One of the most tireless organizers of environmental groups, David Brower served as the first full-time executive director of the **Sierra Club** from 1952 until 1969. He was extremely popular among club members. Membership grew rapidly under his leadership, especially as he steered one of the most well-established conservation organizations in the world toward more radical engagement with the authorities. However, he was forced to resign in 1969 by opponents who pointed to the poor administration of financial resources. In the years prior to his resignation the club had suffered significant financial losses and forfeited its entitlement to tax exemptions following political campaigns against government plans to build two dams in the Grand Canyon. Brower moved on to establish **Friends of the Earth** and devote himself to mobilizing support and influencing public opinion. He was one of the most highly regarded environmentalists at the national and, through the growth of Friends of the Earth, international levels. In 1982 Brower founded the Earth Island Institute, an organization that linked a preoccupation with environmental protection to the question of human rights and economic development in emerging nations.

BRUNDTLAND COMMISSION. *See* **BRUNDTLAND, GRO HARLEM; WORLD COMMISSION ON ENVIRONMENT AND DEVELOPMENT.**

BRUNDTLAND, GRO HARLEM (1939–). Chair of the **World Commission on Environment and Development.** At the time of her appointment, Brundtland was leader of the opposition Labor Party in Norway. She had been prime minister in 1981 and was elected to the same office for the period 1986 to 1989 and from 1991 onwards. As chair of the World Commission on Environment and Development, Brundtland was immensely successful in promoting the concept of **sustainable development,** which was used in dialogue between less developed and more developed countries.

In the early 1990s as prime minister of Norway, Brundtland came under pressure from both environmentalists and Norwegian fishermen. The fishermen argued that their livelihood was being threatened by bans on whaling because the whales were consuming large quantities of fish. Environmentalists and governments of many developed countries have been unwilling to ease restrictions on the hunting of whales after decades of campaigns to protect various species.

C

CAMPAIGN FOR NUCLEAR DISARMAMENT (CND). Formed in January 1958, the Campaign for Nuclear Disarmament paved the way for social movements that protested against the war in Vietnam in the 1960s and campaigned against the deployment of nuclear weapons in the 1970s. All these movements signaled the upsurge of extraparliamentary activities that contributed to the emergence of the green movement. Many of the issues brought up by the CND later became an integral part of the agenda of green political parties. The CND developed in Britain from the disquiet, initially among pacifist groups and prominent intellectuals, writers, and thinkers, about the development of atomic weapons, bombing of Hiroshima and Nagasaki in 1945, and development of the hydrogen bomb. Among the forerunners of the CND were a wide range of local initiatives against the development of nuclear weapons as well as the umbrella organizations the National Council for the Abolition of Nuclear Weapons Tests, created in February 1957, and the Emergency Committee for Direct Action against Nuclear War, formed in April 1957. The latter represented a response to the conducting of nuclear tests on Christmas Island by the British government.

The trigger to the formation of the CND was an article by J. B. Priestley entitled "Britain and the Nuclear Bombs" published in the *New Statesman* on 2 November 1957. Priestley was responding to divisions in the Labour Party over adopting a unilateralist policy as well as to the concern in the international community about the competition between the United States and Soviet Union in the nuclear arms race. Events like the invasion of Suez by the British and the uprising in Hungary in 1956 also provided a focus for those who were anxious to reverse the apparent trends toward confrontation between East and West. Priestley's article served to bring together prominent people. The first executive committee of the CND included Canon John Collins as chair, Bertrand Russell as president, and Peggy Duff as organizing secretary. Groups like the National Council for the Abolition of Nuclear Weapons Tests merged fully with the CND.

Five thousand people attended the inaugural meeting of the organization, held on 17 February 1958 in London. The aims of the campaign were to persuade people that Britain should take unilateral action to cease using and producing nuclear weapons and bring other countries to the negotiating table to do the same. Between 1958 and 1965 the CND organized marches between Aldermaston, the site of an installation for nuclear weapons, and London. These marches attracted tens of thousands of participants and a vast amount of publicity. At the conclusion of the march held in 1961 around 150,000 assembled in Trafalgar Square. Although commitment to the CND waned in the 1960s (due partly to changes in policy like the signing of the Partial Nuclear Test Ban Treaty in 1963 and divisions between militants who favored direct action and those who wanted the organization to remain primarily a pressure group), links were made with protests against the Vietnam War.

Further marches to Aldermaston in the 1970s strengthened the connection between the CND and the **antinuclear protest** movements. The CND was affiliated with the Ecology Party, **Friends of the Earth,** and **Greenpeace,** especially in campaigns against the deployment of nuclear weapons in Europe. CND membership rose sharply, from 4,000 in 1979 to 50,000 in 1982. The number of CND branches or groups around the country increased from 150 in 1979 to about 1,000 in 1982. There were also about 1,000 affiliated organizations. Significant campaigns were conducted against the expansion of the nuclear submarine fleet and placement of cruise missiles. A rally held in Trafalgar Square on 26 October 1980 attracted around 80,000 people. The CND increasingly became part of antinuclear protests throughout western Europe in the 1980s. The focus was not simply nuclear weapons but the entire nuclear industry. *See also* **ANTINU-CLEAR PROTESTS.**

CARBON TAXES. Proposals for the introduction of taxes to modify behavior, in particular to reduce consumption of resources, have arisen in many developed countries. Concern about the **greenhouse effect,** inefficient use of resources like oil and other fossil fuels, unrealistic pricing of resources, and traffic congestion and an interest in applying the **polluter pays principle** have led to proposals for the introduction of carbon taxes in the European Union. There has been strong support for the introduction of carbon taxes among governments represented in the European Union, with the notable exception of the United Kingdom (on the grounds of interference by the European Union in national taxation policy). The coal, oil, metal, and car industries oppose these measures despite the argument by the proponents of the new taxes that there should be reductions in other forms of taxation. However, many developed countries, including the United Kingdom, have introduced taxes, charges, or other incentives that have led to a reduction in emissions (for instance, of lead from gasoline).

CARSON, RACHEL. (1907–1964). The author of *Silent Spring* (1962), a work that is widely credited with providing a major impetus to the birth and growth of a more radical and vigorous form of environmentalism in the 1960s. Carson, following her studies in genetics at Johns Hopkins University and after teaching at that university and the University of Maryland, worked for the U.S. government as a marine biologist. In 1951 she published a best-selling study in natural history entitled *The Sea around Us*. Subsequently, she dedicated herself to writing and in 1955 published *The Edge of the Sea*. In the 1950s she became interested in and deeply disturbed by the impact of chemical pesticides and insecticides on wildlife and its habitat and on the dangers to human life. Using her skills as a writer and scientist, she produced, in *Silent Spring*, one of the most provocative and rousing accounts of the damage done to the natural environment by human beings.

CATLIN, GEORGE. (1796–1872). An artist who traveled around the U.S. West in the 1830s and, in a book entitled *North American Indians*, argued for the protection of American Indians, buffalo, and the wilderness through the establishment of national parks.

CHERNOBYL. A town near Kiev in the Ukraine, formerly part of the Soviet Union, and scene of the worst civilian nuclear power disaster. Following a failed experiment, the nuclear reactor at Chernobyl exploded and for 10 days released radioactivity into the atmosphere. Around 30 people died shortly after the explosion and over 130,000 had to be evacuated from the region. There would have been many more deaths and injuries if the explosion had occurred during the day, rather than at night, because more people would have been working in the plant and many local inhabitants would have been outdoors. The explosion realized the worst fears of opponents to nuclear power and hardened public opinion against the development of nuclear power plants. Programs for the development of nuclear energy for civilian use were either canceled or postponed in Austria, Belgium, China, Finland, Greece, Italy, the Philippines, and Spain. The expectation is that tens of thousands of people will die from cancer as a result of the explosion. Radioactive clouds containing zodine131, caesium134, and caesium137 traveled thousands of kilometers and affected 21 countries in Europe. In Germany, Italy, and the Netherlands bans were placed on the consumption of certain foods. In many countries warnings were issued about the contamination of vegetables and fresh milk. Measures were also introduced to prevent cattle from grazing outdoors. Some of these procedures were short-term, but others were maintained for a long time. Almost a decade after the disaster, there were still restrictions in parts of Wales in the United Kingdom on the sale of sheep. Scientists continue to be concerned about the possibility of another similar disaster.

THE CHINA SYNDROME. The title of a Hollywood film, starring Jane Fonda and Jack Lemmon, which presents a dramatic and plausible story about a disaster in a nuclear power plant. Shortly after the film was first released, the world became aware of the near catastrophe at the **Three Mile Island** nuclear reactor in Harrisburg, Pennsylvania.

CHIPKO ANDALAN. A protest movement involving mainly women in Indian villages. The term *chipko* means "embrace" and refers to protestors who cling to trees in order to prevent loggers from felling them. The aim of the protestors is to protect their livelihoods, since the forests provide food and fuel and prevent soil erosion and flooding. The movement arose in April 1973 in the village of Gopeshwar, Uttar Pradesh. The successful protest against a logging company inspired many others, and the movement spread to different parts of the Himalayas and India. A notable feature has been the adoption of resistance and protest through nonviolence, inspired by the Gandhian concept of *satyagraha*. In 1980 the movement achieved a significant concession from the government, a 15-year ban on green felling in the Himalayan forests of Uttar Pradesh. Though still a long way from effecting fundamental changes in government policies, Chipko Andalan has been celebrated for using nonviolent protest and highlighting the predicament of communities in less developed countries as they address environmental issues and defend a traditional way of life.

CHLOROFLUOROCARBONS. *See* **OZONE LAYER.**

CITIZENS' INITIATIVE. The term "citizens' initiative" has been used to describe the organization of **antinuclear protests** in the early phase of their development. In countries like the Federal Republic of Germany the origin of citizens' initiatives (*Bürgerinitiativen*) can be tracked to the citizens' associations (*Bürgervereine*) of the 1950s and 1960s. The latter were formed by leading figures in local communities to apply pressure for community projects. To a degree, they were an attempt to fill the vacuum left by traditional political parties that tended to neglect local interests. This void became even larger in the 1960s and resulted in the advent of student protest movements. The notion of citizens' initiatives was continued in the 1960s in the wake of these protests for greater participation by the citizens in decision making. Many citizens' initiatives turned to the reformist Free Democratic Party in the hope that it might be more effective than other major parties in articulating the people's aspirations for greater involvement in politics.

Campaigns like those at **Wyhl** and **Brokdorf** against the development of nuclear power were initially carried out mostly by local citizens' initiatives. The citizens' initiatives also had strong connections with the reform-oriented youth wing of the Social Democratic Party. Above all, the campaigns against the development of nuclear power led to the spread of citizens' initiatives that were supported by a powerful umbrella organization, the Bundesverband Bürgerinitiativen Umweltschutz (Federal Association of Citizens' Initiatives for Environmental Protection).

Citizens' initiatives have not only been influential in persuading traditional political organizations to reconsider their policies on the environment, they have also played a pivotal part in the formation of green lists or parties. The candidates for green parties have often gained their political experience and expertise through involvement in citizens' initiatives. Participation in these associations contributed to the desire of activists in green parties to practice **direct democracy** at the local, regional, and even national levels.

CITIZENS PARTY. The Citizens Party resulted from the first major effort in the United States to form a green political organization to contest local and national elections. After informal discussions among prominent environmentalists and expressions of interest from members of environmental and other social movements, the Citizens Committee was formed in August 1979. The aim of the committee was to form a national Citizens Party, and over the next few months thousands of people from around 30 states became members of the fledgling organization and formed local chapters.

The official foundation of the Citizens Party occurred in April 1980 at a gathering of nearly 300 delegates. Despite reservations expressed by some members, the Citizens Party quickly prepared itself for the 1980 presidential elections. This had always been the intention of its founding members. However, this issue soon led to divisions within the organization. Several leading figures who questioned this focus on the presidential campaign subsequently resigned from the party. The first priority for those who remained was to engage in the onerous and expensive task of securing enough signatures to obtain a position on the ballot. Even though the Citizens Party only gained access to the ballot in 29 states and in the District of Columbia, it did cover three-quarters of the total population. At any rate, this was a considerable achievement in the context of the enormous institutional barriers that face any new party that tries to challenge the Republican and Democratic dominance over the political system. Achieving this goal depleted the resources available to the party for the electoral campaign, and in attracting 234,279 votes (0.27 percent), it fell far short of its stated goal of winning 5 percent of the vote. In the 1984 presidential elections the results were even less encouraging. The Citizens Party, which was in a state of rapid decline, attracted only 72,200 votes (0.1 percent). Yet, these results reflected neither the underlying strength of interest in environmental issues nor the much better prospects for the influence of green politicians at the local level.

The Citizens Party's difficulties in mounting effective presidential campaigns were both external and internal. The primary external obstacles were the complicated laws imposed by different states regarding a new party's access to the ballot (for instance, regulations on gathering large numbers of signatures for a petition in support of a new party) and the cost of conducting a campaign that would attract sufficient coverage by the media. The internal obstacles included the haste with which the new party tried to engage in a presidential contest, its failure to attract support from key environmental groups (which were often more interested in exercising influence over the established parties, notably the Democrats), and the divisions between factions that wished to focus on a variety of agendas (including feminist issues, social justice, minority rights, and economic democracy).

The Citizens Party had its greatest impact at the local level. In contests for local seats its share of the vote rose progressively (and on average) from 1.5 percent in 1980 to 19.6 percent in 1981, 22.5 percent in 1982, 23.2 percent in 1983, and 26.2 percent in 1984. In elections to state legislative assemblies the Citizens Party did quite well, polling an average of 11.2 percent in 1980 and 10.4 percent in 1982. Its candidate for Congress in a statewide election in Vermont polled 12.8 percent, and in Burlington, the largest city in the state, they polled 24 percent. Two of its candidates for the state legislature in Burlington polled 20.8 percent and 19.8 percent. In local elections between 1981 and 1984 the Citizens Party secured 11 seats on city councils and school boards in Burlington.

Its primary sources of support were young, white, and middle-class groups. There were also important links with public interest groups, as well as with social movement organizations that had played an influential role in upheavals during the 1960s. Membership of the party rose from around 2,000 in 1980 to a peak of 22,000 in 1981, before declining steadily to 9,000 in 1984. The Citizens Party capitalized on both the growing concern about environmental issues and the reputation of one of its founding members, **Barry Commoner.** Commoner had a national reputation as a scientist and prominent campaigner for environmental protection. Both Commoner and another leading figure, Gar Alperovitz, sought to link their ideas about environmental protection to a profound restructuring of the economic system (including a shift away from the free market system dominated by large corporations to more decentralized and community-based structures). In addition, there were efforts to link these concerns to the questions introduced by social movements, particularly as regards the rights of women and minorities. Hence, in contesting the 1980 presidential elections, the Citizens Party nominated Commoner as its presidential candidate and La Donna Harris, a Comanche Indian, feminist, and campaigner for minority rights, as its vice presidential candidate.

Although leading figures in the Citizens Party realized after the 1980 elections that the prospects for the party at the national level were very poor, further efforts were made to contest the 1984 elections. These were seriously undermined when Commoner, among others, decided to support the Rainbow Alliance presidential campaign of Democrat Jesse Jackson. The nomination of Sonia Johnson, a leading feminist, as the Citizens Party presidential candidate occurred in the context of deep divisions, including those over whether or not to contest the elections and over the influence of feminists on the party platform. The Democrats' nomination of Geraldine Ferraro as their candidate for vice president appeared to undermine the Citizens Party's new emphasis on attracting the support of feminists.

At its inception the Citizens Party sought to combine concerns about the democratization of the economic system and environmental protection. It also profited from the widespread **antinuclear protests** arising from the accident at **Three Mile Island.** The focus on other social issues, notably the rights of women and minorities, had the potential to broaden the base of the party but was not fully realized, particularly as a result of disputes between leading figures. At times the struggles at the national level were reflected in conflicts among local chapters of the party. Yet, it is at this level that the Citizens Party demonstrated the possibilities for political action by green parties in the political system of the United States. *See also* **GREEN PARTIES, UNITED STATES OF AMERICA.**

CLUB OF ROME. At the instigation of Italian entrepreneur Aurelio Peccei, a group of 30 industrialists, scientists, economists, politicians, and bureaucrats met in 1968 to discuss issues of global concern, including environmental and economic issues. As a result of their first meeting, held in Rome, the group named itself the Club of Rome and set out to examine the dynamic interrelationships between economic development, the environment, population, resources, and industrialization. The group was also concerned about the political and social implications of changes in all these spheres. Though dealing with global issues, the Club of Rome was widely regarded as being primarily concerned with the interests of industrial and political regimes in developed countries. In 1970 the 75 members of the Club of Rome were drawn from 26 countries. Most were from more developed countries.

The impact of the Club of Rome on the environmental movement was assured when a report it had commissioned in 1970 was published two years later under the title *The Limits to Growth*. The alarming findings of this report ensured sales of 20 million copies worldwide and secured the Club of Rome a place in the history of the green movement. The Club of Rome exercised significant influence on the agenda for debate over environmental policy, including the **UN Conference on the Human Environment** held in 1972. The Club of Rome, while recognizing the exploratory nature of much of *The Limits to Growth* study, was intent upon provoking debate, especially among political and economic elites. It has since commissioned further reports and continued to exercise significant influence in the area of environmental and industrial policies.

COMMONER, BARRY. (1917–   ). The author of *The Closing Circle: Nature, Man, and Technology*, Barry Commoner is a biologist who has been associated with the University of St. Louis since 1947. Apart from his interest in plant pathology, Commoner has been prominent in campaigns against nuclear testing and for environmental protection. In the 1970s Commoner engaged in a highly publicized debate with **Paul Ehrlich** over the danger of population growth. *See also* **CITIZENS PARTY.**

CONSERVATION INTERNATIONAL. Founded in 1987 in the United States, this organization is primarily concerned with achieving **sustainable development** in less developed countries. Its most significant contribution so far has been in organizing agreements between less developed and wealthy nations; instead of repaying part of their national debt to the developed nations the emerging nations spend an agreed-upon sum on conservation measures. This arrangement is referred to as a **debt-for-nature swap.** The most notable success by Conservation International was the exchange of a portion of Bolivia's national debt for preservation of part of Amazonia. It has been able to replicate this kind of achievement in negotiations with several other countries. *See also* DEBT-FOR-NATURE SWAPS; WORLD WIDE FUND FOR NATURE.

CONVENTION ON INTERNATIONAL TRADE IN ENDANGERED SPECIES OF WILD FLORA AND FAUNA. The Convention on International Trade in Endangered Species of Wild Flora and Fauna is one of the more successful international treaties. It aims to identify and protect both plants and animals by either controlling or preventing trade in them. The convention was signed in 1973. In 1992 over one hundred countries, including those that were most heavily involved in trade in endangered plants and animals, were signatories to the convention. Support for the administration of the scheme was at first derived from the UN Environment Programme (UNEP). Over time, however, the signatories of the treaty supported the scheme with their own financial resources.

CZECHOSLOVAKIA. Until 1989, prior to the "velvet revolution" that destroyed the communist regime, Czechoslovakia was under the influence and control of the Soviet Union. The possibility of an autonomous green movement and green political organizations was severely constrained. The pattern of damage to the environment was similar to other countries in eastern Europe, as environmental protection was accorded a much lower priority than economic development, and there were few or no opportunities for interest groups and other political organizations to influence this ordering of priorities. Several organizations were formed, however, notably Brontosaurus, though they were only tolerated if they were connected to the Communist Party. Later, these organizations were used by activists opposed to the regime.

The communist regime had enacted some laws to protect the environment, notably the 1967 Practical Measures against the Pollution of the Atmosphere. Although the law included penalties for polluters, they were ineffectual. Following the collapse of communism, more stringent measures modeled after international organizations like the World Health Organization and the European Union were introduced. The **polluter pays principle** was reaffirmed and new policies developed on **sustainable development** such as the General Environmental Law and General Act on the Environment enacted in 1992. Other landmark legislation included the 1991 Clean Air Act and the 1992 Act on Environmental Impact Assessment. After a promising start, the Green Party went into decline in the 1990s. However, environmental groups have had access to the government and been able to express their point of view about legislation on issues like protection of the **ozone layer**. Moreover, some groups received support from the Ministry of the Environment for research into environmental protection. On 1 January 1993 the country divided into two separate nations, the Czech Republic and Slovakia. *See also* **GREEN PARTIES, CZECHOSLOVAKIA.**

D

DALY, HERMAN. *See* **STEADY-STATE ECONOMY; STEWARDSHIP.**

DEBT-FOR-NATURE SWAPS. The concept of a "debt-for-nature" swap was invented in 1984 by Thomas Lovejoy, a U.S. biologist, who suggested that less developed and wealthy nations might come to the following arrangement: Rather than repay part of their national debt to the developed nations the emerging nations would spend an agreed-upon sum on conservation measures or social programs. Under this arrangement, a nongovernmental organization purchases the debt of an emerging nation at a large discount. The elimination of the debt is followed by an arrangement between the nongovernmental organization and the emerging nation to ensure that the latter preserves a certain portion of land. *See also* **CONSERVATION INTERNATIONAL; WORLD WIDE FUND FOR NATURE.**

DECENTRALIZATION. *See A BLUEPRINT FOR SURVIVAL.*

DEEP ECOLOGY. Differentiation between "deep" and "shallow" ecology was made by Norwegian philosopher Arne Naess in 1972. The term "shallow ecology" is used to refer to campaigns against pollution and the depletion of resources that have as their principal objective "the health and affluence of people in developed countries." The term "deep ecology" suggests a **fundamentalist** approach or a concern with **spirituality** in relating to the environment. In addition, as formulated by Naess, it focuses on the intrinsic value of nature. It attempts to posit a nonanthropocentric approach, an ideal in which nature is valued for its own sake, and the idea that human beings are located in but separate from the environment is renounced. As in **biocentrism,** the focus is on the possibility of unity with nature and the dangers associated with attempts by human beings to conquer the environment. Naess develops the notion of "biospherical egalitarianism" to open a debate on how we should coexist with other forms of life and avoid killing, exploiting, and suppressing them. He links these ideas to the question of **quality of life** and of how, in overcrowded environments, humans and mammals suffer from neuroses, aggression, and the loss of traditions. He evokes the principles of diversity and symbiosis to support the retention of all species and argues for the principle of "live and let live" to replace the conventional principle of "either you or me" derived from arguments about the survival of the fittest. Deep ecology promotes diversity in all spheres of activity, including the economic, cultural, and occupational. This appears to be consistent with Naess's advocacy of autonomy and decentralization (*see A BLUEPRINT FOR SURVIVAL*).

Although there have been many variations on the model of deep ecology conceived by Naess, his core ideas introduced issues that have remained central to discussions about the core principles and practices that should be adopted by the green movement in its efforts to transform social practices. Among the many objections to the deep ecology approach is the argument that any attempt to posit nonanthropocentric values is still based on attempts by human beings to devise or formulate values. Nonetheless, deep ecology has been influential in changing perceptions about the values attached to the nonhuman natural environment and how it might be preserved and protected through the efforts of the green movement and its sympathizers. *See also* **ECOLOGY**.

DEINDUSTRIALIZATION. A common theme in writings by leading promoters of the green movement has been that of the problems associated with **industrial society**. This has led some to propose a radical shift in direction, away from industrialization that is seen to destroy nature necessarily, toward deindustrialization, preventing the pillage of the environment.

This theme was most explicitly developed by Edward Goldsmith. His book *The Great U-Turn: De-Industrializing Society* opposes all efforts to build cities, factories, highways and airports. Goldsmith also draws a distinction between the "real" world, which comprises the world of living things or the biosphere, and the "surrogate" world, which involves the destruction of forests, soil erosion, and the creation of pollution and toxic wastes. Goldsmith's proposals represent a radical response to the findings of studies like *The Limits to Growth*, which points to the limits of the resources available for maintaining lifestyles in affluent societies.

The argument for deindustrialization is also advanced by writers like Ted Trainer who, in *Abandon Affluence!*, argues that the Western way of life is unsustainable and contributes directly to poverty in less developed countries. In sum, he argues for the "de-development" of wealthy nations in order to ensure that resources are redistributed to the poor and that the economic system can be reshaped in order to meet their needs. However, arguments about deindustrialization have not been widely accepted or promoted by the green movement.

DIE GRÜNEN. Founded in January 1980 following widespread support for social movements opposed to the development of nuclear power and green groups contesting local and state elections, Die Grünen (The Greens) became the most celebrated manifestation of the upsurge of the green movement. Its formation as a political party was anything but a smooth process. At the preliminary meeting in Offenbach in October 1979 divisions emerged over issues like dual membership in Die Grünen and other political parties, the focus on grassroots **citizens' initiatives**, electoral politics, and whether to adopt a conservative or socialist agenda. Prior to the formation of Die Grünen as a federal party, a coalition of green groups, Sonstige Politische Vereinigung: Die Grünen (Alternative Political Association: The Greens), had polled 3.2 percent in elections to the European parliament (June 1979), and a green group in Bremen, Bunte Liste (Multicolored List), had for the first time secured seats in a state parliament (four seats and 5.1 percent of the vote).

Die Grünen's performance in federal elections improved progressively in the 1980s, from a shaky start in the 1980 elections (1.5 percent), to 5.6 percent of the vote and 27 seats in 1983 and 8.3 percent of the vote and 42 seats in 1987. Die Grünen suffered a reversal of fortune in 1990 when it polled only 4.8 percent of the vote, thereby failing to gain any seats in parliament because of the "5 percent electoral hurdle" that applies in the Federal Republic of Germany. The principal reasons for their setback in 1990 were the failure to appreciate the significance of German unification to the electorate and the willingness of the major parties to adopt many green issues in their programs. For a while Die Grünen was represented in parliament only by Bündnis 90 (Alliance 90), a group that had been formed in East Germany. Bündnis 90 represented a coalition of citizens' initiatives concerned about environmental issues as well as the restoration of democracy.

Special rules had been introduced for the 1990 electoral contest, whereby the 5 percent electoral hurdle was applied separately in the eastern and western parts of Germany. Bündnis 90 polled 5.9 percent of the vote in East Germany and thus gained eight seats in parliament. Moreover, the West German greens soon began to reassert themselves in numerous state elections. Die Grünen, in coalition with Bündnis 90, also performed very well in the 1994 federal elections, attracting 7.3 percent of the vote and 49 seats. Its success was doubly significant. It displaced the Free Democrats (who gained 47 seats) as the third largest party and made an unprecedented recovery. No other party in the Federal Republic of Germany had previously succeeded in overcoming its complete exclusion from parliament (following an electoral defeat) and regaining representation.

In elections in 1984 to the European parliament Die Grünen secured 8.2 percent of the vote and seven seats. In 1989 a "Rainbow Coalition" of Greens gained 8.4 percent of the vote and eight seats. At the state level Die Grünen has consistently attracted enough votes to secure continuous representation in most parliaments. Its share of the vote has risen consistently in large states like Baden-Württemberg, North Rhine Westphalia, and Rhineland-Palatinate and in city-states like Berlin and Bremen. In 1996 the party held seats in all the state parliaments of West Germany and in Saxony in East Germany. Apart from regularly dislodging the Free Democrats as the third largest party, Die Grünen has been a member of a coalition government with the Social Democratic Party (as the senior partner), in Hesse between 1985 and 1987 and again in 1991 and 1995, in Berlin from 1989 to 1990, and in North Rhine Westphalia in 1995. Another significant development has been the willingness of the Christian Democratic Party to consider forming coalitions with Die Grünen. In September 1991, following the state election in Bremen, a coalition was formed between the Social Democrats, the Christian Democrats and Die Grünen. In 1992, there was even serious discussion about the possibility of a coalition between the Christian Democrats, and Die Grünen in Baden-Württemberg. Even at the federal level, the Christian Democrats, led by Federal Chancellor Helmut Kohl, began to adopt a much more conciliatory approach to Die Grünen.

Support from the Christian Democrats resulted, for instance, in the November 1994 election of Antje Vollmer, a leading figure in Die Grünen, to the position of deputy parliamentary speaker. The Christian Democrats also became eager to involve members of Die Grünen in parliamentary committees. These changes flowed from the increasingly precarious position of the Free Democrats, who had served as coalition partners for over a decade, and the growing influence of the "realists" or "Realos" rather than the "fundamentalists" or "Fundis" within Die Grünen.

The predominance of the realists followed a protracted process. The transformation of powerful social movements campaigning against the development of nuclear energy (*see* **ANTINUCLEAR PROTESTS**) into a political organization participating in government was fraught with difficulties. As part of a social movement, rather than a political party, the environmentalists were under less pressure to achieve a degree of ideological coherence and provide an alternative set of policies to those proffered by the traditional political parties. Among the most influential people in the early stages of the formation of Die Grünen were Herbert Gruhl, a former Christian Democrat and member of parliament; **Petra Kelly**, who had been active in protests against the Vietnam War in the United States; Rudi Dutschke, a leading radical intellectual in the West German student revolt in the 1960s; and **Rudolf Bahro**, a dissident intellectual who had been expelled from East Germany.

Certain patterns in the sources of support for the party are evident. Backing for Die Grünen is most likely to come from the following groups: people with higher than average levels of formal education, the relatively young, those living in urban residential districts, and white-collar government employees. The percentage of voters who have indicated they might choose Die Grünen has been consistently high (up to 20 percent), though many of its supporters may vote in a tactical manner (in other words, if the prospects for Die Grünen to overcome the 5 percent electoral hurdle appear to be weak, some of its supporters are more likely to vote for the Social Democratic Party).

A significant proportion of the electorate has come to identify Die Grünen as the party most likely to draw attention to and address environmental questions. The issue that contributed most to the formation of Die Grünen was the opposition to the development of nuclear energy that began in the mid-1970s. Concern about the growth of the nuclear power industry has been intensified by misfortunes in other countries, notably at **Chernobyl** in the Ukraine. Die Grünen has also focused on the actual and potential consequences of **acid rain**, the **greenhouse effect**, and the totality of other issues broached by environmental groups. In parallel with these issues, Die Grünen has profited from the mass mobilization against the deployment of U.S. nuclear weapons on German territory and the upsurge in countercultural and alternative lifestyle movements in the late 1970s and early 1980s, particularly in cities like Berlin.

Die Grünen has progressively broadened its focus to include a wide range of economic and social issues. Although it cannot therefore be labeled a "one-issue" party, there is a cluster of issues that serves to differentiate it from the other parties and mobilize electoral support. Apart from environmental issues, which have to some degree been adopted by the other parties, Die Grünen has taken the lead in opposing the use of military force in foreign policy, criticizing patronage and corruption in politics, advancing women's rights, and advocating a looser confederal structure for the European Union. The issues of political reform, rendering decision-making processes more transparent, and combating the problems arising from the concentration of power have both benefited and harmed Die Grünen. Many voters have appreciated the party's efforts to uncover shortcomings in the political system; practice grassroots or **direct democracy**, like the rotation of office holders; and reduce the privileges enjoyed by parliamentarians.

Some of these issues also reflect deep divisions within the party over whether to adopt some of the organizational practices of traditional political parties. Initially, the main ideological division within Die Grünen tended to be between conservative "pure" environmentalists and those who sought to link **ecology** with left-wing politics. Although the latter won out, a new division emerged, namely, between the fundamentalists, who did not wish to make compromises with established organizations as regards specific policies (like the development of nuclear power) or with respect to sharing power (for instance, in a coalition government), and the realists, who adopted a more pragmatic approach to parliamentary politics. The conflict between the fundamentalists and realists has often been blamed for preventing the development of Die Grünen as a major political force.

Following the setback in the 1990 federal elections, the realists, who in the 1980s had already entered coalitions with the Social Democrats in states like Hesse, began to gain the upper hand and remove some of the restrictions placed by the fundamentalists upon tenure of office and styles of political negotiation adopted by parliamentary delegates. Above all, the realists have been more successful than the fundamentalists in attracting support at the ballot box. This trend was reinforced by the coalition with Bündnis 90, which also espoused a pragmatic approach to parliamentary politics and for a time, between 1990 and 1994, was the only green party in the federal parliament.

It is important to emphasize that the focus on coalitions with other parties and a more professional approach to parliamentary politics (including a greater emphasis on achieving coherence and unity at the level of the party elite) does not mean that Die Grünen has abandoned some of its basic long-term goals that continue to set it apart from the major parties. *See also* **GERMANY.**

DIRECT DEMOCRACY. The term "direct democracy," or "grassroots democracy," is widely used by green political groups to distinguish their practices from those of traditional political organizations. The latter are seen as autocratic or promoting representative rather than participatory democracy. The focus on direct democracy in green parties reflects the interest among **fundamentalists** to retain the spontaneous character of the social movements from which they emerged and remain accountable to the grass roots of the organization. Direct democracy is seen as a means of preventing the emergence of a strong bureaucratic and professional culture in green political organizations. It also exhibits the enduring skepticism of many activists about involvement in conventional political action and parliamentary politics. Among the most notable efforts to put direct or grassroots democracy into practice have been the endeavors of the fundamentalists in Germany's **Die Grünen** to limit the tenure of parliamentary delegates by rotating them out of office and to ensure that representatives remained directly accountable to the membership, in effect allowing members to dismiss them from their offices. The latter principle is often referred to as the imperative mandate. Green political organizations have constantly had to decide between their efforts to ensure greater accountability to the membership and the need to develop a higher degree of competence and professionalism to deal with the complex processes and decisions that arise in parliamentary politics.

Apart from the principle of rotation and the imperative mandate, green political organizations have attempted to promote direct democracy by trying to maintain close links with social movements, convening meetings that are open to all members of a political organization, and advocating consensus rather than majority voting on important issues. Another manifestation of the emphasis on direct democracy has been the granting to local and regional groups within green political organizations of a large measure of autonomy to draw up party programs, follow their own procedures for internal organization, and manage their financial affairs. There is a convergence here with notions of decentralization (*see A BLUEPRINT FOR SURVIVAL*). The notion of direct democracy has also been used to bolster campaigns by green political organizations against the accumulation of offices, patronage and corruption in parliamentary politics.

DUBOS, RENÉ. (1901–1983). Born in France, René Dubos worked as a biologist and philosopher in the United States. Renowned as the person who invented the expression "**think globally, act locally,**" Dubos is coauthor, with **Barbara Ward,** of *Only One Earth.* This highly influential book, which took issue with the path of development pursued by advanced industralized market economies, contributed to the shaping of the policy agenda of the United Nations, which had commissioned the work. For most of his career Dubos taught at Rockefeller University in New York. He had also held posts at Rutgers University and Harvard Medical School. A recipient of the Pulitzer Prize, Dubos wrote extensively on the relationships between human beings and their surroundings, and his works include *The Wooing of Earth: New Perspectives on Man's Use of Nature* and *Celebrations of Life.*

E

EARTH FIRST! The radical environmental group Earth First! was formed in 1980 in the southwestern United States. The group has often been compared with and described as more radical than **Greenpeace**. Both organizations focus on direct action, though Earth First! has had nothing like the success enjoyed by Greenpeace in gaining popular support and eliciting a sympathetic response from the news media. This is hardly surprising since Earth First! was formed as a strong reaction against conventional green groups and their ameliorative approach to environmental issues. Earth First! has also espoused **biocentrism** and **deep ecology** as well as an extremely loose organizational structure.

The founders of Earth First!, including David Foreman, its unofficial leader, were also strongly influenced by the ideas expressed by Edward Abbey in his well-known novel *The Monkey Wrench Gang*. Its fictional characters want to protect nature by engaging in acts of sabotage, which involve wrecking equipment and machinery. Earth First! came to the attention of the media and the public in 1981 by scaring the authorities responsible for the Glen Canyon Dam through an imaginative act. They created the illusion of a crack in the wall of the dam by rolling a huge strip of plastic over it. Other actions by some members of the group were less benign and mirrored the ideas of activists Foreman and Bill Haywood, who together edited *Ecodefense: A Field Guide to Monkeywrenching*. The guide promoted "monkeywrenching" (the destruction of machinery and equipment) as part of a campaign to sabotage the infrastructure being used to destroy wilderness areas. The proponents of monkeywrenching argued that it was nonviolent (*see* **NONVIOLENCE**), not subject to any central control or direction, and carefully aimed at vulnerable elements of a project.

The monkeywrenchers regarded themselves as warriors defending the wilderness from industrial civilization. By striking at companies involved in activities like logging they aimed to force them out of business by increasing the costs of equipment repair and insurance premiums. Actions by supporters of Earth First! included the destruction of equipment belonging to loggers and logging companies and, most controversially, the "spiking" of trees (the insertion of metal spikes into trees, damaging the chain saws used to cut them down). The authorities have argued that this poses a serious hazard to the loggers, though this has been denied by the activists. There have been deep divisions among supporters of Earth First! over the tactics used in support of their original motto: "No Compromise in Defense of Mother Earth!" For some, sabotage of power lines and equipment is entirely valid in defending the wilderness. Others advocate much stricter adherence to the principles of nonviolence.

The absence of organizational structures has left activists unconstrained in pursuing a wide range of approaches to achieving their primary objective, namely, the protection of wilderness areas. Earth First! has repudiated organizational structures to a far greater extent than most environmental groups. There is neither a formal leader or a leadership structure nor a formal membership. Communication between members is maintained through a magazine that appears about eight times a year, an annual meeting lasting one week, and, more recently, an annual conference. One indicator of the size of the membership has been the subscription list of the magazine, which by 1990 had 6,000 subscribers plus sales of another 3,000 copies. Following a serious conflict among members in 1990, subscriptions fell to around 3,000. It is difficult to estimate how many people participate in Earth First!, though groups are spread throughout the United States. A following has also developed in Europe as well as in Canada and Australia. Although much attention has been directed to some of the violent tactics employed by Earth First! supporters, their actions usually entail accepted forms of campaigning. These include using music and theater to entertain children and raise their awareness of environmental issues as well as standard approaches to lobbying for changes in policy.

Like other green political organizations, Earth First! has had to grapple with struggles between its founders, who have been fundamentally committed to deep ecology, and those members who have been concerned about the implications of their actions in terms of social justice and economic welfare. Developments within Earth First! parallel the conflict between **fundamentalists** and **realists** in many green political parties. In 1990 David Foreman withdrew from Earth First! on the grounds that the organization had taken on too many economic and social issues. Foreman was also concerned that many members were becoming less enthusiastic about the militant approach, for instance the spiking of trees. Foreman felt that the focus on social issues damaged the initial and fundamental objective of the organization, namely, to focus above all else on the defense of the earth.

EARTH ISLAND INSTITUTE. *See* **BROWER, DAVID.**

EARTH SUMMIT. *See* **UNITED NATIONS CONFERENCE ON THE ENVIRONMENT AND DEVELOPMENT (UNCED).**

ECOFEMINISM. As with many other social movements, sections of the feminist movement have developed a strong interest in **ecology.**

The range of arguments about the connection between the concerns of feminists and the protection and preservation of nature is fairly diverse. Some themes, however, arise quite frequently. They include the assumption by many ecofeminists that women are inherently closer to nature than men. This ties in with arguments, contested within the feminist movement itself, about fundamental traits that can (or cannot) be ascribed to females rather than to males. Some feminist thinkers, like Carolyn Merchant in her book *The Death of Nature*, have suggested that the distinction in Western societies between culture and nature caused women, who are seen as closer to nature, to be regarded as socially and culturally inferior to men.

Some ecofeminists have employed this argument about the proximity of women to nature to suggest that patriarchy, the control of a disproportionately large share of society by men, lies at the core of the devastation of nature. This argument is similar to that posited in **social ecology** about hierarchy as the source of environmental destruction. Some ecofeminists consider women to be more likely than any other group to become aligned with efforts to protect the environment. Not surprisingly, many of these assumptions are challenged by other feminists who question suppositions about the role of women and their potential contributions to all areas of social life.

ECOLO. The Belgian green party that represents the Walloon population. Ecolo was founded in March 1980, and its origins are more diverse and complex than those of **Agalev**. Since the early 1970s a variety of groups had been formed to contest elections either on a platform promoting direct democracy, including a group called Démocratie Nouvelle (New Democracy), or combining democratic and ecological principles, like Combat pour l'Écologie et l'Autogestion. By the late 1970s these groups and others like Ecopol and Ecolog (which partly represented segments of the **Friends of the Earth**) had laid the foundations for Ecolo. Paul Lannoye, who left the Rassemblement Wallon (Walloon Union) in 1971 to form Démocratie Nouvelle, was a central figure in the development of Ecolo. The immediate spur to its creation was the success of a loose association called Europe-Écologie in the 1979 elections to the European parliament. Europe-Écologie did better than any other green party, attracting 5.1 percent of votes cast by the Walloons.

In 1981 Ecolo, with 5.9 percent of the Walloon vote, gained two seats in the Belgian lower house. It improved slightly on this performance in 1985, gaining 6.2 percent of the vote and five seats. In 1987 it gained 6.4 percent of the Walloon vote but only three seats. In the 1984 elections to the European parliament Ecolo secured 9.4 percent of the vote and a single seat. In the 1989 European elections Ecolo did even better, winning 16.6 percent of the vote and two seats. Similarly, at the national elections it secured 13.5 percent of the ballot in Wallonia and ten seats. However, like Agalev, Ecolo lost many supporters in 1995: its share of the national poll declined from 5.1 to 4 percent. The number of Ecolo delegates in the lower house was reduced as a consequence both of the election result and the reduction in the total number of seats available in the lower house from 212 to 150. Ecolo therefore lost four seats compared to 1991. This important reversal in the fortunes of Belgium's green parties has been attributed partially to the fear of many green voters that lack of support for the Socialist Party, which was under siege because of various corruption scandals, would result in the dismantling of many important aspects of the social security system by the conservative opposition. *See also* GREEN PARTIES, BELGIUM.

ECOLOGY. Originally a scientific term, "ecology" has been used to describe new political parties and social movements concerned about environmental issues as well as new ways of conceptualizing politics. In *What Is Ecology?* Denis Owen moves from its straightforward definition as the relationships between plants and animals and the environment in which they live to an argument about how human activities should not be considered separate from the living world, which is composed of both simple and complex systems of interrelationships. The notion of the connection between human beings and the rest of the living world has been a source of inspiration for supporters and sympathizers of the green movement. Owen states: "The first important lesson to learn is that man is part of nature and that the rest of nature was not put there for man to exploit, the claims of business, political and religious leaders notwithstanding." *See also* DEEP ECOLOGY.

EHRLICH, PAUL. (1932–). Best known for his controversial views on population growth and its impact on the environment, Ehrlich is the author of *The Population Bomb*. A biologist who has worked at Stanford University since 1959, his views have always provoked strong reactions, including a fierce debate in the 1970s with another biologist, **Barry Commoner**. *See also* MALTHUS, THOMAS ROBERT; POPULATION GROWTH.

EUROPEAN FEDERATION OF GREEN PARTIES. The European Federation of Green Parties comprised, in 1997, green parties from Austria, Belgium (Flanders and Wallonia), Bulgaria, Denmark, England, Estonia, Finland, France, Georgia, Germany, Greece, Hungary, Ireland, Luxembourg, Malta, the Netherlands (De Groenen and

Groen Links), Norway, Portugal, St. Petersburg in Russia, Scotland, Slovakia, Spain, Sweden, Switzerland, Ukraine, and Wales. Groups submitting applications to join the Federation included green parties from Andalusia and Catalonia, Armenia, and Azerbaijan, as well as from Latvia and Lithuania. European green parties that are not members of the federation include organizations in Cyprus, Jersey, Northern Ireland, Slovenia, and Turkey.

The federation is an ongoing attempt to lend coherence to the efforts of green parties to influence the direction of European politics. In June 1993 at a conference held in Masala, Finland, the federation agreed on a set of "guiding principles." These focused on the economy (patterns of consumption and production), citizenship (including a focus on equal rights for all individuals regardless of gender, age, race, religion, ethnic or national origin, sexual orientation, wealth, and health), democratization, and security. Some of these themes were articulated in a section entitled "the new citizenship," which called for the expansion of civil rights, democratic participation, human rights ("without discrimination on the basis of race, disability, gender, sexual orientation, religion, age or national or ethnic origin"), and protection for the rights of minorities. The federation opposed the strong reactions against newcomers to western Europe and called for a "humane immigration policy." It also supported proportional electoral systems.

The federation's principles included a pan-European strategy of ecological and social reform. Economic development was to focus on "cooperation not competition." Both free market economy and state-controlled economies were rejected, as they assumed no limits to economic growth. The European Greens emphasize "ecological sustainability, equity and social justice" and argue for "the protection of the diversity of ecological resources and the global commons." They also focus on the burden of debt affecting poor countries and the question of **population growth** and how it should be reduced. Europe was to foster more "self-reliant" national, regional, and local economies within a "Europe of Regions." Any attempt to measure the performance of the economy was to include all social and environmental costs, for instance, by imposing "ecological taxes" on resources like nonrenewable energy and activities that threatened the environment (*see* **CARBON TAXES; POLLUTER PAYS PRINCIPLE**). Recycling and repairing products were similarly emphasized.

The federation also proposed the conversion of the economy, for example, from the production of military equipment and the chemical industries toward new sectors like those focusing on reducing the consumption of energy, recycling, public transport, agriculture, forestry, nature protection, and environmentally sound technology.

Other themes included a total ban on the construction of nuclear power plants and the phasing out of existing facilities, as well as measures to reduce all forms of pollution. Forestry and agricultural practices would also be changed to prevent overproduction by the European Union and pollution and to protect endangered species and expand the size of forests.

The greens seek a more equitable distribution of wealth and resources between western, eastern and central Europe and the introduction of environmental safeguards across the continent. The federation also envisions a new European security system that would not be dominated by Western organizations like the North Atlantic Treaty Organization (NATO). Greater parliamentary control of military arrangements would be introduced and "regional security systems" created. Hence, there is a proposal to transform the Conference on Security and Cooperation in Europe into a "regional security organization" and improve funding of this agency as a replacement for NATO. The federation rejects nuclear weapons and calls for a comprehensive test ban treaty.

EXXON VALDEZ. The running aground of the oil tanker *Exxon Valdez* in March 1989 was one of the darkest moments in the succession of disasters of this kind. The responses of traditional political organizations to the related concerns brought up by the green movement have varied immensely. In some instances, there has been a huge effort by governments to shift public opinion in support of new, radical measures to prevent such potential catastrophes. In others, changes have been slow despite the obviousness of the problem. As early as 1922 the International Committee for Bird Protection (later named International Council for Bird Preservation) was worried about oil pollution of the oceans. Oil pollution increased in the 1960s, and incidents like the *Torrey Canyon* spill in 1967 received worldwide publicity.

Despite efforts to regulate the oil industry, there has been a string of disasters. On 24 March 1989 more than 10 million gallons of crude oil spilled into Prince William Sound, Alaska, from the *Exxon Valdez*. For over two decades scientists, environmentalists, and local citizens had warned of the dangers of such an accident in Prince William Sound. The political response to this calamity appeared to be appropriate; the U.S. Congress obtained assurances from the oil companies that they would only use double-hulled ships in Prince William Sound. However, this measure was never enforced by the government, since it was not prepared to challenge the powerful oil companies.

F

FOREMAN, DAVID. *See* **EARTH FIRST!**

FRANKLIN DAM. In Australia challenges to the institutional order by green groups rose in the late 1960s and had gained in intensity by the late 1970s, notably in the form of social movements like the one opposed to the construction of the proposed Franklin Dam in **Tasmania**. The campaign against the Franklin Dam, waged between 1979 and 1983, is one of the most striking examples of a rise in popular awareness of environmental problems and of the tensions between central and regional governments. If the changes that occurred during the 1970s in the government's approach to environmental issues were meant to defuse conflicts, they were a failure. In 1983 environmental issues featured prominently in an Australian federal election for the first time.

The question of states rights (that is, the rights of regional governments), which had preoccupied reformers for decades, now assumed a new significance. In the conflict over the proposed construction of a hydroelectric power system and the subsequent flooding of the Franklin and lower Gordon Rivers, the Tasmanian government confronted environmentalists who pleaded for federal intervention and more central regulation of environmental policy. Though the Australian Labor Party (ALP) supported environmentalists against the Franklin Dam, it refused to address the issue of states rights. In the 1983 federal election the conservative (Liberal and National) parties stood for the individual state's right to set its own environmental policy. The Liberal government sought to avoid confrontation by offering the Tasmanian government A$500 million for the construction of a coal-fired thermal power plant instead of the dam. When this offer was refused, the ALP announced that it would oppose the construction of the dam if it were elected. The party offered help to the Tasmanian government to diversify the methods of electricity production and to expand the tourist industry in order to create employment. These policies were crucial in attracting green votes in the 1983 election.

Once elected, the ALP government offered the Tasmanian Liberal government alternative schemes for creating employment. The rejection of this offer led the federal government to use existing legislation to override states rights. This decision has been interpreted as a major extension of the powers of the federal government. Still, the ALP government was reluctant to clash with state governments and finally came to an arrangement with the Tasmanian government, offering it compensation for money spent on the Franklin Dam project before it was halted, alternative employment programs, and subsidizing the supply of energy.

Though the ALP had sided with the green movement over the Franklin Dam, it was initially unable to respond to growing expectations of a more decisive environmental policy. It remained uncertain about taking sides between established interests, which favored development and the exploitation of states' resources, and the new green movements. Over time, the question of states rights appeared to become less important than the long-term social and economic implications of environmental protection.

The pressure on governments to incorporate environmentalism became apparent during and after the dispute over the Franklin Dam. The expectations of green groups and their supporters exerted a decisive influence on ALP policies in the 1980s. Each new conflict over environmental policy appeared to increase both public awareness of environmental issues and the economic and political stakes.

The battle to protect the Franklin and Gordon Rivers was significant for a number of other reasons. The Tasmanian Wilderness Society, later renamed the **Wilderness Society,** emerged from this campaign and provided a basis for getting the environment onto the national political agenda. The radicalism of the Wilderness Society epitomized the new generation of environmentalists, engaged in political activities. The campaign against the Franklin Dam also created new opportunities for coalitions between environmental groups. In a historic effort to coordinate and render more effective actions against the Franklin Dam, environmental groups formed a coalition that included the **Australian Conservation Foundation,** state conservation councils, national parks associations, and 70 branches of the Wilderness Society. It rallied the support of around 800 conservation groups with up to half a million members. Environmentalists were successful in attracting media attention by inviting international figures like David Bellamy to participate in their campaign. The arrest of 1,340 activists between January and March 1983 attracted widespread attention and accelerated the ascent of the green movement in Australia.

FRIENDS OF THE EARTH. In 1969 **David Brower,** the executive director of the **Sierra Club** since 1952, parted company with this powerful organization and became the founder of Friends of the Earth. Although Brower had effectively been forced to leave the Sierra Club by members who felt that he was primarily responsible for some of its financial problems, he had been very popular, particularly because of his espousal of a more proactive stance in trying to change public policy. Brower was able to shape Friends of the Earth to attract the growing sections of the population that favored more direct forms of political action than those deployed by well-established environmental groups. Moreover, like the student and other protest movements of that era, Friends of the Earth sought a basis for support that transcended the boundaries of nation-states.

In keeping with the spirit of political involvement and participation by the grass roots, Friends of the Earth gave its established branches in other countries a high degree of autonomy in determining their campaign strategies and internal organization. Following the establishment of its first office in San Francisco, Friends of the Earth installed themselves in London and Paris in 1970 and subsequently in most Western democracies as well as in other countries. Among the questions initially raised by Friends of the Earth were the protection of wildlife, prevention of pollution, and the development of **alternative energy** forms such as solar power. However, like many other green groups, they have assumed many additional issues, like **green consumerism**, protection of the **ozone layer**, and the **greenhouse effect**. Some of the leading figures in the green movement, like Jonathon Porritt in England, have served as directors of national branches of Friends of the Earth. In Britain the organization has grown steadily, from a membership of 12,000 in 1980 to 120,000 in 1989 and 200,000 in 1993. Apart from the extension of the Friends of the Earth into many other countries, in 1990, the organization coalesced with the Environmental Policy Institute and the Oceanic Society.

FUNDAMENTALISTS (FUNDIS). The term "Fundi," or fundamentalist, is derived from conflict between factions of **Die Grünen** in Germany. In the early years, the main ideological conflict in Die Grünen was between the more conservative "pure" environmentalists and those who wanted to unite **ecology** with left-wing politics. In the end the latter predominated and created a new division: between the fundamentalists (who objected strongly to any notion of cooperation with a traditional political party like the Social Democrats in order to form a government and were anxious to maintain close links and accountability to social movements and other radical groups operating outside the confines of parliamentary politics) and the **realists** ("Realos").

These terms were gradually absorbed by other countries trying to distinguish between factions emerging in green parties. The fundamentalists are generally credited with being more radical and interested in grassroots involvement in decision making than the realists (*see* **DIRECT DEMOCRACY**). They assume that green movements, as they become more involved in parliamentary politics, are in danger of losing their spontaneous character and being afflicted by processes of bureaucratization and professionalization. Fundamentalists have always questioned elitism and party politics, and both leaders and the rank and file were critical of parliamentary politics. The strength of the fundamentalists appeared to lie in their close contact with activists within green parties.

The two most striking innovations introduced by Die Grünen were the control of delegates by limiting their term in office and allowing members to dismiss them. The first was enshrined in the principle of rotation, which stipulated that a delegate could only serve a limited term in office, although reelection for one term was permitted. The second, the imperative mandate, was designed to make delegates accountable to members and subject them to recall at any time. These principles were not strictly adhered to, and some commentators have argued that rather than achieving direct democracy, Die Grünen created new forms of hierarchy and centralized control by career politicians and leading personalities.

However, Die Grünen has used legislative bodies both to promote some of the issues raised by social movements and to demonstrate the possibility of grassroots democracy, including the convening of open meetings and committees at all levels for all members. Decisions have been predominantly based on agreement of all delegates—the consensus principle—rather than rule by majorities. Although generally the fundamentalists have in recent times been on the retreat in green parties (for instance, following Die Grünen's abolition of restrictions on how long a party leader might remain in office and formation of coalitions with other parties), they have made a significant impact on how green parties approach parliamentary politics. Green parties tend to be more decentralized than the major parties, allowing for a large degree of autonomy in the formulation of local and regional party platforms and financial management. The social movements have contributed considerable expertise in parliamentary activities, especially in enabling parties like Die Grünen to launch inquiries into government activities and assisting in the formulation of the party program.

A striking weakness of the fundamentalists has been their failure to attract the support of ordinary members or sympathizers of the green parties. Most supporters of green parties have tended to express a preference for involvement in government, even if it means forming coalitions with traditional political parties. Although this may result in short-term rather than long-term objectives, most supporters of green parties appear to prefer the possibility of achieving some of their objectives, even if they must compromise on other issues or defer the realization of certain goals. The major strength of the fundamentalists lies in their ability to broaden the agenda and establish principles for long-term change. *See also* **REALISTS**.

FUNDIS. *See* **FUNDAMENTALISTS.**

G

GAIA HYPOTHESIS. The term "Gaia" is derived from the Greek word for earth. The Oxford dictionary definition of Gaia refers to the earth "as a self-regulating system in which living matter collectively defines and maintains the conditions for the continuance of life." The Gaia hypothesis has been promoted since the 1970s by James Lovelock, a British scientist who worked for the National Aeronautics and Space Administration on a project to discover whether or not there was life on Mars. Lovelock, in trying to establish the composition of the gases surrounding Mars, began to speculate about the process of maintaining life on earth. In *Gaia: A New Look at Life on Earth*, Lovelock suggests that "life itself" shapes the composition of the earth, the atmosphere, and the oceans and thereby challenges the customary view that "life adapted to the planetary conditions as it and they evolved their separate ways."

Lovelock acknowledges that his belief in the existence of a complex system that can act as a "single living entity" (Mother Earth) cannot be tested scientifically. Still, his argument, which has attracted considerable interest among some supporters of the green movement, is based on three crucial observations. First, while for about 3,500 million years and despite significant variations in the heat emitted from the sun, there has been very little change in the climate of the earth. Second, the atmosphere appears to be not so much a biological product but a biological construction: "not living, but like a cat's fur, a bird's feathers, or the paper of a wasp's nest, an extension of a living system designed to maintain a chosen environment." Third, the atmosphere has appeared to have always been ideal for supporting life on earth. This, he suggests, must be more than a highly improbable coincidence.

Lovelock therefore defines Gaia "as a complex entity involving the earth's biosphere, atmosphere, oceans, and soil; the totality constituting a feedback or cybernetic system which seeks an optional physical and chemical environment for life on this planet." The conclusion by many writers using the Gaia hypothesis is that nature will survive the onslaught on it by human beings. The question is whether or not human beings will withstand nature's response to their assault on it.

GERMANY. As in other western European nations, the predominance of economic development after World War II led to little emphasis on environmental protection as a core component of the national policy agenda. In the Federal Republic of Germany, the only hint of a change in focus came from the leader of the opposition Social Democratic Party, Willy Brandt. In a 1961 speech Brandt proclaimed the necessity for turning the sky over the Ruhr River blue again. The situation in the German Democratic Republic was even worse.

It was not until the late 1960s, and then in West but not East Germany, that this exclusive attentiveness to economic development began to weaken. The formation of a coalition government between the Social Democratic and the Free Democratic (Liberal) Parties in 1969 was followed by the transfer of control over measures to combat pollution from the Ministry of Health to the Ministry of the Interior, which was eventually, in 1986, named the Ministry of the Environment, Nature Conservation, and Nuclear Safety.

Historically, however, the powers to legislate, manage, and regulate the environment have been vested in the states. There is also an enduring tradition in Germany of a legal basis for the protection of the environment. A key change to the involvement of the states in regulating environmental protection occurred in 1972 in the form of an amendment to the Constitution. This conferred on the federal government the power to enact legislation which in effect overrode the states in areas like air and noise pollution and waste management. In addition, the federal government was able to issue guidelines on the enactment of state legislation on matters such as water quality and planning as well as the preservation and conservation of nature. Another significant action was the formation of the 1974 Federal Environmental Agency.

Despite these important changes, spurred on by key figures in both parties of the coalition, the predominance of economic considerations in policy making and the decision to expand massively the system of nuclear power plants brought a powerful counterresponse. This came in the form of **citizens' initiatives** for environmental protection, **antinuclear protests**, and the formation of a green political organization, **Die Grünen**. There was also increasing concern over **acid rain**, the destruction of forests, and the quality of air and water. By the mid-1980s, following a sequence of successes by Die Grünen at regional and national elections, traditional (conservative, liberal, and socialist) political organizations, trade unions, and business groups realized that a fundamental shift in values and priorities had occurred. Even if economic considerations were still predominant, the environment was now widely regarded as a crucial issue in deliberations over future directions.

Apart from the importance of the federal structure, environmental policy making in the Federal Republic of Germany has been shaped by a tradition of formal cooperation between government and influential interest groups, notably industrial organizations. There is also an enduring and successful practice of informal cooperation between the government, and opposition, and bureaucracy. In the 1970s and early 1980s both the informal approach to cooperation and the formal corporatist system appeared to be working against the inclusion of new political movements. In response to pressure by the green movement and widespread skepticism about the appropriateness of the prevailing approaches to environmental questions, the federal government, led by the Christian Democrats, began to play a more active role than any previous government in considering the possibility of including Die Grünen in the informal processes of deliberation over policy and promoting environmental protection at a national and international level. At the national level, the government made some advances in improving the quality of air and water, even though there is still a great deal to be accomplished in these and other spheres, like reversing the deterioration of forests.

In 1994 the Constitution of the Federal Republic was amended to include a specific commitment to protect "the natural foundations of life for future generations." The government also played a leading role in international fora, notably at the 1992 **UN Conference on the Environment and Development,** in applying pressure on other countries to follow its lead in requiring a total ban of chlorofluorocarbons and pushing other members of the European Union to implement commonly agreed-upon directives on environmental policy.

The federal government has also had to deal with new challenges, notably those arising from the unification of Germany and the environmental problems associated with East Germany. Although the Constitution of the (former) German Democratic Republic did include a clause on the protection of nature and plans for preventing pollution, no regulations were implemented. The most acute problems were the contamination of land and water caused by uranium mining over several decades, the decline in air quality largely due to the use of brown coal in power plants, and the safety of nuclear reactors.

The federal government has taken on these assignments by introducing to the East its own structures for environmental protection and establishing a specific time frame for achieving its objectives. This has led to a huge loss in employment in the East. Apart from subsidies based on higher taxes on citizens in the West, the federal government has funded numerous projects (and thereby created new jobs) to solve environmental problems. In addition, there were rapid moves to close down nuclear power plants in the East.

The government of the Federal Republic has also attempted to raise a considerable amount of revenue specifically to address environmental problems and has been among the leaders in introducing a **carbon tax,** on those who contribute to carbon dioxide emissions. Although, as in most other countries, its focus is still very much on economic growth and production, the Federal Republic has begun to develop long-term strategies and apply the **precautionary principle** in dealing with concerns about the environment. There has been a shift toward more dialogue, a better-informed public, and the introduction of improved procedures for handling environmental issues. The government has also begun to play a more innovative and strategic role in environmental policy and promote international cooperation.

GLOBAL 2000 REPORT, THE. *The Global 2000 Report* summarizes the findings of an investigation by the U.S. Council on Environmental Quality. The report was commissioned by the government and first published in 1980. It contains a critique of previous accounts of the current and future condition of the environment and its own analysis of trends. Like many of the critiques of the **limits to growth** thesis, the study questions prevailing presuppositions about political and social values as well as the availability of mineral reserves and fossil fuels. In particular *The Global 2000 Report* points out that *The Limits to Growth* failed to produce accurate analyses of problems in particular regions and recognize that the type of economic growth that occurs can hugely influence the rate of depletion of natural resources.

In the same vein as *The Limits to Growth* and other reports, *The Global 2000 Report* draws attention to the many possibilities for disaster if prevailing trends are not addressed through cooperation between nation-states. In particular, the report points to the links between **population growth,** the state of the environment, and the depletion of natural resources. The report also gives a number of specific predictions for the year 2000: namely, an increase in the frequency of natural disasters caused by human interventions; the destruction of tropical rainforests, which would lead to the extinction of hundreds of thousands of plant and animal species; a 50 percent increase in the population of the world, with most of the growth taking place in poorer countries; an increase in the gap between rich and poor; and the diminution of resources like land, water, and oil.

The Council on Environmental Quality published a further report, *Global Future: Time to Act.* This outlines measures, like investment in renewable sources of energy and sustainable land use, that could be implemented to address these problems. There is also an emphasis on improved coordination between government agencies as well as the establishment of new structures.

GOLDSMITH, EDWARD. *See A BLUEPRINT FOR SURVIVAL*; **DEINDUSTRIALIZATION.**

GRASSROOTS DEMOCRACY. *See* **DIRECT DEMOCRACY.**

GREECE. Though far less developed than northern European countries, in the 1960s and 1970s Greece experienced very high rates of economic growth. The focus on economic development has left many pressing environmental problems unaddressed both in political debate and policy implementation. Until 1989 the established parties felt no pressure from environmentalist political organizations, and the poor performance by the latter since then has allowed the major parties to retain their focus on economic rather than environmental issues.

In policy, there is a conspicuous difference between legislation, or intent, and implementation, or practice. To a degree, Greece's 1981 affiliation with the European Union placed some pressure on the government to enact new legislation. The obstacles to its implementation were substantial, however. The Greek constitution, framed in 1975 after the resignation of the military junta in 1974, provided for "the protection of the natural and cultural environment" by the state (Article 24). There were also pledges to protect forests. In addition, the government established a National Council for Physical Planning and Protection of the Environment in 1976. In the 1980s various governments formed ministries that combined the administration of environmental issues with other areas of responsibility. The net outcome of these initiatives, including the attempts to implement directives issued by the European Union, has been far from favorable.

There are at least two major obstacles: first, the focus on economic development and the pressure to maintain the pace of industrialization and second, the divisions in the structure of public administration and lack of coordination among government agencies. Many different ministries have had responsibilities pertaining to environmental protection. Often, protection of the environment is regarded as of secondary importance if there is a potential for dispute with industrial or economic interests. Still, there are indications that some government agencies, particularly at the local level, are exploring possibilities for **sustainable development**, particularly in the area of tourism and the need to prevent pollution in order to maintain this industry. Among the most pressing problems affecting Greece are air pollution (particularly the smog over Athens), deforestation, and noise pollution. Other issues that the government needs to address are the disposal of wastes, water pollution, and soil erosion.

A difficulty in dealing with these issues is the lack of public awareness about their urgency. The growth of environmental groups may alert more people to these problems and is certainly a novelty in the political life of the country. However, their access to policy making is limited. Government agencies, through membership in the European Union and international meetings, have nonetheless become more aware of measures that can be adopted to influence both business and industrial organizations, as well as individual citizens, to give greater consideration to the environment. *See also* **GREEN PARTIES, GREECE.**

GREEN-ALTERNATIVE EUROPEAN LINK. *See* **GREEN PARTIES, EUROPEAN PARLIAMENT.**

GREEN BELT MOVEMENT. The driving force behind this movement is **Wangari Maathai**, who grew up in Kenya and studied in the United States. On her return to Kenya Maathai became interested in altering the trend toward desertification of the landscape. An active member of the Kenyan National Council for Women, Maathai also has connections with prominent people in **UNEP.** The first step toward the Green Belt movement was taken on 5 June 1977, the day set aside for World Environment Day. Seven trees were planted in Nairobi. Apart from securing corporate sponsorship for tree-planting, for instance from Mobil Oil, Maathai ensured that her initiative was backed by organizations like UNEP and by local political elites.

Organizations like the Danish Voluntary Fund for Developing Countries, the Norwegian Forestry Society, and the Spirit of Stockholm Foundation also provided valuable financial support. Hundreds of tree nurseries were established, employing thousands of people, mainly women, and involving participation by hundreds of thousands of schoolchildren. Apart from the success in reversing some of the damage inflicted on the landscape through the planting of millions of trees, the movement has raised awareness about the connection between development and environmental protection. It has also promoted a number of other goals, including the creation of employment opportunities in agriculture, improving the status of women, and undertaking research in collaboration with universities.

GREEN CONSUMERISM. Green consumerism entails enjoying a prosperous lifestyle without destroying the environment. For instance, in a bestseller entitled *The Green Consumer Guide*, John Elkington and Julia Hailes suggest that the choices we make in purchasing goods contribute significantly to the quality of the environment. Apart from offering specific advice on products, these advocates of green consumerism describe how major corporations have implemented radical changes in the manufacture of products like aerosols to ensure that they do not contain chlorofluorocarbons that destroy the **ozone layer.** They also make several key points about how green consumers should select goods. For instance, the products should not pose a danger to anyone's health; have a critical impact on the environment as a result of their manufacture, use, or disposal; require large amounts of energy to manufacture, use, or dispose of; expend materials from species or environments that are at risk; entail cruelty to animals; or be counter to the interest of developing nations.

Some of the critics of green consumerism, like Sandy Irvine in her book *Beyond Green Consumerism,* have recognized that the approach advocated by Elkington and Hailes can enable the green movement to exert immense pressure on business and industrial groups to change dramatically the entire process of production or risk losing their customers. However, along with many other proponents of **the limits to growth** thesis, Irvine is skeptical about the possibilities for overcoming some of the fundamental problems of our economic and social system. These critics argue that it is impossible, even for highly educated green consumers, to be fully cognizant of the involvement by a particular manufacturer or corporation in a wide range of activities, some of which may have an adverse impact on the environment. More significantly, they develop the following argument: in order to address environmental questions we will need to do much more than substitute goods that have been produced, will be used, and will be disposed in ways that damage the environment with those that have a less deleterious impact on it. Rather, we will need to consume less.

Green consumerism, they maintain, perpetuates the illusion that we can maintain affluent lifestyles without harming the environment. In addition, the critics suggest that only fairly affluent people can afford the selectivity and lifestyle implied by the proponents of green consumerism. The main issue, however, centers on the limits to growth, diminution of energy and raw materials as a consequence of **population growth,** and reduction in land available for waste disposal (see also the arguments by Herman Daly for a **steady-state economy**). At present, however, there is growing support for green consumerism, especially in the context of arguments for **sustainable development** and the possibility of combining economic development with environmental protection.

GREEN PARTIES, AUSTRALIA. The recent origins of green political organizations in **Australia** can be traced to the appearance in the 1970s of community group opposition to specific developments. A striking example of a popular protest movement was the radical Green Ban movement, which involved cooperation between industrial workers and middle-class environmentalists in New South Wales. Workers from the militant Builders Labourers Federation joined in protests against plans for development and the destruction of parklands, established communities, and historical buildings. The unions imposed work-bans on projects they considered to be environmentally hazardous. Forty-two bans were applied over a four-year period (from 1971 to 1975) and blocked development projects valued at hundreds of millions of dollars.

These protests in Sydney were predated by a momentous campaign that arose on the island state of **Tasmania**, in response to the impending destruction of Lake Pedder to promote a hydroelectric scheme. **The United Tasmania Group (UTG)**, which was created in response to the failure by traditional political parties to consider the full implications of this action, was among the first green political organizations in the world to compete in state elections. The conflict over the flooding of Lake Pedder is widely believed to have contributed to the upsurge of green political organizations and is regarded as a source of inspiration for many leading activists in more recent campaigns. In addition, it gave rise to associations like the Save Lake Pedder Committee (1967), a group with a far more radical orientation than environmentalist associations of the past. Although the protest groups were ultimately unsuccessful in preserving Lake Pedder, they precipitated the growth of a movement that eventually influenced the national agenda on environmental policies.

The program of the UTG contained some of the classic tenets of green political organizations, including a critique of the "misuse of power" as well as a focus on social justice and on participatory democracy (*see* **DIRECT DEMOCRACY**). The emphasis on values like grassroots participation had a far-reaching impact on organizations that followed the UTG, for example the Tasmanian Wilderness Society (later renamed the **Wilderness Society**). This organization, formed in 1976, became one of the most influential groups in the development of the green movement and provided a loose, yet highly effective, organizational structure for mobilizing protestors. Groups like the Wilderness Society helped get the environment onto the national political agenda, as in the campaign, between 1979 and 1983, to prevent the creation of the **Franklin Dam**.

Another association that has played a crucial part in mobilizing support for green political organizations is the **Australian Conservation Foundation**. Both the Wilderness Society (through its mobilization of activists) and the Australian Conservation Foundation (through its adoption of a more radical stance) were to influence environmental policies, first of the Australian Labor Party (ALP) and later of other established parties, notably the **Australian Democrats**.

Apart from providing a focus for green campaigns, Tasmania also had an electoral system that made it easier than in most other states for minor parties to secure representation in the state parliament. The breakthrough came in 1989, when five green independent candidates, who polled 17 percent of the vote across the state, were elected to the House of Assembly, which is made up of 36 members. The independents also held the balance of power and signed a momentous "accord" with the ALP. The greens agreed to support an ALP government in exchange for some major policy concessions, notably the extension of wilderness and forest areas covered by World Heritage protection and national park status, guarantees of staffing and other resources for the green parliamentary delegates, access to parliamentary committees and reforms in parliamentary procedures, and standing orders to ensure greater transparency of the financial interests of parliamentary delegates.

Many of these measures were implemented, particularly those pertaining to the protection of forests and wilderness. The accord accelerated a shift in values; environmental considerations were taken into account much more consistently than in the past in political and other institutional processes and decision making. The accord did not entail the formation of a coalition government, however, and the ALP was able, in effect, to govern on its own. The party remained constantly under pressure by green delegates who questioned the slow pace of reforms. After 18 months the accord fell apart after a dispute over the closure of schools and differing perceptions on how to deal with economic and environmental issues, notably the question of whether to apply quotas on the export of wood chips from Tasmania. The formal disintegration of the accord in September 1991 was directly linked to arguments over the wood chip quota.

The ALP remained in government until February 1992, and by then many voters had become disillusioned with the Labor-Green experiment. Although the vote for the ALP in the 1992 election was its lowest ever, the green independents retained their five seats. However, the latter's share of the vote was reduced to 13.4 percent, and a new Liberal government was elected on a platform that opposed many green reforms. In 1996 the greens lost another seat in Tasmania, and their share of the vote declined to 11 percent.

Tasmania and Western Australia are the two states in which green political organizations have managed to secure sufficient support to send representatives to the federal upper house, the Senate. The origins of the Western Australia Green Party reflect both failures and successes of other green political associations, including the short-lived upsurge of the **Nuclear Disarmament Party (NDP)** in the early 1980s. The demise of organizations like the NDP contributed to the long delay in the formation of a national green party. For a long time the gap was filled by the Australian Democrats.

In 1991 there was speculation that a national green party would emerge prior to the 1993 federal election, following discussions between conservation groups, the Australian Democrats, and Green Independents in states like Tasmania and Western Australia. However, a number of factors hindered the development of a full-fledged national green party. These include the electoral system which creates a disincentive for minor parties to enter elections to the lower house, the House of Representatives; the desire of green political activists in state organizations to maintain their independence from any federal structures; and the ability of other parties to adopt many aspects of the green agenda. In addition, the negative experiences of the NDP have made environmentalists wary of transforming a social movement into a vehicle for parliamentary politics.

By 1996 a new political organization called the Australian Greens, which formed a "confederation of like-minded groups" in various states, had emerged. Though the branches in each state are "autonomous," they contribute to the formulation of policy at the national level and are supposed to "accept the positions of spokespeople from the Australian Greens." However, the state organizations are "not bound by any national policy or decision of the Australian Greens or other state groups." In 1996 organizations that were associated with the Australian Greens covered all states expect Western Australia, though there was a "working arrangement" with groups operating there.

Proposals for the formation of a green party that includes the Australian Democrats have not come to fruition even though there is a high level of correspondence between the aims of both organizations. Following the March 1996 federal election, a member of the Western Australia Green Party, Christabel Chamarette, lost her seat in the Senate, though Bob Brown, a leading figure in the Australian Greens, secured a second seat for green political parties.

Green political organizations are still regarded with suspicion by political activists who are uneasy about traditional forms of parliamentary and electoral politics. They have also been aware of the difficulties of moving from focus upon a single issue to addressing a wide range of questions and the problems of organization. At the state level, particularly in Tasmania and Western Australia, green activists interested in electoral politics have been relatively successful in coordinating their activities. However, prior to the 1990 federal elections, the overriding impression, particularly in states like New South Wales, was one of disorganization. National associations like the Australian Conservation Foundation and the Wilderness Society responded to this situation by recommending that their supporters vote for the Australian Democrats. The Australian Conservation Foundation and the Wilderness Society made two exceptions: in 1990 voters in Tasmania were urged to support the UTG and in Western Australia, the Western Australia Green Party.

Apart from the UTG and the Western Australia Green Party, the Democrats are the only other minor party that has succeeded in exploiting the environment as an election issue. In 1990 the Democrats appealed to environmentalists by adopting, in their advertising, the widely recognized triangular symbol used in the campaign against the Franklin Dam almost a decade earlier. They also claimed to be "the original environmental party" and to have fought consistently for environmental protection. In the first assertion they ignored the formation of the UTG in 1972. On the issue of consistency, their leader, Senator Janine Haines, suggested that the Democrats had always been far ahead of other parties on environmental matters. Haines drew attention to initiatives by the Democrats like the introduction of the first bill to save the Franklin, the first bill to ban all ozone-depleting substances by 1995, and a bill to rescind the sales tax on recycled paper and to campaigns in the 1970s to combat soil salinity and degradation.

Support for green independent senators as well as for parties like the Democrats reflects the concern of many people, including a number of those voting for other parties, that the traditional parties either do not have answers or lack the will to face many of the central problems confronting society. For some, the preoccupation of traditional parties with maximizing votes is related to their failure to develop appropriate policies. There is a widespread perception that independent green senators and Democrats are more likely to address issues like environmental protection or to apply pressure on the traditionals to do so. Although all political parties now devote considerable attention to environmental issues, they are expected to demonstrate a greater consistency in securing protection of the environment. *See also* **AUSTRALIA.**

GREEN PARTIES, AUSTRIA. The Vereinte Grüne Österreichs (VGÖ) (United Greens), a moderate and reformist green party, was formed in 1982. It gained its main basis of support from campaigns against nuclear power. The Alternative Liste Österreichs (ALÖ) (Alternative List), a more radical green party, was also formed in 1982. Support for this party arose principally from social movements, including those that campaigned for peace and nuclear disarmament and on issues directly affecting less developed countries.

As early as 1977 citizens' lists (*Bürgerliste*) contested local elections in Salzburg and attracted 5 percent of the vote. These results anticipated the emergence of green parties in the 1980s. Following the referendum on nuclear power in 1978, green groups did not form a political party in time for the 1979 national elections. When they competed in the 1983 national elections the VGÖ and ALÖ only attracted 1.9 and 1.4 percent of the vote, respectively. Consequently, they did not obtain any seats in the national parliament. By contrast, in 1986, by presenting a united front under the title Die Grüne Alternative (Green Alternative) the two parties gained 4.8 percent of the vote and eight seats in the national parliament.

The unity between the two parties was short-lived due to their diverse origins. The ALÖ was, in many respects, not dissimilar to **Die Grünen** in Germany, and borrowed heavily from its platform. It had close links to new social movements and emphasized participation by activists. The VGÖ was a much more conservative organization, and much of its program, apart from environmental questions, resembled that of traditional political organizations. However, most of its supporters, like those of the ALÖ, voted for the coalition rather than their individual party.

In 1990 Die Grüne Alternative again received 4.8 percent of the vote and secured 10 seats. The VGÖ only gained 2 percent of the vote. Die Grüne Alternative also performed well in the 1991 state elections in Vienna (9.1 percent and seven seats) and 1992 presidential elections (5.7 percent went to their candidate Robert Jungk). In 1994 Die Grüne Alternative increased its share of the vote to 7 percent and its representation to 13 out of 183 seats in the national parliament. However, the party suffered a setback in 1995 when it attracted only 4.8 percent of the vote and lost four seats. The outcome of the elections to the European parliament was somewhat more favorable; the party attracted 6.8 percent of the vote and acquired one of the 21 allotted seats.

The organizational structures of the VGÖ and ALÖ differed in the following respects. The VGÖ was more like conventional political parties, with close ties between the national and regional organizations. By contrast, the ALÖ regional organizations were relatively independent of the national organization and had a profound distrust of hierarchical forms of association. The emergence of Die Grüne Alternative appeared to represent a compromise and reflected a keen awareness of the problems experienced by Die Grünen in Germany. At first, Die Grüne Alternative vigorously avoided what it regarded as the weaknesses of a professional political party. Thus limitations were imposed, for example, on simultaneously occupying a seat in parliament and an executive position in the party. Die Grüne Alternative did not, however, adopt the principle of rotation of delegates or subscribe to the imperative mandate, and it permitted delegates to serve several terms in parliament or in executive office (*see* **DIRECT DEMOCRACY**).

Moreover, Die Grüne Alternative rapidly developed a pragmatic approach once it secured representation in parliament and made a greater effort than other parties, relative to the number of seats it held, to introduce new legislation and launch inquiries into the activities of the government. It drew attention to patronage and corrupt practices in politics and business. Above all, in the 1990s, Die Grüne Alternative adopted a more professional approach with an eye to expanding its electoral base and gaining favorable coverage by the media for its policies and programs.

There was initially a clear contrast between the respective programs and policies of the VGÖ and ALÖ. The former concentrated on the individual citizen, support for the family, and civil liberties. It had, in many respects, an antistatist program, emphasizing deregulation and privatization in economic affairs and a less interventionist role in social policy. By contrast, the ALÖ favored statutory intervention in all these areas, including such measures as nationalization and regulation of incomes. Moreover, the ALÖ seized on issues articulated by social movements, notably their preoccupation with peace and nuclear disarmament. Die Grüne Alternative took up some of the concerns expressed by the VGÖ, though it also developed more fully ALÖ policies on the economy, reforming the political system, health and social security, peace, and many other questions.

In the 1990s the question of reform of the political system included issues like greater citizen involvement in policy making, as well as in determining the direction of schools; work conditions; and strengthening the role of parliament. Special attention was paid to the rights of social minorities and disadvantaged groups. Die Grüne Alternative opposed Austria's application for membership in the European Union. Once this effort failed, it did not undertake to work for the withdrawal of Austria, but to influence the union from within.

The formation of Austria's green parties is significant, since it disrupted the constant dominance of the political system by the established parties. At the local level, citizens' lists achieved some notable successes in the early 1980s. The same applies at the regional level, for example, an alliance between the VGÖ and ALÖ attracted 13 percent of the vote and four seats in elections to the regional council of Vorarlberg. The citizens' list in Salzburg was one of the most successful in Austria, gaining 5.6 percent of the vote (and two seats) in 1977, 17.7 percent (and seven seats) in 1982, and 10.1 percent (and four seats) in 1987. In Graz an alternative list polled 7 percent and secured four seats on the city council. In the late 1980s the fortunes of green parties did not improve much due partly to internal disputes and partly to the proliferation of people and groups claiming to represent green interests at local, regional, and national levels.

In 1986, one of the leading figures in the green movement in Austria, Freda Meissner-Blau, competed in the presidential elections. Although she received only 5.5 percent of the vote, this was sufficient to force a second-round contest between candidates for the conservative People's Party and the Socialist Party.

Backing for green parties has come largely from younger voters and the well educated. The strongest bases for support are in the city, not the country. The potential support for green parties has been estimated at up to 20 percent during the 1980s and even higher by the end of the 1980s and early 1990s. Apart from being relatively young and well educated, supporters of the greens are more likely than other voters to have postmaterialist values (*see* **POSTMATERIALISM**). In the 1994 parliamentary elections there was also much greater support for Die Grüne Alternative among women than men. Protests against energy policies have long been used to mobilize support for green parties. In one campaign, people succeeded in blocking the construction of a nuclear power plant at Zwentendorf near Vienna. In a referendum conducted in 1978 most people voted to ban nuclear energy. In 1984 the green movement was triumphant in a campaign that was crucial to its development when it succeeded in preventing the building of a hydroelectric power plant at Hainburg on the Danube.

The prospects for Die Grüne Alternative to implement its ideas at a national level are still slim, though it can continue to bring about changes in its policies that are eventually adopted by the major parties. At the state or local level there are possibilities for directly influencing policy making and its implementation. In the city council of Salzburg Die Grüne Alternative became part of the coalition in power. In 1994 Die Grüne Alternative also secured a ministerial post in the provincial government in Tyrol. There are also other prospects for the formation of coalitions, notably in the city government of Vienna.

GREEN PARTIES, BELGIUM. Because of ethnic and cultural divisions, there are no longer any truly national parties in Belgium. Mirroring these divisions, two green parties were formed: **Agalev** ("for an alternative way of life") representing the Flemish community and **Ecolo** representing the Walloons. The most high-profile and well-known member of Agalev was Ludo Dierickx, a founding member of the party who initially became a member of the lower house and later, from 1987, a member of the Senate. An important factor in the success of Agalev was the influence of its party secretary, Leo Cox, who exercised shrewd political judgment in dealing with the issues confronting it.

As with most other green parties, the bases of support of Ecolo and Agalev are primarily among the young and well educated living in urban rather than rural locations. Like many other green parties Ecolo and Agalev have been suspicious of conventional party structures. Both trace their roots to a variety of social movements and are extremely wary of developing hierarchical structures. However, Agalev has been much more insistent than Ecolo on maintaining a grassroots approach. Ecolo, while maintaining fairly strong party discipline, has remained conscious of the demands of its membership for autonomy in decision making. The issue of organizational structure and democratic decision making has caused more difficulty for Ecolo than for Agalev. Efforts by leading figures in Ecolo to strengthen the power of the party executive met with opposition from within. There have also been several resignations by parliamentarians, some of whom became frustrated by problems associated with the organizational structure of the party.

Both green parties have criticized the Belgian system of political patronage whereby major parties are heavily and directly involved in the appointment of civil servants. Another goal of the green parties is participatory democracy (*see* **DIRECT DEMOCRACY**). The greens regard referendums and greater decentralization of power, through a more federal structure, as important means of achieving this objective. Although Agalev and Ecolo mirror ethnic and cultural divisions, unlike the other parties in Belgium they reject the dominant nationalistic ideologies. This has not led to the creation of a unified green party, but rather to an unprecedented degree of collaboration between parties representing different linguistic groups. Unlike any other pair of parties, Agalev and Ecolo have formed a unified parliamentary group.

Insofar as it is based on proportional representation, the Belgian party system favors green parties, but other aspects of the electoral system make it extremely difficult for a minor party to influence the formation of coalitions at the national level. The nationalistic divisions that characterize Belgian politics are reflected in the electoral system. No party can gain an absolute majority of seats, and coalitions have to be formed between the larger parties. At the regional level, Ecolo has had opportunities to influence government because of the delicate balance of power in Wallonia. The greatest chances for involvement in government have been at the local level, where candidates from Agalev and Ecolo have entered coalitions, though these have so far not rendered significant changes in policy. The strong performances by Agalev and Ecolo in the early 1990s have created further possibilities for coalitions with the dominant parties and the introduction of new issues onto the political agenda.

Among the major environmental issues taken up by green parties and political organizations are the concern about the development of nuclear energy, especially after the catastrophe at **Chernobyl**, as well as **acid rain** and the **greenhouse effect**. Green parties have also managed to broaden their program for change to include social and economic concerns, notably in the area of social justice, education and economic management. In addition, green parties have proposed significant reforms to the political and administrative structures of the country, especially as regards practices of political patronage and the involvement by established parties in the hiring of public officials. *See also* **AGALEV; BELGIUM; ECOLO.**

GREEN PARTIES, BRAZIL. The foundation of the Gaucha Association for the Protection of the Natural Environment in 1971 marks, in certain respects, the appearance of a social movement directly concerned about green issues. The rise of a green movement was connected to diffuse protest actions over questions like the rights of women and indigenous groups and, above all, the restrictions on freedom imposed by the military regime between 1968 and 1974. With the easing of these restrictions in 1974, hundreds of environmentalist groups emerged over the following decade. Apart from addressing the problems connected with extremely rapid expansion in the size of cities and with industrial development, the green movement concentrated on the defense of the rainforests and drawing attention to the immense problem of soil erosion. The extent of some of these problems has meant that many traditional organizations, notably trade unions or professional associations, have often articulated popular concerns about damage to the environment. Support for the green movement itself came largely from the middle classes, especially from the growing number of people living in cities and those who were obtaining a university education and entering white-collar occupations.

The military regime's relaxation of some of its control over political activity allowed environmentalists to contest elections, and beginning in 1982 members of the green movement were elected to state assemblies. In 1985 several prominent personalities gave serious consideration to the formation of a green party. They facilitated dialogue among environmental groups and in 1986 agreed to form a national green party, though it was not formally registered until 1988. In the interim, it campaigned on a joint platform with the Workers' Party and received much favorable coverage in the media. In the November

1988 municipal elections several candidates were successful in gaining seats in Rio de Janeiro, São Paulo, and Santa Catarina.

GREEN PARTIES, BULGARIA. As in other former communist countries, the ascent of the green movement in Bulgaria was connected to concern about the exclusive focus on economic development, exploitation of natural resources, and the struggle against an oppressive regime. Once the old communist regime weakened, there was less emphasis on environmental protest and a new focus on economic development and social welfare. Nonetheless, the political and social movements for environmental protection were genuine and had a lasting impact. The most important manifestations of action for the environment are the formation of the Independent Union of Ekoglasnost and the Bulgarian Green Party and the advent of a protest movement that originated in the city of Ruse on the Danube and along the border with Romania. Like the protests in Ruse, which subsequently led to the formation of the Ruse Committee, Ekoglasnost emerged under the communist regime.

The main problem at Ruse was pollution from chlorine emissions at a factory in Giurgiu, a town across the Danube in Romania. The contamination, especially from 1986 onwards, was so severe that thousands of people were hospitalized, and a significant proportion of the population either left Ruse or wanted to (but were prevented from doing so by the authorities). Eventually, in February 1988, approximately 2,000 local citizens staged a protest rally and thereby contributed to the formation of similar protest groups throughout the nation. The national focus on this issue prompted the March 1988 creation of the Ruse Committee by intellectuals, scientists, and artists (many of whom were members of the Communist Party). Most of these activists were based in the capital city, Sofia. The objectives of the association were to lobby the government to address the problems identified at Ruse, to draw on the assistance of national and international scientific experts, and to demand openness in government, especially in divulging the truth about environmental problems.

Members of the committee had to endure harassment and intimidation to such a degree that they were unable to organize any activities. Most went on to form The Independent Union Ekoglasnost on 22 March 1989. The authorities found it harder to suppress this organization, though it was severely restricted in some of its activities and often had to operate in a clandestine manner in order to disseminate information about environmental problems, particularly to the international media. Ekoglasnost even managed to carry out small-scale protests and lobby against larger projects that were causing pollution and endangering the health of citizens, notably the pharmaceutical industry.

Still, the demise of the old communist regime at the end of 1989 meant that the focus on environmental issues was overshadowed by an interest in political reforms. Ekoglasnost played a pivotal role in the formation of the Union of Democratic Forces in December 1989. However, the process of political liberalization presented Ekoglasnost not only with new opportunities to bring about social change but with dilemmas about how to organize itself. Over a period of two years it experienced three kinds of schism. In April 1990, after some argument, the association formed a parliamentary wing. In June 1991 the parliamentary delegates who had formed the Political Club Ekoglasnost found themselves under pressure by Ekoglasnost to withdraw from parliament because of the dangers associated with signing a constitution that was being shaped, to a large degree, by the Communist Party. The parliamentary delegates then split from the social movement. Following the October 1991 elections fortunes were reversed when the delegates associated with the Political Club Ekoglasnost failed to overcome the 4 percent electoral hurdle, while four delegates from the Ekoglasnost social movement were elected as part of the United Democratic Front.

The other main division among environmentalists seeking political reforms was the December 1989 foundation of the Green Party by a leading member of Ekoglasnost. This move, which appeared to have taken place with no prior discussion among members of Ekoglasnost, came as a surprise and was regarded as divisive. Despite opposition by Ekoglasnost the party joined the United Democratic Front and in the June 1990 elections secured 12 seats in parliament. Other highlights for the Green Party included the election as mayor of Sofia (October 1990 to October 1991) of the leader of the party, Aleksandar Karakacanov; the 1991 election of another leading member of the party, Filip Dimitrov, to the post of president of the Coordinating Council of the United Democratic Front; and the appointment of two members to ministerial positions in the coalition government.

In 1990 the Green Party had formed a network with 90 branches across the nation and 20 groups in Sofia. The membership of the party, in 1998, numbers approximately 10,000. Despite these early successes and the actuality of numerous environmental problems (notably the pollution arising from industrial plants), focus on economic development and social welfare has once again supplanted interest in environmental protection and thereby diminished the prospects for the Green Party and the green movements that emerged in the 1980s.

GREEN PARTIES, CZECHOSLOVAKIA. The rise and decline of Czechoslovakia's Green Party was linked as much to the rapid political changes that occurred from 1989 onwards as to concern about damage to the environment. Formed in November 1989, the party was closely associated with the displacement of the communist regime. Its program for reforms focused primarily on the political system and democratic change rather than on the environment.

The connections between the new party and environmental organizations were slender. A very large proportion of the members of the new party had never belonged to environmental associations. These organizations had often been anything but subservient to the communist regime and included groups like Brontosaurus, the Czech Union of Nature Protectionists, and the Slovak Union of Protectionists of Nature and the Countryside. In addition, they were used by many activists as a platform for opposing the Communist government.

The formation of the Green Party in Prague was followed by the creation of green political organizations throughout the country. In February 1990 over 300 delegates attended the inaugural national congress of the new party. The fragmentation of the new political organization reflected divisions between ethnic groups and the difficulty that has confronted many other green parties in reconciling a focus on national politics with the emphasis on the grass roots.

Divisions within the nation were mirrored in the structure of parliamentary representation. Elections to the two chambers of the federal assembly were structured along the following lines: in the Chamber of People seats were allocated according to a ratio of the Czech and Slovak population. Of the 150 seats in the Chamber of Nations, half went to the Czechs and half to the Slovaks. Elections were also held to a Czech National Council and to a Slovak National Council. The electoral system was structured to include both an element of proportional representation and one of multimember constituencies. There was one important rider: in the federal assembly and the Czech National Council seats would only be allocated to parties that secured 5 percent of the vote. For the Slovak National Council the hurdle was only 3 percent. In June 1990 elections to all these bodies, the Green Party did not fulfill its promise. It polled only 3.3 and 2.9 percent of the vote for the two assemblies, 4.1 percent in the election to the Czech National Council, and 3.5 percent (and six seats) in the Slovak National Council.

The environment had rapidly been eclipsed as an electoral issue by the focus on how to reinforce the rapid changes in the political system by developing the economy. The inherent weakness of the Green Party, its slight connection with environmental groups, made it ineffectual in mobilizing a large number of potential voters. In local elections in November 1990 the Green Party, on average, did not perform much better than it had in June of that year. It did quite well, however, in areas that had suffered high levels of damage to the environment.

In order to compete in the 1992 elections and overcome electoral hurdles, the Green Party, representing primarily Czechs and Moravians, joined a Liberal Social Union, which included the Socialist and Agrarian Parties. From then on, the party split into various groupings and suffered further decline. To make matters worse, a large proportion of the Green Party had been opposed to the coalition with the Agrarian Party. The latter was in favor of cooperative agriculture, which, in the eyes of many, had been largely responsible for immense damage to the landscape. For many environmentalists, the Agrarian Party was too left-wing in orientation.

A further difficulty, which afflicted the Green as well as other parties, was the tension between the Czechs and Slovaks. The Slovak wing of the party contested the 1992 elections on its own and secured 2.5 and 2.1 percent of the vote for the federal assembly and Slovak National Council, respectively. The Liberal Social Union polled 6 and 6.5 percent in the federal assembly and Czech National Council, respectively. Although several green deputies were thereby elected to these assemblies, the Green Party lost most of its members because of the coalition it had formed with other parties. Moreover, it was harmed by internal conflicts, its loose and deficient organizational structure, and the dominance of nonenvironmental questions on the political agenda.

The most significant of these issues was the nationalist tension between Czechs and Slovaks, which culminated in the division of the country into the Czech Republic and Slovakia on 1 January 1993. Other issues included the revival of the economy and, beginning in 1992, social problems like unemployment, crime, and poverty. While the prospects for the Green Party were bleak, the possibilities for reforms in environmental policy were greatly enhanced following the transition from Communism. *See* **CZECHOSLOVAKIA.**

GREEN PARTIES, DENMARK. The Danish greens, De Grønne, were founded in October 1983 and first competed in local elections in 1985, attracting 2.8 percent of the vote and gaining 12 seats on municipal councils and six on provincial councils. In the 1987 and 1988 national elections they attracted only 1.3 percent of the vote. In the 1990 elections the figure was even lower (0.9 percent). The relatively weak performance by De Grønne is partly attributable to the competition from other minor parties that had championed the goals of various new social movements in the 1970s. Another explanation is that other parties, notably the Socialist People's Party, had already shown a keen interest in environmental issues. Unlike some of its neighbors, Denmark did not have a nuclear power program. The greatest support for De Grønne comes from younger people, those with higher levels of education, and urban dwellers. In its organizational structure De Grønne has attempted to promote internal democracy and accountability to the membership. With this objective in mind, it holds several national congresses each year to which local branches of the party can send delegates. Like **Die Grünen** in Germany, De Grønne has based its platform on four principles: **ecology, nonviolence, direct democracy,** and social security. There is also an emphasis on peace and disarmament. Like many other green parties, De Grønne has developed policies on the economy, social issues, and international relations, with a focus on unilateral disarmament, the abrogation of NATO, and the repudiation of Denmark's membership in the European Union.

GREEN PARTIES, EUROPEAN PARLIAMENT. In 1979, when the first elections to the European parliament were held, the green movement had only recently begun to make an impact on the political agenda, and none of the new green parties were successful in gaining seats. In 1984 green parties succeeded in capturing 12 seats. The dominant group in what came to be known as the Green-Alternative European Link was from the Federal Republic of Germany, with seven delegates from **Die Grünen.** The Netherlands and Belgium each had two representatives, and Italy had one.

In 1989 green parties achieved their best-ever results in elections to the European parliament, gaining 32 seats. Although Die Grünen acquired eight of these seats, they were no longer the dominant group. There were nine delegates from France, seven from Italy, three from Belgium, and two from the Netherlands. Portugal, Spain, and Denmark had one each. Although among the most successful green parties in terms of share of the national vote, the UK Green Party gained no seats because of the constraints imposed by the electoral system in that country.

In 1994 environmental issues were less prominent on the political agenda than they had been in 1989. As a result there was a decline in the green parties' share of the European parliament vote, and only 22 candidates were successful. Unlike most other green political parties, Die Grünen improved on their previous performance and once again emerged as the most powerful group, with 12 seats. Italy had three representatives, Belgium had two, and the Netherlands, Denmark, and Luxembourg each had one. The Danish delegate was not the representative of a green party. However, her party, the Socialist People's

Party, became part of the Green Group in the European parliament in 1992.

The ambivalence that has characterized the approach of many green parties to parliamentary politics has also influenced their attitude toward the European Union and the relationship between various green parties. Green parties have always opposed any tendencies toward centralization and, since the 1984 congress of green parties held at Liège in Belgium, have advocated a "Europe of the regions." This corresponds to their emphasis on decentralization and autonomy and arguments against hierarchical forms of governance. Green parties have also regarded with suspicion the development of large, centralized bureaucracies. Questions that have united green parties include their opposition to any attempts to achieve greater central control and coherence of the military, focus on the arms race, the goal of protection of the environment, and advocation of the rights of women and minority groups.

However, some of the divisions that have prevailed at the national level have manifested themselves at transnational meetings. During their first term in office, between 1984 and 1989, most members of Die Grünen refused to adhere to the principle of rotation out of office on the grounds that this would undermine their efforts to gain and make use of their newly acquired expertise in operating within the political system. Green delegates also disagreed about the value of working in the institutions of the European Community: whether to attempt, in a pragmatic manner, to transform the institutions (to make them more transparent and accountable) or refuse to change fundamentally flawed structures. There are strong parallels here with the division in green parties between **realists** and **fundamentalists**.

Further conflict arose between members of Die Grünen (who wanted to promote both environmental protection and traditional left-wing themes like social justice and democratization) and other green parliamentarians (who wanted to focus first and foremost on environmental issues). Following the 1989 elections these conflicts intensified with the election of delegates from countries like France and Italy who were able to challenge the dominance of the German representatives. There were also serious divisions among the latter over how they should implement forms of **direct democracy** and the question of the professionalization of politics.

As a result of these conflicts the Green-Alternative European Link was dissolved, and in July 1989 a new association called the Green Group, supported by 29 green parliamentarians, emerged in the European parliament. This group focused much more on environmental policy than on attempts to promote both environmentalism and a left-wing agenda. The question of the adherence of the green parties to a common program remained problematic, though there have been efforts to improve the structures for dealing with this issue. Nonetheless, on some questions, particularly policies for peace and protecting the environment, the green parties in the European parliament have demonstrated a high level of solidarity. There have also been attempts by the **European Federation of Green Parties** to lend greater coherence to the agenda for change.

GREEN PARTIES, FINLAND. Throughout the 1980s green groups contested elections without attaching themselves to a formally constituted green party. In February 1987 the Green Association was formed, though this subsequently divided into two separate strands, Vihreät (the Greens) and Vihreä Liitoo (the Green Association). The main reasons for this division were the difficulties leading figures had in getting along with each other. There appeared to be little difference on policy issues between the two organizations.

In the mid-1970s green groups began to contest municipal elections in Helsinki and in the 1980 elections gained a seat on the council. At the 1983 national election a green list of candidates was put forward and received 1.5 percent of the vote and two seats in parliament. They improved on this in the 1987 national elections, with 4 percent of the vote and four seats. In 1991 Vihreä Liitoo secured 6.8 percent of the vote and 10 out of 200 seats. They achieved a similar result in 1995 (6.5 percent and nine seats). Following this, Vihreä Liitoo joined a coalition of five political parties and held the portfolio for the environment. The minister, Pekka Haavisto, was thus the first green parliamentarian ever to hold such a post in a national government. In 1995 the party obtained one of 16 seats allocated to Finland in the European parliament (based on the results from the 1991 parliamentary elections) and in October 1996 was again allocated one seat, attracting 7.6 percent of the vote.

Green political organizations originated from a variety of social movements in the late 1970s preoccupied with environmental issues including the dangers of nuclear power. Among the major concerns were the preservation of Lake Koijärvi, a haven for many species of birds, which came under threat. Other issues that were important in the mobilization of support for green groups included the problem of sulphur emissions and acid rain and opposition to the development of more nuclear power plants and the wood pulp industry.

GREEN PARTIES, FRANCE. The origins of the green movement in France are as diverse as those in many other countries. There is a strong tradition of nature conservation associations, and in the 1960s these groups became more politicized as they focused on issues like the *Torrey Canyon* disaster (which affected the coast of Brittany) and government plans to develop Vanoise National Park for commercial gain. Further impetus was provided by the student uprisings of May 1968, which questioned traditional political parties and modes of political behavior. In the 1970s a strong **antinuclear protest** movement emerged as France became more dependent than almost any other country in the world on this form of energy. In 1977, at the height of these protests, a demonstrator was killed during a rally against the proposed site of a nuclear reactor at Creys-Malville.

Until 1984 green political groups were organized under two umbrella organizations, the Confédération Écologiste and Les Verts–Parti Écologiste. Other significant groups were the French section of **Friends of the Earth,** Réseau des Amis de la Terre, which was founded in 1970; a group called Écologie et Survie (Ecology and Survival), formed in March 1973 in Alsace; and the Mouvement Écologique, which like all the other groups was principally concerned about the expansion of the nuclear industry. The foundation of Les Verts (The Greens) in 1984 was an attempt to unify the diverse green groups.

In 1981 Brice Lalonde contested the presidential elections on a green platform and obtained 1,222,445 votes (3.9 percent). This was a significant improvement on the 337,800 votes (1.3 percent) for Réné Dumont who, as the representative of environmental groups, had contested the 1974 elections. In the 1988 elections Antoine Waechter gained 1,145,502 votes (3.8 percent). In elections to the European parliament, green groups attracted 888,134 votes (4.7 percent) in 1979. However, partly due to internal disputes, their share of the vote in the 1984 elections dropped to 3.4 percent (680,080 votes). By contrast, they performed well at the 1989 elections, with 10.6 percent of the vote. Les Verts became the largest group, with nine delegates, of all the green parties represented in the European Parliament.

One of the earliest attempts by green groups to compete in elections to the national assembly occurred in 1973, when Écologie et Survie attracted 3.7 percent of the vote. However, in general, green groups have fared worse in national assembly elections than in presidential contests, attracting only 2.2 percent of the assembly vote in 1978, 1.1 percent in 1982, and 1.2 percent in 1986. At the local level around 270,000 votes were cast for green groups in the 1977 elections, winning 30 seats on town councils. Due to changes in the electoral system, green groups gained 757 seats in town councils following the 1983 local elections, even though they attracted fewer votes (around 148,000) than in 1977. In 1989 green groups gained nearly twice as many votes as in 1983 and 1,369 seats on town councils. These elections were a significant breakthrough in the advance of green politics.

At the 1992 regional elections, following the 1990 formation of Génération Écologie, under the leadership of Brice Lalonde, as a competing party to Les Verts, both parties secured a similar proportion of the vote, 7.1 and 6.8 percent, respectively. Despite important differences in their organizational structure, compounded by the different styles of their leaders, Les Verts and Génération Écologie resolved to join forces in the 1993 elections to the legislative assembly and present a single candidate in each constituency. Though the greens secured a respectable 7.6 percent of the vote, they failed to obtain any seats in the national assembly. Thus, in addition to internal problems, they continued to have difficulty in overcoming the hurdles set by the electoral system. However, in the 1997 elections, they finally succeeded, gaining eight seats in the national assembly.

Support for Les Verts has come largely from young people and those employed in the academic sector, as well as from managers and white-collar employees who have acquired high levels of formal education. The structure of Les Verts is decentralized, and regional groups enjoy a high level of autonomy. As in many other green parties, members have shown distrust of leading personalities in the party, and several of these figures have had to make way for others.

Autonomy, solidarity, and **ecology** are key principles in the platform of Les Verts. They embrace the central green themes of the protection and preservation of "life" in the face of advanced **industrial society's** fundamental threats to the existence of human beings, plants, and animals. Les Verts have also presented an alternative economic program that explores the possibilities for work-sharing schemes in order to address the problem of unemployment, a **guaranteed minimum income**, and greater control of the economy by workers. There has also been an emphasis on cooperation with less developed countries and on peace and disarmament. Like other green parties, Les Verts has adopted **nonviolence** and civil disobedience as alternatives to conventional approaches to security.

By contrast, Génération Écologie adopted policies that could be regarded as antagonistic to Les Verts. Brice Lalonde supported the efforts of the West in the **Gulf War**. In addition, his group has given far less emphasis, at least initially, to participatory democracy (*see* **DIRECT DEMOCRACY**). Many of the supporters of Génération Écologie came from the socialist party, and the tendency was to create an organization that resembled the dominant parties rather than one that articulated the style and objectives of new social movements.

The green parties represented have recently also begun to adopt a more pragmatic approach. Apart from an appreciation of the gains made by Génération Écologie, there has been a realization that the state of the environment, although not displacing the economy as the major preoccupation of voters, does concern most people and could be linked to dissatisfaction with the political system as a whole.

GREEN PARTIES, GERMANY. *See* **DIE GRÜNEN; GERMANY.**

GREEN PARTIES, GREECE. Thus far environmental issues have not formed a significant part of Greek political life though, as in most European countries, attempts have been made to create new political organizations to address these questions. In 1986 environmental groups participated in local elections without much success. In 1988 some groups tried, without any lasting effect, to form a citizens' union. In 1989 some of these groups managed to form the Ecologists-Alternatives Party and competed in the June elections to the European parliament. They polled only 1.1 percent of the vote and failed to secure any seats.

In October 1989 a large number of environmental groups formed the Federation of Ecological Organizations, with a view to competing in a national election the following month. They retained the name Ecologists-Alternatives, and although they polled only 0.6 percent, they secured one seat in parliament. In the national elections held in April 1990 their share of the vote rose only to 0.8 percent, and they retained one seat. In local elections in 1990 the environmentalists managed to gain seats on some municipal councils.

The Federation of Ecological Organizations had a loose structure that failed to unify a number of highly diverse groups. Apart from arguments about organizational structures (centralized versus decentralized), there were disputes over fundamental principles (shallow versus **deep ecology**). These quarrels delayed the founding congress of the party until February 1992 and then came to dominate it. To confound matters, the sole parliamentary representative of the party detached herself from the organization and sat as an independent delegate.

Support for the party comes largely from urban residents, particularly from Athens, as well as from the young and well educated. Although Greece has numerous environmental problems, green groups have been ineffective in mobilizing the population to support them in very large numbers. Much of the difficulty in developing the green movement lies in the focus by government and the population on economic development and political structures that appear to inhibit the growth of new social movements into powerful forces in political life. *See* **GREECE.**

GREEN PARTIES, IRELAND. The Ecology Party of Ireland was formed in 1981 by a Dublin schoolteacher, Christopher Fettes. The party received only 0.2 percent of the vote in national elections held in November 1982. In 1983 it was replaced by Comhaontas Glas (Green Alliance). However, it continued to have little impact in electoral terms. Christopher Fettes secured 1.9 percent of the vote in the 1984 elections to the European parliament. In the 1985 local elections, the Green Alliance only gained 0.6 percent of the vote.

As in many other countries, the basis of support for green groups is largely the young and well educated. Although Ireland does have environmental problems, some of the issues associated with high levels of industrialization and development that have led to the mass mobilization of citizens in other countries are lacking, one explanation for the relatively poor standing of the Green Alliance. Green groups affiliated with the Green Alliance are permitted a large degree of autonomy. Apart from environmental protection, the Green Alliance campaigned on a platform of more democratic and local forms of decision making and on issues like disarmament and support for less developed countries. Among its economic policies were proposals for a **guaranteed minimum income** and a strong focus on employment.

GREEN PARTIES, ITALY. In November 1986 green groups in Italy formed the Federazione delle Liste Verdi (Federation of Green Lists). This national federation has widely come to be known as "the Greens." Other political organizations have also campaigned successfully on a green platform. They include the Radical Party and Worker Democracy, which had been formed long before the green party. The Radical Party has also collaborated with green groups in electoral campaigns.

Green groups began to contest municipal elections in 1980 in the towns of Este, Lugo di Romagna, Mantove, and Usmaate. In 1983 they contested elections in 16 locations. At the 1985 local elections green groups put up 150 lists. They also competed in the regional elections, receiving 636,000 votes (2.1 percent). They gained 115 seats at the local level, 16 at the provincial level, and 10 at the regional level. In 1988 the Greens polled an average of 3.7 percent in local, regional and provincial elections.

The Italian electoral system, which used to be based on proportional representation, provided genuine opportunities for minority parties to gain seats. In the 1987 elections to the national parliament, green groups received around one million votes (2.5 percent) and gained 13 seats in the lower house and two in the Senate. In 1992 they procured a similar vote (2.8 percent) and thereby won 16 seats in the lower house and four in the Senate. They attracted a similar share of the vote in elections to the House of Representatives in 1994 (2.7 percent and nine seats) and 1996 (2.5 percent and 14 seats in cooperation with parties like the Democratic Left Party). Their share of seats in the Senate was seven out of 325 in 1994 and 14 out of 325 in 1996.

In the 1989 European elections the Greens received 3.8 percent of the vote, and a coalition of green associations, Verdi Arcobaleno (Rainbow Greens), gained a further 2.4 percent. The latter represented and reflected the connection between environmental issues and left-wing groups. In the 1994 elections to the European parliament the Greens attracted over a million votes (3.2 percent of the ballot) and secured three out of 87 seats.

The profile of supporters and voters for green groups is similar to that in many other European countries. In other words, the young and better educated are more likely than other sections of the community to support green groups. Green organizations are also more likely to do well in the more prosperous northern part of Italy than in the south. A pivotal issue in the emergence of a green movement in Italy was the plan, announced by the government in 1975, to develop dozens of nuclear power plants. This attracted strong opposition both from elite groups (scientists and intellectuals) and the public. Amici della Terra (**Friends of the Earth**) played an important role in organizing the campaign against the development of nuclear power. Prominent members of the Communist Party, which had become one of the dominant parties in Italy in the 1970s, joined in the campaign and even formed the Lega per l'Ambiente (Environmental League). Following the nuclear accident in 1986 at **Chernobyl**, the Lega per l'Ambiente organized a protest rally against the development of nuclear power with up to 150,000 people attending.

In 1987 environmental groups initiated a national campaign for a referendum on the development of nuclear power, and the overwhelming majority of citizens voted against the nuclear plans of the national government, voting instead for a decision that would be made at the local level. A majority also opposed the development of the Super-Phéonix nuclear reactor project. Apart from the focus on environmental protection and opposition to the development of nuclear power, green groups have campaigned on social justice issues and improving participation through the extension of democracy and self-government (*see* **DIRECT DEMOCRACY**).

As in other countries, there has been considerable tension between attempts to organize the party at a national level and the strong demand for regional autonomy. Liste Verdi is made up of representatives elected from regional and local associations. There is also a coordinating committee of 11 people. The results of the 1987 national election, though satisfying for the Greens, aggravated tensions between the upholders of regional and local autonomy and the advocates of a stronger national organization for future campaigns. Since the state funds political parties in Italy, the national organization of the Greens received substantial sums of money following its electoral gains in the 1987 elections.

In terms of their programs the various green political organizations have had difficulty in agreeing on a common approach. Some, like the Liste Verdi, have tended to focus exclusively on environmental issues. Others, which are more strongly connected with left-wing organizations, present a platform that includes social justice issues, peace and disarmament, the right of minorities, and aid to developing countries. A further difficulty for small parties like the Greens arises from the reform to the electoral system, away from proportional representation. In 1994 Liste Verdi therefore joined a coalition of left-wing and socialist groups called the Progressive Alliance. Its share of the vote was consistent with previous elections (2.7 percent), and it was allocated 11 seats in the lower chamber and seven in the Senate.

GREEN PARTIES, LUXEMBOURG. In 1979 green groups formed an umbrella organization, the Alternative Leescht: Wiert Ich, to compete at elections. As in several other European countries, the formation of a green party in Luxembourg (Dei Greng Alternativ) was an effort to articulate at the electoral level the protests of social movements, notably those concerned about the development of nuclear power. The party was founded in 1983, and a year later gained 6.1 percent of the vote in elections to the European parliament. In concurrent elections to the national parliament, two deputies won seats: Jean Huss with 5.7 percent and Jup Weber with 6 percent of the vote. The average across the nation was 2.9 percent. The main issues that concerned supporters of Dei Greng Alternativ were nuclear power, damage to the environment caused by industrialization, and the corporatist structures for determining policies, which involved business, labor, and the state but appeared to exclude other groups.

Decisions within the party are made at the district, local or regional, and national levels. Members at the district level elect representatives for the National Coordinating Group, a key body that oversees the democratic processes within the party and its financial and administrative affairs. At the national level there are three conventions, the National Convention (which has a broad agenda), the Full Convention (which takes place four times a year and focuses on specific policy issues), and the Extraordinary Convention.

Dei Greng Alternativ, like **Die Grünen** in Germany, has practiced the rotation of parliamentary delegates and party officers, stipulating that they may only serve a limited term in office. The aim is to ensure that power does not become entrenched. Parliamentary delegates are also subjected to the imperative mandate, a principle that is designed to make them accountable to members and decisions passed at the party conventions and to subject them to recall at any time. Delegates also have to give their parliamentary salaries to the party, which remunerates them according to its own formula. All these issues caused great difficulty within the party; delegate Jup Weber even eventually ended up as an independent in the parliament.

Dei Greng Alternativ espouses five core principles, **ecology**, **direct democracy**, social reforms, solidarity, and peace. The main emphasis in the party program has been on the consequences of industrialization, particularly pollution caused by the steel industry. However, Dei Greng Alternativ has argued not so much for deindustrialization as for the exploitation of new opportunities and combining of development and environmental protection, for example, through the production of goods in ways that do not cause damage to the environment. Dei Greng Alternativ has been critical of other aspects of **industrial society**, notably the pollution caused by vehicles, destruction of communities resulting from poor planning of housing development, and the inefficient use of energy, particularly the failure to develop renewable sources of energy (*see* **ALTERNATIVE ENERGY**). Apart from environmental issues, Dei Greng Alternativ has focused on the rights of women and minorities and on democracy, particularly on how local communities can have a greater say in decisions about development. As with many other green parties, Dei Greng Alternativ has not participated in government but has played a crucial role in accelerating the process whereby major parties address environmental issues.

GREEN PARTIES, NETHERLANDS. Two green parties have recently been formed in the Netherlands. The first, De Groenen (The Greens), was founded in December 1983 and has generally failed to make much of an impression in elections. The second, Groen Links (Green Left), was an electoral alliance of left-wing parties in 1989, before turning itself into a new political party in November 1990. The history of the two organizations and the parties that existed prior to the formation of Groen Links are closely linked.

Although Groen Links was formed much later than De Groenen, it was composed of political organizations that arose much earlier. De Groenen was formed in 1983, partly as a reaction to the possibility that these (left-wing) organizations would exercise considerable influence over the direction of green politics. However, De Groenen failed to prevent this; the political organizations that came to form Groen Links comprised the left-wing political parties feared by De Groenen. They included the Communist Party of the Netherlands; the Pacifist-Socialist Party, which had gained seats in parliamentary elections since the 1950s; and the Political Radical Party, which had been formed in 1968 and represented in parliament since the early 1970s. Another, minor, party that joined this group was the Evangelical People's Party, founded in 1981.

The Pacifists opposed the military and began to engage in protests against environmental destruction in the 1960s. The Radicals had also concentrated on environmental issues. Both Pacifists and Radicals objected to the development of nuclear energy in the 1970s. Nonetheless, each of the minor parties in Groen Links retained its adherence to particular ideologies. The Communists remained loyal to many of the tenets of Marxism and Leninism. The Radicals and Pacifists espoused libertarian ideas. The main impetus to the merger between these parties was the growing evidence of their decline and the hope that they would make a far better showing in electoral politics as a united group. The combined membership of these political organizations had declined from a peak of around 36,000 in 1981 and 1982 to about 18,000 in 1989.

The existence of fairly coherent, small left-wing parties, let alone of a coalition between them based on a pro-environment platform, has always made it difficult for De Groenen to establish itself as an influential minor party. In elections to the European parliament in 1984, De Groenen polled 1.3 percent of the vote, whereas the coalition of left-wing minor parties, which then called itself the Groen Progressief Akkoord (Green Progressive Accord), secured 5.6 percent of the vote and two seats in the European Parliament. In the 1986 national elections De Groenen polled only 0.2 percent of the vote, in 1989 0.4 percent, and in 1994 only 0.1 percent.

By contrast, Groen Links secured 4.1 percent of the vote and six seats in the 1989 elections. In 1994, when environmental issues played a much less important part in the campaign, it polled 3.5 percent and secured five out of the 150 seats. De Groenen has always stood on a platform that attends first and foremost to environmental issues and links this to notions of self-sufficiency, decentralization, and grassroots democracy (*see* **DIRECT DEMOCRACY**). De Groenen has not, however, been able to overcome its own problems in establishing a coherent organizational structure or the perception that Groen Links represents a much more viable and credible platform for addressing environmental issues.

Groen Links attempts to combine diverse convictions (including beliefs about control by the state of many large enterprises, the withdrawal of the Netherlands from NATO and the introduction of a **guaranteed minimum income**) with many of the aspirations of green parties throughout the world. The dissolution of the minor parties that formed Groen Links and development of environmental policies in the 1990s indicate that concerns about the environment are likely to dominate the agenda of the new political formation. Supporters of Groen Links share many of the characteristics of supporters of many other green parties: most are younger and/or have high levels of formal education and large proportions are employed in the public sector. They also appear to be more concerned about environmental than other issues.

GREEN PARTIES, NEW ZEALAND. *See* **VALUES PARTY.**

GREEN PARTIES, SLOVAKIA. *See* **GREEN PARTIES, CZECHOSLOVAKIA.**

GREEN PARTIES, SWEDEN. Green groups in Sweden have attracted support in local elections since the early 1970s. The Stockholm Party, which focused on environmental issues, gained three seats in the 1979 municipal elections. Miljöpartiet de Gröna, the Swedish Green Party, was founded in September 1981. In the 1982 and 1985 national elections it polled only 1.7 and 1.5 percent, respectively. By contrast, in municipal elections held at the same time, it received a significantly higher proportion of votes and gained 167 seats in 1982 and 240 seats in 1985. In 1988, however, Miljöpartiet de Gröna overcame the 4 percent threshold for parties to enter parliament and was the first new party in 70 years to gain representation. It was allocated 20 seats after acquiring 5.6 percent of the national vote. This success can be attributed to the significance attached to the environment during the election campaign, dangers posed to the Swedish population by the **Chernobyl** disaster in 1986, and strong reaction against the style of professional politics that characterized the major parties.

In 1991 Miljöpartiet polled only 3.4 percent and lost all its seats. The environment was not a major issue during this election campaign, and many voters were apparently deterred from supporting the party because it had become more explicit in leaning toward the left. However, in 1994, the party recovered in a convincing manner by obtaining 5 percent of the vote and 18 seats. Among the main factors that contributed to the revival of Miljöpartiet were its strong stance in opposing Sweden's membership in the European Union, the general mistrust of professional politicians, and, paradoxically, its ability to present itself as a conventional party and avoid some of the difficulties associated with divisions between **fundamentalists** and **realists** that have troubled other green parties.

Since the late 1980s Miljöpartiet has polled well enough at the local (municipal) and regional levels to gain seats in all local councils and enter coalitions in local governments. The most impressive results for the party have been at the local level and in the 26 county councils. In the 1980s the number of seats gained by Miljöpartiet in municipal councils rose from 127 in 1982 to 237 in 1985 and 698 in 1988. At the county council level the number of seats increased from three in 1982, to six in 1985 and 101 in 1988. Beginning in 1994, the party came to hold the balance of power in numerous districts. As a consequence, it began to play an important role in the administration and provision of services like health care, education, and housing, as well as in supervising arrangements for environmental standards. Another important success of Miljöpartiet was its showing in the September 1995 elections to the European parliament, when it polled 17.2 percent and gained four seats.

A large proportion of Miljöpartiet's members had formerly been supporters of the Center Party and the Social Democrats. Most are young, middle class, and well educated. Women and people employed in the public sector are among its most numerous members. However, like other green parties, Miljöpartiet has been vulnerable to the propensity of voters to switch parties between elections.

As in many other western European countries, **antinuclear protests** paved the way for the formation of green political parties, including Miljöpartiet. Sweden relied heavily on the development of nuclear power for its energy needs, a policy championed by the Social Democratic Party that had governed Sweden for several decades. In 1976, however, a decisive shift in electoral politics occurred. The Center Party, led by Thorbjörn Fälldin, campaigned on an antinuclear platform. It gained 24 percent of the vote and displaced the Social Democrats in the government after forming a coalition with the Conservative and Liberal parties.

However, these two parties did not share the same goals as the Center Party, at least on the question of nuclear power. The unwillingness of the Center Party to confront its coalition partners over this question undermined its credibility among environmentalists, and disagreement over the development of nuclear power eventually led to the collapse of the coalition.

In 1979, following the **Three Mile Island** accident in the United States and changing climate of opinion on the issue of nuclear power, the Social Democrats agreed to hold a national referendum. The March 1980 referendum offered three options. The Center Party and the Communist Party advocated an end to the expansion of nuclear power and phasing out of the six reactors in operation within 10 years. By contrast, the Social Democrats and the Liberals agreed to phase out nuclear power, subject to the following conditions: the twelve reactors in operation, completed or under construction, could be used and would be held under state control. The Conservatives agreed with the phasing out of nuclear power but, like the Social Democrats and the Liberals, argued for the utilization of the 12 reactors in operation, completed, or under construction. The position of the Center and Communist Parties attracted 38.7 percent of vote, that of the Social Democrats and Liberals, 39.1 percent, and that of the Conservatives, 18.9 percent. Following the referendum, the decision to close down all nuclear reactors by the year 2010 was made. However, the referendum also allowed the government to proceed with the construction of six more nuclear power plants, thereby strengthening the dependence of the country on this form of energy.

Following this disappointing result, the antinuclear movement lost faith in the Center Party and began to concentrate its efforts on creating a new party that would focus principally on environmental issues. Miljöpartiet de Gröna was organized at several levels. Local branches provided the foundation of the party. Above these were the regions, which elected representatives to the Annual Congress and national Representative Committee. As in other green parties, a key principle was to ensure as much participation as possible. This was epitomized by the focus on decentralization and **direct democracy**. The principle of rotation of delegates highlights the party's emphasis on addressing the problem of the concentration of power.

The Annual Congress elects members to a variety of committees, including a political bureau and an administrative bureau. The idea is to reduce the concentration of power. For example, the political bureau focuses on policy making in general, whereas the administrative concentrates on economic policy. Again, symbolizing the effort by Miljöpartiet to present itself as a clear alternative to the major parties, there is a tendency against the emergence of strong party leaders. In 1995 Miljöpartiet did elect two spokespersons, though they remain representatives who deal with the media rather than serve as party leaders. There are also numerous rules to ensure equal representation of men and women, especially at the highest levels of the party.

Miljöpartiet established itself as an antinuclear party and has taken on many other issues, including self-government at a local level, decentralization of the state, peace and disarmament, and a reduction in economic growth. Most people regard the party as first and foremost a voice for environmental concerns, though there are several possibilities for it to develop a distinctive profile on other issues. Above all, Miljöpartiet did not share the view of most major parties that Sweden should join the European Union. The party also challenged assumptions about the state's involvement in owning enterprises, creating wage-earner funds, and promoting the arms industry and spending on defense. Miljöpartiet has continued to espouse collectivist goals like social justice and fairer and more equal distribution of income and wealth. *See also* **SWEDEN.**

GREEN PARTIES, SWITZERLAND. A proposal in the early 1970s to build a highway through the city of Neuchâtel mobilized the local population. Opponents of the project, unable to persuade the authorities to reverse their decision, entered the communal elections in 1972 and won eight of the 41 seats in the local parliament. This paved the way for the foundation of the first green party in Switzerland, the Mouvement populaire pour l'environnement (MPE).

Inspired by the activities of the MPE in Neuchâtel, Jean-Jacques Hédiguer founded an MPE in the canton of Vaud. The organization attracted 5.6 percent of the vote in Lausanne and won five of the 100 seats in the town council and 15 other seats in various communes. Divisions within the MPE-Vaud led to the formation of the Groupement pour la Protection de l'Environnement, which, in 1977 attracted 8.2 percent of the vote and won eight seats on the town council and in 1979 gained a seat in the national parliament. Another green party, in the German-speaking part of Switzerland, was founded in 1978. The Grüne Partei Zürich made steady progress, and in 1987 won 22 out of 180 seats in the cantonal parliament.

Before the 1987 national elections a federation of green groups (Föderation der Grünen Parteien der Schweiz) formed a national Swiss Green Party (Grüne Partei der Schweiz, GPS) in May 1986. In 1987 it secured 119 seats in cantonal parliaments, and by 1991 the number had risen to 154 seats. This is only a partial measure of the strength of the green movement. The total number of seats held by all green and alternative parties was somewhat greater. In 1991, despite some pessimistic predictions about the influence of environmental issues on voting behavior, the GPS polled 6.2 percent and secured 14 seats at the national level. This was an improvement on the 5.1 percent it received in 1987, which procured nine seats, and the 2.6 percent of 1983 (and four seats). In 1987 a coalition of leftist environmental groups, the Grüne Bündnis Schweiz, polled 4.3 percent nationally and secured five seats. However, this was a fairly loose coalition, and by 1991 the GPS had become the most influential and well-known green party.

Over time different environmental issues have been prominent on the political agenda. In the 1970s a powerful social movement against the development of nuclear energy arose. The most famous protests emerged in 1975 against the proposal to construct a nuclear power plant at Kaiseraugst. Eventually, environmental groups and other political organizations succeeded in persuading the government to offer compensation to the developers responsible for not completing this project and introduce a moratorium, lasting 10 years, on nuclear power.

Since the 1970s environmental groups have campaigned to reduce pollution by automobiles, for example by attempting to prevent the construction of new highways. By the 1990s a strong reaction against the restrictions imposed on motorists by the government occurred, expressed in significant support for the AutoPartei (Car Party) and for the Lega Ticinese (Ticino League). Both these political parties were also opposed to the loosening of restrictions on immigration and the admission of asylum seekers to Switzerland.

Support for environmental groups and political organizations has remained strong. In the 1980s the destruction of forests by **acid rain** and the nuclear disaster at **Chernobyl** focused attention on the environment. Moreover, there is an enduring concern about air pollution and the contamination of water supplies.

Over time dominant parties have adopted significant components of the green agenda. In addition, the well-established conservation groups and new social movements that maintain a watchful eye on environmental issues operate at a distance from both the GPS and dominant parties. This allows groups like the **World Wide Fund for Nature**, which has well over 100,000 members in Switzerland, to gain better access to government and develop an independent stance on many issues. The program of the GPS covers many of the issues brought up by environmental groups while trying to articulate a broader agenda for political reform.

Apart from the environmental issues mentioned above, the GPS has sought to develop policies on how to check economic growth and focus on **sustainable development**, using taxation, especially energy taxes (*see* **CARBON TAXES**), instead of indirect taxes; transportation (particularly on promoting public transport); and a range of social justice measures (including a **guaranteed minimum income**, more equitable distribution of wealth and resources, and the protection of minorities and disadvantaged groups). The GPS has also attempted to gain support by focusing on two issues that have preoccupied many people: first, the system of political patronage and control exercised by established political elites and interest groups and, second, concern about the impact that membership in the European Union would have on the environment as well as on certain valuable elements of Swiss culture and political life.

The GPS has, like other green parties, embraced the principles of decentralization (*see* *A BLUEPRINT FOR SURVIVAL*), a precautionary approach (*see* **PRECAUTIONARY PRINCIPLE**) to development projects, and the idea of government and industry on a small scale (*see* **SMALL IS BEAUTIFUL**). Coalitions with other parties in order to form a government commonly occur in municipal and cantonal settings. There has been successful collaboration, for instance between 1986 and 1990, in the canton of Bern over issues like the conservation of energy, nuclear power, education, and transport.

Above all, the GPS has developed a pragmatic approach to politics along the lines espoused by the **realists** in other green parties. It has taken full advantage of entitlements to membership in parliamentary committees and participated in the formulation of policies as well as in the negotiation of compromises with other parties. The GPS, like many other green parties, seeks to balance a fundamental commitment to environmental protection with achieving changes in policy within the prevailing political structures and to meet the challenge of retaining a distinct identity as other parties adopt substantial elements of the green political agenda.

Although support for the GPS comes mainly from people with higher than average levels of education and training, a significant proportion have only a basic education. The older persons are less well represented than the younger ones, and most supporters are less than 45 years old. Membership reached around 6,000 in the early 1990s.

The organization of the party reflects the emphasis of the Swiss political system on federal structures. Regional bodies have immense flexibility in determining their own policy platforms. The national governing body is the Assembly of Delegates, which is drawn from all cantons and meets twice a year. This meeting elects the party president and other officials. The GPS has applied the principle of rotation to its officers. The party has been successful in combining some of the principles of **direct democracy** with the need to achieve a degree of coherence in all its operations, including the formulation of policy and electoral contests.

GREEN PARTIES, UNITED KINGDOM. Influenced by the debates about *The Limits to Growth* and by publications like *A Blueprint for Survival* as well as by predictions of impending doom by writers like **Paul Ehrlich**, a small group founded a party called People in 1973. In 1975 it became known as the Ecology Party. At the two 1974 general elections the party called People presented five and four candidates, respectively. Until 1979, there was little emphasis on electoral activity. In a further attempt to improve on poor electoral results, it was renamed the Green Party in 1985.

The simple plurality electoral system in Britain, often referred to as a first-past-the-post system, makes it difficult for minor parties to gain any representation since the candidate with the most votes in a particular constituency is automatically elected, and there is no means for minor parties to have any representation in the Parliament unless they can secure a majority of votes in that electorate. The system does not allow for any element of proportional representation. However, at the 1979 general election, the Ecology Party presented 53 candidates in order to boost its public profile and take advantage of the access to national television that was permitted to parties contesting at least 50 seats. The party attracted on average only 1.5 percent of the vote for the 53 seats; however, it did gain national recognition as a result of the campaign. In the 1983 general elections the party attracted on average only 1 percent of the vote for 108 seats.

The disappointing performance was attributed to the emergence of another new party, the Liberal/Social Democratic Party Alliance. The alliance attracted many people who were disillusioned with the major parties. Even with a change in its name, in the 1987 elections the Green Party received on average only 1.4 percent of the vote in 133 seats. In 1992, with 256 candidates, it polled only 1.3 percent. The only consolation was the success of Cynog Dafis in the Welsh constituency of Caredigium Gogledd Penfro. Dafis had campaigned as a candidate for both the Welsh nationalist organization Plaid Cymru and the Green Party and thus became the first ever green member of the Westminster Parliament.

In the 1984 elections to the European parliament the Green Party contested only 16 of 78 divisions. In these divisions it polled 2.6 percent on average. In 1989, the party profited from the prominence of issues like the **greenhouse effect** and the depletion of the **ozone layer,** as well as from disillusionment with the dominant parties, notably the Conservatives, to win about 15 percent of the vote in elections to the European parliament. As in many of these elections, the turnout was low (36 percent).

Overall, electoral prospects for the Green Party remain bleak. As in many other countries, the dominant parties have successfully adopted many aspects of the green political agenda. In elections to district councils in 1980 the Ecology Party attracted on average 5.8 percent of the vote. The party received over 10 percent of the vote in several seats and 40.8 percent in one. In Caistor, Lincolnshire, it gained one seat. In the 1991 elections to county councils the party, represented by Jeremy Faull, retained the seat of Bodmin after attracting 50.1 percent of the vote. At the 1983 local council elections the party won several seats. In council elections in 1986 and 1987 it won three positions on district councils. In 1987 it secured 5.9 percent of all votes in local elections, and many candidates won office in local councils.

Between 1989 and 1992 Green Party candidates continued to gather similar levels of support, and in the 1993 county council elections it fielded 566 candidates who on average gained 5.7 percent of the votes.

Jonathon Porritt is one of the most well-known members of the Green Party. In the 1979 European elections he gained 4.1 percent of the vote in London Central, and was one of the few figures in the Green Party to attract attention from the national media. However, like other leading figures in the party, he has had to deal with the inherent suspicion with which many high-profile activists are viewed. He has also experienced difficulties in retaining the membership base of the organization. In 1979 the Ecology Party had only 650 members. However, within two years membership had grown to around 6,000, mainly as a result of a deliberate strategy to raise the party's electoral profile and partly because of widespread concern about the development of nuclear power and weapons that began around 1979. Membership of the Green Party has fluctuated enormously, from a pinnacle of around 20,000 in 1990 to 6,500 in 1992 and 4,500 in 1993.

These fluctuations can be partly attributed to the internal conflicts over the organization of the Green Party and to the difficulties associated with the highly restrictive electoral system. As in other green parties, there has been tension between the imperative to organize the party along professional and more centralized lines and the abiding wish to grant autonomy to local associations. Local branches have considerable control over their own organizational structures. So long as the process is democratic, local branches are permitted to develop their own methods for selecting candidates for elections. Although there is some coordination of activities at the national level (through a party council comprising people elected from the regional organizations through a national ballot of all members and at an annual conference), there is little control over what occurs at the local level. The tension between central and local control is fairly weak in Britain, because there is widespread agreement on the current arrangements and the prospects of electoral success are very limited.

However, the success of the party in the 1989 European elections and the recognition of its fragile basis of support, especially in light of the constraints imposed by the simple plurality electoral system, led to pressures for reform of the organizational structure. In 1990 a group called Green 2000, led by prominent figures who wanted to increase the influence of the Green Party in national politics, advocated more centralized and professional organizational structures. At the 1991 Party Conference Group 2000 succeeded in concentrating the central structures (reducing the size of the party executive) and introducing other organizational reforms.

These successes only served to widen the gap, however, between Group 2000 and activists who espouse decentralization. Coupled with the decline in membership and poor electoral fortunes of the party, these changes caused an acrimonious struggle between those who favored decentralization and those who wanted to concentrate on making the party more professional in order to have greater success in elections. Although members of Green 2000 were successful in gaining seats on the national executive at first, they were soon drawn into disputes with those in favor of decentralization. In 1992 the chair of the national executive, Sara Parkin, and five other members relinquished their positions as a result of these conflicts. At any rate, by the end of 1991 Green 2000 had already vanished as a force for reform in the party.

The development of the party called People was deeply influenced by the notion of "the limits to growth." A cornerstone of the new party was the use of decentralization as a means for addressing this and other questions. Among the issues that emerged in the late 1970s was the development of nuclear power, which became the focus for the Windscale Enquiry into the development of facilities to process nuclear waste, and the deployment of nuclear weapons, as in the "dual track" decision by NATO in 1979 and the decision by the British government to acquire the Trident nuclear submarine as part of its own strategy for deterrence.

The party called People was founded on a platform derived from *A Blueprint for Survival*, which included its emphasis on a sustainable society based on stable **population growth**, a minimum of interference in ecological processes, and more efficient use of energy with a focus on conservation of resources (*see* **ALTERNATIVE ENERGY**). The Green Party articulates themes similar to those of other parties, notably disquiet about nuclear power and the deployment of nuclear weapons. Its energy policy is a focus on renewable resources.

A pivotal concept in both its energy policy and various other policies, including assistance to less developed countries, is the notion of self-reliance. The 1987 manifesto of the Green Party advocated the creation of a **"steady-state**, sustainable economy." Employment policy would focus on job-sharing, and there would be general measures like a **guaranteed minimum income**. There would be a much greater emphasis on the informal sector and small communities and networks. Underlying much of this is the concept of decentralization of government and the economy. *See also* **UNITED KINGDOM**.

GREEN PARTIES, UNITED STATES OF AMERICA. Following the dissolution of the Citizens Party, which was the first large-scale attempt by social movements to contest elections on a platform that combined a focus on environmental questions and socialist ideas for restructuring the economy, green political activists became even more convinced of the value of focusing on local politics. In 1984, many of these activists, who had been members of the Citizens Party, formed Committees of Correspondence. Although the committees wanted to achieve a degree of coordination and coherence at the national level, they differed from the Citizens Party by focusing principally on local political campaigns and shedding the preoccupation with left-wing agendas. To some degree this weakened any efforts to develop broad platforms for political campaigns.

It also created new opportunities for local and regional green parties to emerge throughout the United States over the following years. Eventually, in August 1991, these groups came to form the Green Party USA. The party recognized the Committees of Correspondence as the basis for the new political organization. It also drew directly on the undertaking by parties like **Die Grünen** of **ecology, nonviolence,** social justice, and grassroots democracy (*see* **DIRECT DEMOC-RACY**). An effort was again made to broaden the agenda from a narrow focus on environmental protection to the discussion of economic and social policies.

The new party recognized that most green political activists preferred to exercise influence at the local level, though the possibility of campaigning at state and national levels was seen as desirable once the organization had gathered enough support. The party has described itself as "a weak commonwealth of autonomous Green Parties in several states." The Green Party USA has therefore seen its role as facilitating coordination among the Committees of Correspondence and the local and statewide green parties. There has also been discussion of adopting the model of coordination developed by the **European Federation of Green Parties** for the purpose of contesting elections under a more unified banner. The possibility of forming coalitions with other minority parties has also been mentioned. The intent, however, has been on creating a powerful grassroots movement. Though this is often presented as being consistent with the need for participatory democracy, it is also partly dictated by the difficulties of forming a new party that can overcome institutional obstacles to compete effectively with the two major parties (*see* **CITIZENS PARTY**).

The formation of the Green Party USA had partly been prompted by the emergence of hundreds of green party chapters and successes at the local level. By the early 1990s green parties had secured numerous seats on local councils and boards of education. In the November 1992 local elections the greens secured over half a million votes and

11 seats, increasing their representation to 58 seats in local government across 14 states. The average nationwide total for green parties in these elections was around 16 percent.

In elections to the Senate a Green Party candidate, Linda Martin, gained around 50,000 votes (14 percent) in a contest that included an influential senator, Daniel Inouye, representing the Democrats in Hawaii. In California, green candidates polled around 340,000 votes (an average of 13 percent across the state). The performance of green parties in the 1994 elections was even better. They presented 75 candidates who polled over a million votes. Five candidates gained more than 100,000 votes. In New Mexico and Hawaii several green candidates polled between 30 and 60 percent of the vote in local elections.

Despite the diversity of green parties and their focus on local concerns, some consensus on basic principles, which have been adopted from the platforms of European green parties like Die Grünen, has emerged. Apart from the core principles noted earlier, they include a focus on decentralization (*see A BLUEPRINT FOR SURVIVAL*), feminism, respect for diversity, **stewardship**, the needs of future generations, and ecologically sustainable lifestyles. There is strong emphasis on organizing the economy and social services on a community basis and for much greater sharing of ownership and control than is presently the case.

Green parties in the United States have also adopted ideas about taking into account fully, through taxation and other means, the environmental and social costs of pollution (*see* **POLLUTER PAYS PRINCIPLE**) and the use of energy and other resources (*see* **ALTERNATIVE ENERGY**). They also call for a reform of the electoral system, particularly the introduction of proportional representation, to enable more parties to compete effectively in elections.

GREENHOUSE EFFECT. Concern about the warming of the earth's atmosphere as a result of industrial development has become widespread since the 1980s. The term "greenhouse effect" has been used to characterize the warming of the atmosphere as a result of the emission of gases that prevent the escape of heat from the earth's surface. Carbon dioxide in the earth's atmosphere functions like a greenhouse; in other words, it provides a passage for light waves from the sun but restricts the escape of radiation from the earth into the atmosphere. The main sources of carbon dioxide emissions are the burning of fossil fuels like oil and coal, though other processes like the burning of wood also contribute to the problem. Over the past century there has been a steep increase in the rate of carbon dioxide emissions.

One effort to evaluate changes in temperature was the World Climate Program, initiated in 1979 by the World Meteorological Organization with the support of bodies like **UNEP.** By the mid-1980s scientists had become increasingly aware of the possibility of the warming of the earth's atmosphere as a result of carbon dioxide emissions. At the Villach Conference in 1985 scientists publicized the fact that there had been a slight increase in the average temperature across the world over the past century and that there did appear to be a correspondence between this finding and the rate of emissions of carbon dioxide and other gases. The most alarming finding was that if this trend continued, there could be significant increases in average temperature across the earth and severe consequences. Drastic changes in weather patterns including droughts, floods, and storms would occur. Above all, scientists have speculated on the impact of climate change on regions covered with ice, notably the Arctic, and the consequent impact on sea levels. A vast proportion of the world's population living in coastal regions could be forced to relocate, and some countries, notably small islands in the Pacific Ocean, would vanish under seawater.

In 1988, at a conference held in Toronto, more than three hundred scientists and policymakers from nearly fifty countries and international organizations noted that a 50 percent reduction in carbon dioxide emissions would have to be achieved in order to stabilize the atmospheric concentration of greenhouse gases. They suggested, as an initial target, a 20 percent reduction in carbon dioxide emissions by the year 2000. Coincidentally, in 1988 and 1989, many countries experienced exceptionally warm weather. In the United States and Canada there was a severe drought. Though there was no necessary connection between these experiences and the greenhouse effect, some scientists and the media did speculate on the link between the two. Fears about the greenhouse effect also coincided with speculation about the impact of chlorofluorocarbons on the depletion of ozone at high altitudes and the potential catastrophe that could be unleashed by the hole in the **ozone layer.**

For the first time, leaders from traditional political parties in countries like the United States and the United Kingdom, as well as many other nations, put the environment high on the political agenda, and there was a marked shift in public concern. There were also efforts, in the context of the **UN Conference on the Environment and Development (UNCED),** held in Rio de Janeiro in 1992, to bring together nation-states as well as business, industry, and nongovernmental organizations to combat problems like the greenhouse effect. The Framework Convention on Climate Change, which had been initiated by the UN General Assembly in 1991, was signed by 153 nations and by the European Union at the 1992 UNCED.

However, the agreement, though legally binding on the signatories, could be construed in many ways and allowed governments to determine whether the measures for handling the greenhouse effect were economically feasible. Critics have pointed to the failure by some governments to take the initiative on the emission of greenhouse gases and to their efforts to avoid being restricted in industrial development by defined targets for emissions.

GREENPEACE. The origins of this environmental protest organization can be traced to the 1969 formation of the Don't Make a Wave Committee in Vancouver, Canada. This group, which included people who had protested the Vietnam War, launched a campaign against the testing of nuclear weapons over the atmosphere in the Aleutian Islands. The Greenpeace Foundation was created in 1971, the year in which protesters sailed an old fishing boat into the vicinity of Amchitka Island off the coast of Alaska, an area being used by the U.S. government to test nuclear devices. Apart from effecting a postponement and ultimately the abandonment of these tests, the protestors attracted media attention and a considerable amount of popular support. These events set the pattern for future successful action by Greenpeace. The organization would focus on a particular issue with a view to receiving maximum attention from the media. It would then conduct its protest in a highly organized and professional manner.

In 1972 Greenpeace carried out one of its most memorable protests when, backed by major volunteer associations like the **Sierra Club, Friends of the Earth,** and the World Council of Churches and by the Canadian government, it launched a campaign against the testing of nuclear weapons by the French government in the Mururoa Atoll in the Pacific. Led by **David McTaggart**, a Canadian who later became director of Greenpeace International, a group of activists embarked on a voyage sailing right into the nuclear test zone.

The risks undertaken by McTaggart and his crew, who sailed to within 50 miles of the site where a bomb was detonated, drew an enormous amount of attention to their cause. This was followed, in August 1973, by another attempt to enter a zone for testing nuclear weapons. On this occasion, French troops set upon the crew with force. Photographs of the beatings brought further adverse publicity for the French government which, in November 1973, declared a pause in the tests. Greenpeace profited immensely from these events.

The determination of the French to continue with the tests provided an ideal focal point for exact and professional campaigns over the next 20 years. The most critical moment in this battle was the death of a member of Greenpeace in 1985 when the French intelligence service bombed the *Rainbow Warrior*, a ship owned by Greenpeace, while it was moored at Auckland harbor in New Zealand. The incident led to the resignation of Charles Hernu, the French minister of defense. It also increased the popularity of Greenpeace, which by now had conducted international campaigns on issues like the protection of seals and whales as well as the transportation and disposal of nuclear waste. At the national level, Greenpeace carried out highly visible campaigns against pollution, for example, against the contamination of rivers by chemical companies. For instance, following its inquiries into the Ciba-Geigy factory in New Jersey in the United States, the company had to face numerous criminal charges and pay fines of more than U.S.$4 million.

Support for Greenpeace grew at a rapid rate, especially in the late 1980s. Between 1981 and 1989 Greenpeace increased its worldwide revenue, raised largely from private donations, from U.S.$1.2 million to U.S.$100 million. In the early 1990s it had around 40 branches in 30 countries and claimed around five million supporters in 158 countries. Approximately half of its supporters live in the United States. In Europe, the two largest concentrations of supporters are in the Netherlands and Germany. In 1990 there were about 750,000 supporters in Germany alone.

Supporters do not have any direct say in the running of Greenpeace. The success of a national organization depends both on local conditions and management structures. For instance, in 1990 Greenpeace International sent Steve McAllister, one of its most talented executives, to Australia to breathe new life into the organization. McAllister, a Vietnam veteran who joined Greenpeace in 1981, stressed the importance of developing a highly skilled cadre of activists.

Unlike many environmental groups, Greenpeace places a strong emphasis on professionalism and hierarchical structures. According to Greenpeace, its active members are recruited on the basis of their specialized knowledge in areas like the media, politics, or economics. In addition, it has established scientific laboratories to back its campaigns. The approach by executives like McAllister to improving the effectiveness of Greenpeace in Australia is illustrative of these policies. McAllister chose the brightest activists and trained them to become highly competent organizers.

McAllister and other executives regard Greenpeace as a franchise organization. Its hierarchical organizational structure, which tries to ensure that all key initiatives are sanctioned by the head office, is similar to that of many multinational corporations. The management style has been predominantly autocratic. Reforms of the management and public relations strategies pursued by Greenpeace in Australia, along with growing global concern about the destruction of the **ozone layer** and the **greenhouse effect,** led to an increase in Greenpeace supporters in Australia from 9,000 in 1988 to nearly 50,000 in 1990. By the end of 1991 the number of its supporters had grown to 130,000 in response to sophisticated marketing techniques including door-to-door personal appeals, direct mailings, and advertising in national newspapers.

Greenpeace describes itself as "an independent, campaigning organization which uses nonviolent, creative confrontation to expose global environmental problems, and to force the solutions which are essential to a green and peaceful future." On the whole, Greenpeace has focused on direct protest actions. It has been more successful than any other organization in breaking the law and attracting the implicit support of the media and explicit approval of millions of people.

In recent years, Greenpeace organizers have become aware of the necessity of including lobbying and offering advice to the highest levels of government. In response to an initiative by the Australian Labor government to implement ecologically **sustainable development** policies, Greenpeace took the unprecedented step of becoming involved in dialogue between environmental groups, business and industrial interests, and government agencies. Even though Greenpeace eventually withdrew from the process, its initial participation marked a significant shift from a purely confrontational approach. However, Greenpeace has maintained its stance, which distinguishes it from most environmental organizations, of not procuring financial assistance from government agencies.

In adapting to changing perceptions about what constitute crucial environmental issues, Greenpeace has declared that its objectives include the preservation of life in all its diversity (*see* **BIODIVERSITY**). It has also retained some of its core objectives, like preventing all forms of pollution and bringing an end to "all nuclear threats" as well as the promotion of "peace, global disarmament, and nonviolence."

The strengths and weaknesses of Greenpeace have often been compared with those of other environmental organizations. Greenpeace has usually been regarded as more radical than most environmental groups with respect to its focus on direct action and tendency to break the law. In that respect only groups like **Earth First!**, which have had a far smaller following, can be classed as more radical. However, Greenpeace has been far less interested than other green groups in developing internal democratic structures and has been criticized for valuing passivity among its supporters.

Greenpeace, in describing its own decision-making structures, refers to the role of the council, which is made up of representatives from each of the 40 or so Greenpeace offices. The council meets once a year to approve the budget and plan long-term policy directions.

Still, the overall impression is one of a situation in which most supporters tend to be regarded as bystanders who furnish the occasional professionals with the required resources to carry out spectacular actions and bring about changes in government policy or industrial practices.

By contrast, Earth First!, which has placed even more emphasis on direct action, has attempted to promote the maximum involvement of its supporters. In recent years, Greenpeace has had to deal with reproaches both from its own supporters and outside the organization about its hierarchical structures and confrontational style. It remains, however, one of the most well-known and successful environmental groups in terms of its impact on policy and in attracting the support and sympathy from millions of people for environmental causes.

GROSS NATIONAL PRODUCT (GNP). Concern about the limits to growth and damage inflicted on the environment by **industrial society** has given rise to a variety of suggestions for reconceptualizing economic performance. Green economists have called into question the conventional measures of performance, notably the use of GNP. The principal limitation of the exclusive focus on GNP is the failure to consider factors like health, social, and some **quality of life** indicators, the neglect of the informal economy, which varies immensely in size in different countries and, above all, the disregard for the environmental costs of economic development.

Instead of GNP, the traditional measure of wealth, green economists have argued for the inclusion of the above indicators and a more differentiated approach to promoting economic growth. In some sectors of the economy, economic growth may be highly advantageous, and in others it may be undesirable, especially because of damage to the environment. The green movement has begun to influence some governments and international agencies to the extent that greater effort has been applied both to measuring and publicizing performance along the lines suggested by green economists. Furthermore, techniques like **carbon taxes** and **pollution charges** have been proposed for placing a value on the impact of various processes on the environment (*see* **VALUING THE ENVIRONMENT**). *See also THE LIMITS TO GROWTH*; **STEADY-STATE ECONOMY.**

GUARANTEED MINIMUM INCOME. A guaranteed minimum income is central to the platform and policies of many green political organizations. The guiding principles of the **European Federation of Green Parties** (as resolved on 20 June 1993 at the conference at Masala, Finland) stated that "every person has the right to free education, social protection, and a guaranteed social minimum income."

The connection was then made between the maintenance of a comprehensive social security system (which covered "the basic needs of all people" and did not rest on the notion of paid work) and the notion of "sustainability": "Sustainability will not be possible as long as poverty persists, or people live in material insecurity. We will ensure a guaranteed minimum income for every citizen through either a social assistance scheme or minimum wage legislation, or improved welfare benefits or the introduction of the basic income, or a combination of the above mentioned" (Clause 4.4). **Die Grünen** in Germany have long argued for a guaranteed minimum income that excludes any attempt to measure the financial assets of individuals or their employment record.

A comprehensive defense of such schemes has been elaborated by Paul Ekins in *The Living Economy*. Ekins states that a "basic income scheme" would have the following aims: to prevent rather than just relieve poverty, replace the prevailing system of social security and tax relief, and abolish some of the traps that arise from the current operation of the welfare state. These include, according to Ekins, the poverty trap (an increase in pay can lead to the withdrawal of crucial social security benefits), unemployment trap (if you do not work for low wages you lose all entitlements), idleness trap (which has apparently prevented people from undertaking voluntary work because they would otherwise be seen as technically not seeking formal employment, and thereby lose entitlements), and spendthrift trap (if you save above a certain amount of money you lose entitlements to social security benefits).

There are two fundamental criticisms of this universal scheme that aims to provide benefits at a higher level than the existing system. The first is that it would be very costly and thereby lead to higher taxes for everyone. The second is that for many people at the lower end of the socioeconomic ladder, it may provide a disincentive to seeking employment. At any rate, these ideas about a guaranteed minimum income reflect the strong emphasis in green political organizations on social justice and egalitarianism. The hope cherished by many green political activists is that the guaranteed minimum income scheme, with its strong emphasis on universal rather than individually means-tested forms of social benefits, will engender a spirit of cooperation and serve as a defense against the forces of competition, which are often regarded as responsible for the destruction of the environment.

GULF WAR. Apart from the loss of hundreds of thousands of lives, one of the most striking consequences of the Gulf War waged between 1990 and 1991 was the destruction of the environment on a huge scale. The war between Iraq and a coalition led by the United States followed Iraq's invasion of Kuwait. During their retreat from Kuwait the Iraqis set fire to approximately 600 oil wells, and other installations like oil storage depots and refineries. The scale of pollution caused by burning millions of barrels of oil every day was unprecedented. The main constituents of the pollution were sulphur dioxide and nitrogen oxide, the principal elements in the formation of **acid rain**. The oil fires created havoc with the weather in the region, reducing the temperature and visibility. They also had a serious impact on the health of the local population, particularly people who were prone to respiratory diseases like asthma. Further damage was caused by the considerable spillage into the Gulf of oil, estimated at between two and four million barrels, with devastating consequences on marine life.

H

HARDIN, GARRETT. See *TRAGEDY OF THE COMMONS.*

I

INDUSTRIAL SOCIETY. The term "industrial society" has been used by leading figures in the green movement to criticize a wide range of established political regimes, whether communist, capitalist, or liberal-democratic. The argument is simply that whatever their differences, these political regimes are committed to economic growth tied to industrialization, technology, and the expansion of the means of production. This theme has been articulated by prominent personalities like **Jonathon Porritt** and **Rudolf Bahro**.

INGLEHART, RONALD. See **POSTMATERIALISM.**

INTERNATIONAL UNION FOR THE CONSERVATION OF NATURE AND NATURAL RESOURCES (IUCN). Founded in 1948 and known until 1956 as the International Union for the Protection of Nature, the IUCN is one of the most influential associations in promoting dialogue between national governments and nongovernmental organizations. The primary objective of the International Union for the Protection of Nature was to promote education and research with a view to protecting the environment and raising awareness of how much we rely on nature, including natural resources, for our well-being. Max Nicholson and Julian Huxley were among the leading players in the foundation of the organization.

The focus on conservation, and hence the change in name, came in 1956. The IUCN began to concentrate on conserving wetlands and the creation of national parks. Lacking funds for these initiatives, Huxley and Nicholson, among others, established an international fundraising organization for nature conservation, the **World Wildlife Fund.** Early work by the IUCN targeted conservation in Africa. The **African Special Project,** initiated by the IUCN, had two important results. It rendered effective assistance to African governments concerned about the preservation of wildlife and development of land and it established the credibility of the IUCN as an agency capable of providing guidance and expertise to less developed nations in their efforts to conserve and protect the environment. The IUCN was also instrumental in framing of the **African Convention on the Conservation of Nature and Natural Resources** signed by 33 African states in 1968.

The IUCN also demonstrated a capacity to adapt to changing perceptions of how to protect the environment. Apart from special projects, it developed a vision of the interdependence of development and the environment (*see* **SUSTAINABLE DEVELOPMENT**). One of the most important initiatives by the IUCN in the 1970s was the formulation of a **World Conservation Strategy.** Another was its pivotal role in helping to convene the **UN Conference on the Human Environment** in 1972.

The IUCN, while not part of the more militant green movement that emerged in the 1970s, has played a crucial role in maintaining and articulating green issues. Though not formally a part of the United Nations, it has influenced that body's environmental policies. Recently, the IUCN has had to deal with the tensions that arise between business and environmental interests. Members of the IUCN must reconcile business groups' interests in contributing with environmentalists' suspicion of the involvement of business in environmental protection organizations.

K

KELLY, PETRA. (1947–1992). Born in West Germany, Petra Kelly grew up in the United States and engaged in protests there against the Vietnam War. After returning to Germany, she took part in the Social Democratic Party before becoming a founding member of **Die Grünen** in 1980. Kelly became the most famous member of Die Grünen and was invited to many countries to promote green political organizations and their causes. For a time she was also regarded as the leading figure in the green movement worldwide. From 1983 to 1990 she served as a parliamentary delegate for **Die Grünen,** though she always maintained that she was skeptical of the use of parliament as a means for confronting environmental problems.

In a 1982 *Der Spiegel* magazine interview, she explained that parliament was not where decisions were made about the arms race and it was important to continue to work at the grassroots level to develop alternative social and economic structures based on principles of self-help and environmental awareness. She felt that parliamentary democracy had to be broadened to include a party that was fundamentally opposed to war and committed to **nonviolence** and ecological principles (*see* **ECOLOGY**). Later, in her book *Fighting for Hope*, she referred to Die Grünen as an "anti-party" party. The idea was for Die Grünen to use parliament as a forum for publicizing issues and simultaneously maintain the strong connections between the party and grassroots social movements. Kelly also insisted that Die Grünen not enter coalitions for sharing power with the major parties. In this respect, she appeared to be closer to the **fundamentalists** than to **realists** in the party. Kelly promoted the use of parliament as a means to initiate inquiries and hearings into issues that concerned the public, and Die Grünen used this mechanism effectively.

Despite her insistence on **direct democracy** and her apparent proximity to the fundamentalists, she fought with her colleagues over the issue of the rotation of delegates out of office after they had served either in executive positions in the party organization or in parliament. The argument presented by Kelly and the realists was that they should be allowed to retain their positions because of their accumulated knowledge, experience, and skills. She had numerous well-publicized disagreements with other members over what she perceived to be a lack of professionalism and factional brawling in the party. By 1990, she and her partner Gerd Bastian, a former army general who also served as a delegate for Die Grünen, had become detached from the party. They also withdrew from public life. In October 1992 both Kelly and Bastian were found dead in their home. Bastian had apparently shot Kelly in her sleep before taking his own life.

L

LALONDE, BRICE. *See* **GREEN PARTIES, FRANCE.**

LEOPOLD, ALDO. (1886–1948). Born in 1886 in Iowa, Aldo Leopold is celebrated for a work entitled *A Sand County Almanac*, which has been highly influential in the development of the green movement and a source of inspiration for the perspective on the environment known as **deep ecology**. Leopold graduated from the Forestry School at Yale University and was then employed by the Forest Service in Arizona. His book *Game Management* (1933) focused on the effective management and conservation of forests and wildlife within them. His work on this topic was widely used by professionals.

In writing *A Sand County Almanac*, published in 1949, a year after he died, Leopold became recognized as a key figure in the development of an ethic for the relationship between human beings and their environment. He sought to develop a system of values that went beyond the predominant focus on economic relationships. The notion of a land ethic was meant to extend "the boundaries of community" to cover soil, water, plants, and animals. Leopold argued that the time was ripe for developing a land ethic and like **Rachel Carson**, in her 1962 bestseller *Silent Spring*, painted a bleak picture of the damage being inflicted on the environment. Leopold pointed to the destruction of many species of plants and animals, soil erosion and the utilitarian approach that regarded water as a resource just "to turn turbines, float barges, and carry off sewage."

Above all, his land ethic sought to change perceptions of the role of human beings from that of "conqueror of the land-community to plain member and citizen of it." This would be based on love, respect, and admiration for the environment. There are strong parallels between the idea of a heightened awareness of the value of the "land" (which includes animals, plants, water, and the soil) and **biocentrism** and **spirituality**.

LIMITS TO GROWTH, THE. The title of a book published in 1972 based on a study commissioned by the **Club of Rome** and written by Dennis L. Meadows, Donella H. Meadows, Jorgen Randers, and William W. Behrens III, a team of researchers at the Massachusetts Institute of Technology (MIT). The study tried to realize the goal of the Club of Rome to develop a better understanding of economic growth, industrialization, environmental degradation, population change, and natural resources. Above all, it investigated the complex interaction between these factors rather than examining them in isolation.

In its methodology, the study was deeply influenced by Jay Forrester who, in the 1940s and 1950s, developed a dynamic model of social and economic change. *The Limits to Growth* used computers and complex models to predict the pattern of economic change over the next century. Originally, Forrester had assumed that computer models were superior to mental ones, because they were better able to analyze patterns and predict outcomes of the interaction of complex systems. Critics of these computer models pointed precisely to their inability to take into account the complexity of mental processes and the ways in which human perceptions could change rapidly.

In their computer models Dennis Meadows and his team examined four principal determinants of economic growth: **population growth,** pollution, industrialization, and natural resources. The study predicted that if the prevailing patterns of exponential economic growth were to continue, humankind would be faced with a catastrophe by the end of the twentieth century. The principal causes of the imagined calamity were a rapid depletion of resources, the threat to human existence by pollution of the environment, massive shortages in the food supply, and the rapid growth in world population.

The findings were somewhat alarmist but noted several possibilities for avoiding catastrophe. The principal conclusion was that if the prevailing trends in the expansion and growth of population, industrialization, pollution, food production, and resource consumption were not altered, the basis for **industrial societies** would be eroded within a hundred years. The study went on to argue that these trends could be altered particularly if there was a focus on sustainable systems of economic development and environmental protection (*see* **SUSTAINABLE DEVELOPMENT**).

Among the main recommendations of the study were huge reductions in industrial and agricultural investment as well as a significant decrease in the birthrate and the transfer of wealth from more developed to less developed countries.

In both its assumptions and recommendations *The Limits to Growth* was not dissimilar to concerns expressed during the previous century, notably by **Thomas Malthus** in *An Essay on the Principle of Population. The Limits to Growth* also appealed to people who, in the 1960s, had led or been influenced by the new wave of concern about environmental protection as well as the antiauthoritarian and anti-Vietnam War protest movements.

The Club of Rome acknowledged that the report's findings were tentative; however, it welcomed the opportunity to engage the community in a heated debate about the implications of the study. They were entirely successful; media coverage of the book and arguments stimulated by it helped boost sales of the work. Within a few years, about four million copies of the book had been sold in 30 languages. Worldwide sales eventually amounted to 20 million. The report made an immense contribution to raising awareness of environmental issues. It also generated a great deal of opposition.

One line of attack against the study was that it failed to consider how changes in technology, alterations in consumer behavior, and the discovery of new resources and forms of energy might avert the predicted outcomes. Other critics have argued that the limits to growth thesis outlines the interests of managerialism and reformist capitalism. In other words, the underlying concern is the sustainability of capitalism and industrialism with no attempt to imagine a qualitatively different society and culture. Although *The Limits to Growth* argued for a fairer redistribution of wealth and resources toward less developed countries, critics of the study were unhappy about what they regarded as an attempt by more developed countries to prevent less developed countries from attaining wealth and prosperity through economic growth. In the more developed countries business was angered by recommendations for reduction in industrial growth.

One of the most comprehensive critiques of *The Limits to Growth* was carried out by a group of researchers in the Science Policy Research Unit at the University of Sussex in England in a study entitled *Thinking About the Future: A Critique of* The Limits to Growth. Apart from focusing on the methods used in *The Limits to Growth* and gaps in basic information about certain variables, the Sussex team drew attention to some of the assumptions made by the MIT team, about political and social values. Subsequent studies have also demonstrated that the availability of mineral reserves and fossil fuels is much greater than estimated in *The Limits to Growth*. Apart from echoing some of these criticisms, *The Global 2000 Report* pointed out that *The Limits to Growth* failed to produce specific, detailed analyses of problems in particular regions and recognize that the type of economic growth can make a significant difference in whether natural resources deplete at a rapid or slow rate.

Despite its serious shortcomings, *The Limits to Growth* stimulated awareness of the fragility of the environment, motivated many people to join social and political movements concerned about environmental issues, and eventually prompted changes in the behavior of consumers and in government policies. Regardless of its deficiencies, *The Limits to Growth* accelerated efforts to develop more efficient technology, look for new reserves of natural resources and become more creative in dealing with environmental problems.

LOVELOCK, JAMES. *See* **GAIA HYPOTHESIS.**

M

MAATHAI, WANGARI. (1940–). Born in Kenya, Wangari Maathai founded the **Green Belt Movement**, which promoted, with huge success, the planting of trees in order to prevent soil degradation and enhance the **quality of life** in cities. Maathai was awarded a doctorate in 1971 from the University of Kansas. In 1976 she became head of veterinary anatomy and in 1977 associate professor of anatomy at the University of Nairobi. In 1980 she was appointed chair of the Kenyan National Council of Women. In 1989, when she opposed plans to develop a huge multistory building in a park in the capital city of Nairobi, she angered the political authorities and in November 1990 was prevented from returning to her country after a trip overseas. In 1989 she was named Woman of the World in a ceremony presided over by Diana, Princess of Wales.

MALTHUS, THOMAS ROBERT. (1766–1834). Arguments about *The Limits to Growth*, the *Tragedy of the Commons*, and the problems of **population growth** have frequently recurred in debates articulated by the green movement. These controversies correspond to concerns expressed since the eighteenth century, notably by Thomas Malthus in *An Essay on the Principle of Population* (1798). Malthus was born in Guildford, England, in 1766 and died in 1834. After being educated at Cambridge University, he served briefly as a curate before becoming a professor of political economy at Haileybury College in 1805. In his famous essay, Malthus argued that a sharp increase in population (as experienced by Britain in the transition from an agrarian and feudal to an industrial economy) was likely to outpace the capacity of the community to provide food for it. Should the provision of food be plentiful for the existing population, a further increase in the size of the population was unavoidable. However, if a community were unable to provide for a growing population, the consequences would include famine, disease, and armed conflicts. Malthus's essay was used as the basis for an attack on the system of poor relief. It was argued that the poor laws increased the population, lowered the general standard of living and raised the number of paupers. This in turn had a harmful social effect, undermining the spirit of independence of individuals and destroying their will to work hard.

Although these arguments are not widely accepted among environmentalists today, the basic concern about **population growth** and the possibilities of armed conflict has generated considerable discussion, as in the popular work by **Paul Ehrlich** entitled *The Population Bomb* (1968). Ehrlich has often been described as a neo-Malthusian for his views. Among the measures proposed by some environmentalists to deal with the question of population are financial incentives to discourage procreation and educational campaigns to change beliefs and perceptions about this issue. There is, however, no general agreement in the green movement and in other political and social organizations about the desirability or necessity of introducing various measures to curb population growth.

MAN AND THE BIOSPHERE PROGRAM. An initiative started by UNESCO in 1970 with the aim of gathering reliable scientific data on the state of the environment. The program relied on the cooperation of several governments and was developed by research teams working in various disciplines. It focused on questions like the relationship between human beings and ecological systems, the connection between the evolution of ecological systems and social and economic change, the creation of standards for the measurement of changes in the environment, and the conception of models for the management of resources. Above all, this initiative entailed cooperation between researchers in different countries in order to improve the reliability of information available to planners and politicians. The researchers were thus in a position to contribute to arguments about issues like the preservation of forests, soil erosion, and **biodiversity.**

McTAGGART, DAVID. (1933–). Born in Vancouver, Canada, David McTaggart was a leading badminton player in the 1950s. In the 1960s he became a highly successful entrepreneur in the U.S. building industry. After losing most of his fortune, he sailed around the South Pacific before responding to an appeal by **Greenpeace** for supporters to participate in actions against nuclear testing by the French government at Mururoa. McTaggart led a group of activists into the nuclear test zone, drawing the ire of the French government, leading to serious assaults on the protestors, and succeeding in attracting immense publicity for Greenpeace. McTaggart went on to become director of Greenpeace International and was largely responsible for ensuring that the organization developed a very high level of professionalism and competence in carrying out research and conducting campaigns over numerous environmental issues.

MENDES, CHICO. (1944–1988). The son of a rubber tapper in Brazil, Chico Mendes followed his father's trade and then became the leader of a protest movement against the activities of developers, particularly cattle ranchers and settlers in the Amazon region in the 1970s. While the activities by Mendes and his fellow workers were conducted on a sustainable basis, that is, they allowed for the renewal of the trees, the actions of the cattle ranchers had a devastating impact on the environment. Mendes conducted an electoral campaign in 1986 as a candidate of the Worker's Party and secured a significant proportion of the vote. In 1987 he focused his efforts on lobbying the U.S. Inter-American Development Bank, which was instrumental in providing funds to the developers for constructing highways through the Amazon region. He succeeded in persuading the U.S. Senate Appropriations Committee to reduce significantly the amount of funds allocated to the bank on environmental grounds. He also persuaded the Brazilian government to create reserves for protection of the traditional extractive trades in the region. His successes prompted a violent response from the ranchers who murdered him in December 1988. Mendes left a strong legacy as others organized the defense of the rainforests.

MUIR, JOHN. (1838–1914). Born in Dunbar, Scotland, John Muir moved with his family to Wisconsin in 1849. In 1863, after three years at the University of Wisconsin, where he did well but did not complete his studies, he began to travel around the United States, taking on casual jobs and exploring the countryside. Beginning in 1867, following a serious eye injury from which he recovered, he embarked on lengthy journeys across America before settling in California, first in San Francisco and then in Yosemite. In 1874 he became well known as a writer of "studies in the Sierra." His interest in travel extended to numerous journeys to Alaska as well as trips to South America, Australia, Europe, and Africa.

He became a prolific writer, focusing on his travels, the dangers to the natural environment, the need for protection and preservation of nature, and the spiritual qualities of the wilderness. Muir played a central role in the campaign that led to the creation of the Yosemite National Park in 1890. In 1892 Muir and other preservationists formed the **Sierra Club** to protect areas like the Yosemite National Park as well as the Petrified Forest and Grand Canyon National Parks in Arizona. Muir was elected the first president of the club and guided it through several important campaigns until his death in 1914. In 1903 President Theodore Roosevelt went to visit Muir in Yosemite and undertook several plans for conservation.

N

NAESS, ARNE. *See* **DEEP ECOLOGY.**

NATURE CONSERVANCY. The primary objective of the Nature Conservancy in the United States is to buy land in order to protect it. Formed in 1951, the organization has, over a forty-year period, been able to protect over 5 million acres, which include over 1,000 sanctuaries and many endangered species. Its nonconfrontational approach to environmental protection has made the organization attractive to the more conservative members of American society, many of whom would consider the tactics of some environmental groups as too radical and conflictual. In 1995 the Nature Conservancy had over 600,000 members.

NETHERLANDS. Although, as in other advanced industrialized nations, there is a strong awareness of environmental problems and significant support for social movements concerned about issues like the development of nuclear energy, there have been many obstacles to the successful implementation of environmental protection measures in the Netherlands. Economic development in the 1950s and 1960s led to considerable pollution of the air and water. The location of petrochemical industries in the Netherlands has further contributed to these difficulties. In addition, the Netherlands has both contributed to and been the recipient of pollution flowing through the Rhine River.

Another major problem has been how to deal with the consequences of the enormous success of the agricultural sector in producing more livestock (notably cattle, pigs, and poultry), relative to the territory available, than any other country in the world. The principal difficulty is the damage caused by the nutrients from the manure generated by the livestock. Nitrogen and phosphate have damaged surface waters and groundwater and contributed to air pollution in the form of ammonia acids.

In the early 1970s concern about air and water pollution caused by heavy industry led to the formation of a Ministry for the Environment and introduction of the **polluter pays principle**. In addition, subsidies and levies were introduced to fund new technologies to deal with contamination and assist with the regulation and inspection of levels of pollution. Public opinion was generally supportive of these measures, as was the Christian Democratic Party, which dominated the coalition governments that had to be formed in the context of a multiparty system. Although environmental groups attracted many supporters and sympathizers, green political organizations were unable to exert a great deal of influence in the 1970s and 1980s due to their fragmentation and the particular circumstances surrounding their development in the Netherlands (*see* **GREEN PARTIES, NETHERLANDS**).

Pressure on the major parties to address concerns about the environment resulted in the government's 1989 National Environmental Policy Plan. It recommended targets for reducing pollution, particularly **acid rain** and the depletion of the **ozone layer**. Other proposals were how to reduce drastically the use of pesticides and handle the transportation of hazardous wastes. The government used the findings of the **World Commission on Environment and Development** on

sustainable development to justify drastic action. Summarizing the problems facing the Netherlands and many other industrialized countries, the plan reflected some of the deepest concerns expressed by environmentalists and green political organizations. To fund the plan, the government proposed additional levies on fuel and the withdrawal of tax concessions given to homeowners. This led to the fall of the coalition government (led by the Christian Democrats and supported by the Liberal Party). However, a new government, led by the Christian Democrats and supported by the Social Democrats, did introduce the plan.

Reflecting an enduring trend in the Netherlands, there was considerable resistance by vested interests to the implementation of the plan and reluctance by government to take steps to realize policies aimed at considerably reducing levels of pollution. Large corporations have been able to hinder the introduction of effective measures or to gain exemptions to plans to combat problems like the **greenhouse effect** and energy taxes (*see* **CARBON TAXES**). However, the introduction of new and fairly drastic proposals reflects the growing demand for environmental protection and the possibility for the enactment of specific changes in the future.

NEW POLITICS. The term "new politics" has been used to identify the articulation of issues that had previously been accorded relatively low status on the political agenda. Since the 1960s concern about the environment has been linked by social scientists to the emergence of the new politics. The new politics also includes preoccupation with **direct democracy, decentralization,** and **postmaterialism.** Postmaterialism provides clues to the difference between the old and the new politics. The old politics is concerned with questions of material prosperity, security, and law and order. The new politics focuses on a different set of considerations, aesthetic and intellectual development, and questions of **spirituality** and the **quality of life.** Nonmaterial values have been central to the new politics and reflect an attempt to move away from the focus on economic growth and material prosperity, including the production and consumption of goods.

The new politics also marks the entry of new social groups onto the political stage. Since the 1960s participation in these new movements has been high among women, minority groups, the young, the relatively affluent, and the well educated. New styles of political action have been adopted by these movements, hence the focus on participation and direct democracy, attempts to avoid hierarchical structures, and critique of the political patronage that characterizes traditional political organizations. In the green movement the new forms of political organization have included the formation of **citi-**

zens' initiatives and green political parties that have attempted to introduce innovative practices into conventional political settings.

NEW ZEALAND. *See* **VALUES PARTY.**

NONVIOLENCE. The principle of nonviolence is an axiom espoused by many green political organizations. Some people believe that green political activists should renounce all forms of violence in the manner suggested by Mahatma Gandhi and his followers in the campaigns against British rule in India. There have been numerous suggestions for how to put nonviolence into practice. Green activists have argued that, in certain situations, it is necessary to engage in campaigns of civil disobedience, which could include noncompliance with tax regulations (for example in protest against the use of taxes to purchase military equipment and fund wars) and passive resistance, like blocking the entrances to nuclear power plants to prevent the transportation of nuclear waste. There are also controversies over whether or not to sabotage nuclear plants in order to try and achieve similar objectives, and a small minority have carried out such threats (*see* **EARTH FIRST!**).

Some green activists have suggested that no efforts should be made to arm citizens, even for their own defense, since this would already sow the seeds for violence. Others, however, have developed detailed proposals for eliminating "offensive" weapons that might be used to invade another country; maintaining "defensive" weapons (for instance, antiaircraft units); and preparing citizens to engage in resistance to armed invasion.

NUCLEAR DISARMAMENT PARTY (NDP). The principal objectives of the Nuclear Disarmament Party (NDP) in **Australia** are the closure of all foreign military bases, a ban on the stationing in or the passage through Australia of any nuclear weapons, and, of particular relevance to environmentalists, a halt to the mining and export of uranium. The NDP emerged from the peace and environment movements and represents one of the earlier efforts by green political activists to form a national political organization (*see* **GREEN PARTIES, AUSTRALIA**).

The peace movement has a longer history (as a new social movement) than the environmental movement and can be traced back to campaigns for disarmament in the 1950s both in Australia and in countries like those in the United Kingdom (*see* **CAMPAIGN FOR NUCLEAR DISARMAMENT**). In the 1960s the Vietnam War provided a further focus for the peace movement. The young, better edu-

cated, middle class, and those with left-wing orientations have joined
all these movements and the NDP in great numbers.

The NDP has had strong support among these social groups and
endeavored to combine some of the ideas from both the peace and
environmental movements. Uranium mining was one of the core issues that occupied the NDP, and this reflected an interest in both preserving the environment and peace and nuclear disarmament.
However, the circumstances surrounding the formation of the NDP
were favorable in some respects but problematic in others. The party
was created in response to a 1984 decision by the Australian Labor
Party to permit the operation of a uranium mine. This was a breach
of a pledge to proceed more cautiously in this domain and provoked
a very strong response from opponents of uranium mining, many of
whom were members of the ALP.

In a very short period of time, just six months after the formation
of the NDP, 8,000 people had signed up as members, and 643,061
people, representing 7.2 percent of voters, had cast a first preference
vote for the party in elections to the Senate. There were, however,
numerous disadvantages associated with this momentary shift in fortune. Although the profile, in social and economic terms, of those
who voted for the NDP was similar to that of supporters of green
political organizations in other countries, the party also shared some
of their weaknesses. Apart from a pledge to rid the world of nuclear
weapons and nuclear power, there had been an ineffectual debate in
the NDP about how to implement policies. Little effort had been
made to explain more fully the connection between policies about
nuclear disarmament or uranium mining and questions relating to foreign policy and economic development.

In addition, the catalyst for the formation of the NDP was first and
foremost a momentary reaction to the policies of one of the traditional
political organizations, the ALP. The rapidity of the response to the
policies of the ALP meant that there had been little debate about
political differences among supporters of the NDP. These were
largely repressed because of the need to compete hastily in an election
campaign. Although there was much unity around the notion of nuclear disarmament, there had been little time to develop positions on
other issues. Like many green political organizations the NDP also
lacked a coherent organizational structure. Party branches had been
created in all states, yet there were no mechanisms to facilitate organizational coherence, the exchange of political ideas, and a dialogue
with various social movements.

The overarching appeal to nationalism in a policy on nuclear weapons that was not influenced by the interests of foreign countries lasted
for only a short while. Similarly, complaints against the ALP re-

mained just a protest. Members of the traditional parties that had defected to the NDP felt they had achieved what they wanted simply by registering a protest vote against ALP policies. There had also been insufficient time and reflection for supporters of the green movement to become or remain loyal to the NDP. Many activists from the peace and environmental movements regarded the NDP as a useful adjunct to their campaigns, which took the form of social movements, lobby groups, mass political protests, and political networks.

Among those committed to the new party, conflicts arose between some who were solely concerned with the single issue of nuclear disarmament and others who wished to emulate the broader approach of **Die Grünen** in Germany. The failure by party activists to agree on basic organizational and political principles further undermined the chances of retaining the support of voters who had protested the traditional parties and of activists from social movements. A final obstacle to the further development of the NDP was, as in countries like those in the United Kingdom, an electoral system for the lower house, the House of Representatives, that disadvantaged minor parties. There were also hurdles to entering the upper house. After the 1984 elections, the NDP was allocated one seat in the Senate, following a favorable distribution of preferences to Jo Vallentine, its sole parliamentary delegate, in Western Australia. Yet, in New South Wales, where it attracted 249,722 votes, it was unable to secure another seat because of an unfavorable distribution of preferences by the ALP. Although the NDP continued to contest elections in the 1980s, it never recaptured the position it held in 1984.

The first national conference of the NDP, held in April 1985, was set up only to make recommendations that would be voted on by the membership at a later stage. The conference was not representative either of the membership or state branches. It had no mandate to draw up a constitution, form cohesive organizational structures, or decide on appropriate tactics for Jo Vallentine. Two issues prompted the exit of its only senator, along with about forty other delegates, during the first conference. First, there was disagreement over procedures for the ratification of recommendations made by the conference. Those who walked out of the conference had argued that the entire membership should be involved through a postal ballot. Their preference for this method of voting rather than for ratification by branch meetings of the party was tied in with the other major stumbling block, the question of dual membership. There was concern over the disproportionate influence of the Socialist Workers Party over the NDP. To combat this threat the NDP in Western Australia had introduced a proscription clause that allowed members of other parties into the NDP but prevented them from holding key positions. Postal balloting was regarded by many as a complementary mechanism to the proscription clause. The delegates in favor of postal balloting were, however, unable to secure a majority and walked out of the conference. Among them was Jo Vallentine, who went on to become an independent senator.

At the 1987 elections the NDP attracted only 102,480 votes, and Vallentine, as West Australian senator for nuclear disarmament, attracted 40,048 votes (4.8 percent) compared with 52,365 votes in 1984 (6.8 percent). Overall support for the NDP and for Vallentine dropped from 7.2 percent to 1.5 percent, yet the design of the electoral system ensured that both she and an NDP candidate from New South Wales were elected to the Senate.

O

OWEN, DAVID. *See* **ECOLOGY.**

OZONE LAYER. A term used to describe the concentration of a gas called ozone that occurs in the earth's atmosphere, especially at a height of about 12 to 30 miles above the surface of the earth. Ozone in the atmosphere is vital to the survival of life on earth as we know it because it creates a protective shield against nearly all of the ultraviolet radiation emanating from the sun. The principal danger arising from any depletion of the ozone layer is a startling rise in skin cancer. Other dangers associated with any increase in radiation entering through the earth's atmosphere include damage to the immune system of humans and animals and threats to plant life both on land and in the oceans. An increase in ultraviolet radiation is likely to contribute to chemical smogs and health problems, notably respiratory illnesses.

The principal cause of depletion of the ozone layer has been the production, mainly in industrialized countries, of chlorofluorocarbons (CFCs). Chlorofluorocarbons are artificially made gases comprised of chlorine, fluoride, and carbon. They have been used since the 1930s as an inexpensive and effective way of propelling substances in aerosol cans like deodorants, perfume, and paints. They are also used in a wide range of plastic foams for packing, in furniture, in the production of Styrofoam containers for fast-food outlets, and, in a liquefied form, as a coolant in refrigerators and freezers. Production of the most commonly used CFCs, chlorofluorocarbon 11 and chlorofluorocarbon 12, rose from around 5,000 tons in the 1930s to 45,000 tons in 1951, 750,000 tons in 1971, and over one million tons per annum in the early 1990s.

As far back as 1974 two researchers at the University of California,

F. Sherwood Rowland and Mario Molina, discovered that the release of large volumes of CFCs into the atmosphere would probably destroy a significant proportion of the ozone layer. Studies by the U.S. National Academy of Sciences in 1976 and 1979 supported these findings. The U.S. government did respond to this information by prohibiting, in 1978, the use of CFCs in nearly all aerosols. Sweden, Canada, Norway, and Finland took similar steps. These five countries, thereafter referred to as the Toronto Group, presented a variety of proposals for eliminating, across the world, the use of CFCs in aerosol cans and for phasing out their use in other products.

Initially, action by the Toronto Group had limited impact. First, their own ban on CFCs in aerosol cans did not lead to a reduction in the production of CFCs since they could be put to many other uses. Second, the Toronto Group faced opposition, notably by countries in the European Union, on the grounds that more evidence was needed to prove the connection between CFCs and depletion of the ozone layer. The European Union also perceived a variety of threats to its economic interests.

Major breakthroughs for those concerned about the depletion of the ozone layer occurred in the late 1970s and early 1980s. Scientists engaged in the British Antarctic Survey announced in 1982 a significant reduction in the concentration of ozone over the Antarctic. There remained, however, uncertainty over the reliability of this finding and whether CFCs, rather than other factors, were the cause of ozone depletion. The British scientists carried out exhaustive tests for two more years and by the end of 1984 were convinced that there had been a 30 percent reduction in or thinning of the ozone layer in this region.

The threat to the ozone layer provided a huge impetus to the development of the green movement in the 1980s, as governments and industrialists became involved in negotiations on how to handle the problem and environmental groups like **Friends of the Earth** launched highly successful campaigns all over the world to persuade consumers to boycott products that contained CFCs. Apart from bringing about considerable pressure on governments, public opinion and consumer boycotts led to swift changes in the practices of major corporations. In the United Kingdom, some of the leading corporations removed CFCs from aerosol cans. In a campaign led by Friends of the Earth in the United States and over 30 other countries, environmental groups targeted the use of CFCs in Styrofoam packaging. In 1987 McDonalds, along with other fast-food outlets, agreed to eliminate packaging that was made with CFCs. However, the most significant steps in phasing out CFCs were to occur as scientists made further discoveries about their deleterious impact on the atmosphere and pressure mounted on governments to introduce drastic measures.

Despite the uncertainty over the precise cause of the thinning of the ozone layer, meetings were held in 1987 at which agreements were reached between delegates representing the countries most heavily involved in the production of CFCs. The so-called Montreal Protocol on Substances that Deplete the Ozone Layer was signed on 17 September 1987. Around 50 developed countries agreed to reduce their consumption of CFCs by 50 percent by the year 2000. Less developed countries, which contributed only marginally to the production and consumption of CFCs, were permitted to increase their consumption up to the end of the century.

Within a fortnight, on 30 September 1987, flights by the National Aeronautics and Space Administration over the Antarctic appeared to indicate that the problem of ozone depletion would need to be addressed in an even more radical manner. The scientists found that the "hole" in the ozone layer was roughly equivalent in size to the surface area of the United States and in depth to the height of Mount Everest. At certain levels and points there was almost no ozone left at all. Above all, the connection was made between huge volumes of chlorine monoxide, a by-product of CFCs, and the depletion of ozone.

Scientists soon became convinced that there would have to be a 100 percent reduction in CFCs. They were also aware that even if this were implemented, it would not be until well into the following century that the level of chlorine in the stratosphere would return to the levels registered in 1985. In 1988 and 1989 scientists discovered large volumes of chlorine monoxide in the Northern Hemisphere, over the Arctic. Though they could not identify any significant depletion in the ozone layer, they predicted a similar outcome as had occurred in the Southern Hemisphere. In 1989 the United States and countries belonging to the European Union committed themselves to abandoning all production of CFCs by the year 2000.

In June 1990 the signatories to the Montreal Protocol met in London (London Conference of the Parties to the Montreal Protocol), and 80 countries now agreed to phasing out, by the year 2000, CFCs and other chemicals that were contributing to the depletion of the ozone layer. However, all these measures will not prevent further depletion of the ozone layer. Some countries have not signed the Montreal Protocol, and the phasing in of reductions will mean that the effects of CFCs will continue well into the next century. Emissions of some substances, like carbon tetrachloride, which can cause severe damage to the ozone layer, are not covered by the Montreal Protocol. Although the United States has banned this chemical, it is still produced by other countries.

One of the persisting central issues is how alternatives for CFCs can be introduced worldwide. Countries like India insisted that the more developed nations make accessible to the less developed ones any alternatives at a low cost. Any reductions in CFCs achieved as a result of the Montreal Protocol could be easily reversed by the production of CFCs in less developed countries.

P

POLLUTER PAYS PRINCIPLE. The polluter pays principle has been evoked by environmentalists and economists to address the consequences of damage to the environment. In essence, it refers to the idea that the full costs of goods and services, including the cost of repairing any damage inflicted on the environment, should be taken into consideration. For many governments this means trying to ensure that the price of products includes the entire social and environmental costs of their production. The Federal Republic of Germany has recognized this principle since 1971. More recently, following the Maastricht Treaty on European Union in 1991, this principle was meant to apply to all member states. According to the Maastricht Treaty, the cost of damage to the environment should be met by the producer. Governments set the standards, and polluters pay the relevant costs. The idea is that consumers will pay a price for products that reflects the full environmental and social costs.

POLLUTION CHARGES. In response to growing concern by expert communities and the public at large, governments either have begun to consider the possibility of or have actually implemented taxes and charges on products in order to reflect the costs to the environment. Green economists have long been concerned that the costs of goods and services have failed to reflect the real costs in terms of damage to the environment and have therefore argued and presented various mechanisms for **valuing the environment.** *See also* **CARBON TAXES; POLLUTER PAYS PRINCIPLE.**

POPULATION GROWTH. The notion of population growth as a central problem in modern societies has been a controversial one within the green movement. It underlies arguments about the *Tragedy of the Commons* and *The Limits to Growth*. The theme of overpopulation has been publicized in best-selling works by **Paul Ehrlich** and by activists in green parties like Sandy Irvine and Alec Ponton, members of the British Green Party. In *A Green Manifesto* Irvine and Ponton declared that the expansion in human population represented the greatest of all threats to the survival of the living world. There is also a strong parallel to the arguments of Thomas Malthus in the nineteenth century. Irvine and Ponton outlined detailed measures, including financial disincentives to procreation and educational campaigns that lead to changes in perceptions about this issue. There is, however, no general agreement in the green movement and other political and social organizations about the desirability or necessity of introducing various measures to curb population growth.

PORRITT, JONATHON. See **GREEN PARTIES, UNITED KINGDOM.**

POSTMATERIALISM. The concept of postmaterialism has been used by many writers to explain the change in values that has precipitated the advance of the green movement. The contrast between material and postmaterial values is as old as the study of politics. Aristotle suggested that once people had satisfied their basic material needs they might aspire to fulfill "higher" spiritual needs (see **DEEP ECOLOGY; SPIRITUALITY**).

More recently, in empirical studies conducted since the 1970s, the political scientist Ronald Inglehart interpreted public opinion data from several European nations to suggest that materialist and postmaterialist values were strongly associated with new conflicts in society. Although scholars interested in the rise of postmaterialist values were initially concerned about the protest movements of the 1960s (the student and civil rights movements) rather than the green movement, the connection has often been made between postmaterial values and the ascent of the greens. Studies have repeatedly shown a strong connection between postmaterial values, as measured by Inglehart, and support for the green movement.

The term "postmaterialism" has been used to draw attention to a shift in value priorities from materialism to postmaterialism, from a prevalent way of thinking (oriented to economic growth) to an alternative environmentalist approach. Initially, Inglehart measured materialist and postmaterialist values by presenting survey respondents with a list of four goals for their country over the next 10 years and asking them to rank these goals in order of priority. The four items were "the maintenance of order in the nation," "giving people more say in government decisions," "fighting rising prices" and "protecting freedom of speech."

The second and fourth items were designed to find out who identified with the 1960s protests for more civil rights and liberty. Respondents who chose these two items as their first and second priorities were classified as postmaterialists. Those who chose "the maintenance of order" and "fighting rising prices" were deemed to be materialist. A third "mixed" category was used for those (namely, the majority) who were neither outright materialists nor postmaterialists. (Inglehart has added eight more items to the list, though the original four items are most commonly used).

The scale identified the tendency of some to stress participation and individual freedom rather than economic and personal security. It has also been used to assess the connection between values and political behavior as well as economic and social circumstances. Like groups in the green movement, the 1960s social movements emphasized participation and freedom of speech in Western democracies. Numerous studies have shown that many of the backers of social movements in the 1960s also played a leading role in the green movement that began to attract many supporters in the 1970s. Inglehart's analysis of the impact of these earlier movements has proved to be of lasting importance, despite some shortcomings in his approach.

Inglehart adopted from the psychologist Abraham Maslow the notion of a "hierarchy of needs." At the base of this hierarchy we find primary or basic needs for survival like food, shelter, and security. They are labeled material needs. Once they have been met, people are more likely to seek fulfillment of secondary needs, including intellectual, aesthetic, and social needs. In affluent societies basic material needs for food and shelter are usually met, if not by individuals receiving income as wage earners, at least by the welfare state, which is supposed to provide a basic safety net. People in affluent societies are therefore more likely than those in societies experiencing relatively high levels of material deprivation to be able to pursue intellectual, aesthetic, and social—postmaterialist—goals.

However, during an economic recession, there is likely to be a diminishing emphasis on postmaterial values. Inglehart has postulated that this decline is not inevitable. The effect of poverty on values can be held in check by the **socialization** of individuals into certain values during particular phases of the life cycle. In other words, Inglehart has presented a parallel hypothesis based on the notion of socialization.

Although this and other arguments by Inglehart have been subject to many challenges, the distinction between materialism and postmaterialism has been influential in discussions about the rise of the green movement. Materialism is associated with economic growth, nonmaterialism is connected to self-fulfilment and self-actualization. The natural environment is valued either as a resource to be exploited for material ends or for its intrinsic or essential qualities (*see* **DEEP ECOLOGY**). Though the notion of intrinsic qualities may appear somewhat nebulous, many argue that people are able to appreciate nature for aesthetic, spiritual, or even religious reasons (*see* **SPIRI-TUALITY**). For many activists in the green movement it is not so much a question of dominating but of living in harmony with nature.

PRECAUTIONARY PRINCIPLE. The precautionary principle refers to the possibility of applying very stringent standards before permitting human interventions that may affect the environment. Governments like those of the Federal Republic of **Germany** apply strict standards to minimize the dangers of pollution. In some cases, the application of the precautionary principle may entail a decision not to proceed with a project for development, say the construction of a nuclear power plant. Most green parties have espoused the precautionary principle in debates over large-scale development projects. Some writers have argued that a concentrated emphasis on the precautionary principle may actually deprive human beings of the possibilities of dealing with certain problems. Since it is impossible to anticipate all the risks that might arise from the use of chemicals, a stringent application of the precautionary principle could lead to the denial of medical and other forms of relief to most people. In sum, there may be a need to consider the social and economic costs of implementing the precautionary principle.

PRICE MECHANISM. *See* **CARBON TAXES; POLLUTER PAYS PRINCIPLE; POLLUTION CHARGES; VALUING THE ENVIRONMENT.**

Q

QUALITY OF LIFE. Following the Great Depression and World War II there seemed little prospect of challenging predominant views about the connection between the quality of life and achievement of economic growth and industrial development. However, the green movement's challenging of established beliefs about economic development has led to a much broader definition of the quality of life. Apart from a strong focus on environmental protection and preservation for aesthetic, spiritual, recreational, and cultural reasons, the definition of quality of life includes, and goes beyond, the enduring concerns about security of employment, food, and shelter.

Interest in the quality of life impinges on the symbiotic relationship between formal employment and the informal sector (the home, family, and other social networks). Questions are brought up about the location and character of employment (a job that offers the possibility of self-realization, safe work conditions, a setting that is relatively free of fear and harassment, a reduction of time spent commuting to work, and telecommuting), a more flexible approach to the working day (or night), how work relates to involvement with family and other commitments, and new arrangements for monitoring actual work performance. Pressure for reform in the workplace is occurring in parallel with changes in how we perceive family life, relationships between spouses, and the raising of children.

The broader definition of quality of life advocated by the green movement has often been adopted by traditional political parties that have become preoccupied not only with the economic welfare of those in formal paid employment and their dependents but with the social, economic, and political concerns of minorities, immigrants, single parents, homosexuals, and women. Although some of these issues are not directly related to environmental protection, they reflect concerns about the quality of life introduced by environmentalists. Above all, the preoccupation with the quality of life reflects doubts about some of the definitions, categories, and dichotomies that have been used to influence human behavior over the past century.

Concerns with economic survival (the so-called traditional economic issues of unemployment, prices, inflation, and taxation) continue to play a significant and fundamental role in politics. Yet, a growing number of people view economic and other issues in terms of improving the quality of life. Issues like the health system, education, and care for the aged are deemed important not purely for the sake of survival, but in the context of improvements in the quality of life. Rather than accept traditional social reformers' dichotomy between the market and the state or the economic and the social, the definition of quality of life is being extended beyond meeting basic needs for survival. Environmentalism, along with concerns about the quality of health care, employment, and education, reminds us of this shift in priorities as certain needs have been met for growing sections of the population.

The rise in environmentalism is linked to much more than the obvious signs of deterioration in the physical environment. It is associated with changes in the social structure, efforts to adapt to technological change, and rising levels of education. *See also* **POSTMATERIALISM.**

R

REALISTS (REALOS). The term "Realo" (or "realist") was coined to depict the faction of **Die Grünen** in Germany that attempted to combine the desire for change by green social movements with the pursuit of power. The realists are usually counterposed to the **fundamentalists** or "Fundis," and the terms have been used to describe the divisions in many other green parties. The realists focus on the possibility of achieving effective and immediate political reforms through participation in parliamentary politics and coalition governments at any level. Whereas the fundamentalists argue that green parties will lose their spontaneous qualities by processes of bureaucratization and professionalization, the realists feel that it is possible to achieve many of the goals espoused by social movements through parliamentary action.

It is important to emphasize that the realists do not reject the value of extraparliamentary activities. Although they argue that parliament is one of the most effective forums for enacting change, parliament has been regarded as the domain for influencing the style of traditional politics. Realists have tended to reject the more radical demands of the fundamentalists for grassroots democracy (*see* **DIRECT DEMOCRACY**), including decisions based on agreement of all delegates, the principle of rotation (which stipulated that a delegate could only serve a limited term in office), and the imperative mandate (which made delegates accountable to members and subject to recall at any time).

The leading personalities in green parties have generally come under attack from the fundamentalists, who are suspicious of party elites and hierarchies. While the fundamentalists have attempted to set the agenda for green politics in terms of what they regard as the insurmountable differences between traditional political parties or their programs and oppositional groups arising from social movements, the realists have accepted many features of parliamentary democracy and the market economy while seeking to reorganize them in a manner that meets the demands of people concerned about environmental protection, democracy, and social justice. Although they share many of the long-term goals of the fundamentalists (like improved political participation, the closure of nuclear power plants, or governing in their own right without needing to form coalitions), the realists have tended to adopt a more flexible approach to most issues and focus on short-term gains. Above all, the realists on the whole enjoy much greater support than the fundamentalists among supporters and sympathizers of green parties.

The greatest threat to the realists is that traditional political parties may adopt many of their policies for environmental protection and thereby deprive them of their newly found electoral support. In that respect, the ability of the fundamentalists to draw attention to long-term goals and the principles underlying action by the green movement may prove invaluable to the realists. *See also* **FUNDAMEN-TALISTS.**

REALOS. *See* **REALISTS.**

REGAN, TOM. *See* **ANIMAL RIGHTS.**

RESOURCE ASSESSMENT COMMISSION (RAC). The Australian Resource Assessment Commission was established in 1989 as a response to the conflict over development and the environment. Headed by Justice Donald Stewart, in 1990–91 it had a staff of 50 and a budget of A\$6.2 million. The RAC emphasized its "independence" as well as its role in helping the government "to integrate environmental and economic factors into its decisions about the use of Australia's natural resources." The role of the RAC was to identify environmental, cultural, social, industrial, economic, and other values placed on resources. It also emphasized public participation and education.

Another important consideration in the formation of the RAC was to create a means of defusing political conflicts not only between developers and environmentalists but between powerful cabinet ministers. The RAC itself became a source of controversy and conflict, not between cabinet ministers but between government agencies over their respective roles as mediators in disputes over environmental protection. Senior officials in the Department of Arts, Sport, the Environment, Tourism, and Territories saw the Resource Assessment Commission as a threat on several counts. Not only were they concerned about the involvement by the RAC in mediating between developers and environmentalists, they were also unhappy, given their own funding situation, about the apparently generous amounts of money expended on the RAC. The agency was eventually disbanded in the mid-1990s after carrying out a series of highly influential inquiries into the conservation of national parks, forests, and coastal zones.

ROYAL NATIONAL PARK. Formally dedicated in April 1879, the National Park (later renamed the Royal National Park) was the first national park in Australia, formed by an initiative of a former premier, Sir John Robertson. The park comprised 18,000 acres on the southern shores of Port Hacking, about 13 miles from the city of Sydney. The construction of a railway link in 1886 facilitated access to the park and there was a rapid rise in the number of visitors.

S

SAHABAT ALAM MALAYSIA (SAM). Founded in 1978 by S. Mohamed Idris, Sahabat Alam Malaysia represents the **Friends of the Earth** organization in that country. SAM is best known for its campaigns to prevent the destruction of tropical rainforests. The main focus of these activities has been in Sarawak, where indigenous people like the Kayan, Penan, and Pelabit have been engaged in an enduring struggle with logging companies. The rapid destruction of the forests led in the 1980s to blockades by the native people of routes used by the logging companies. SAM assisted in these campaigns to defend the lifestyles and livelihood of the indigenous people and ensured that their concerns received a huge amount of publicity across the world. SAM has also been involved in legal battles over the land rights of the native people. Apart from these campaigns, SAM has focused on issues like the depletion of resources, pollution of the soil, and reporting on the state of the environment through its publications.

SCHUMACHER, E. F. (1911–1977). Born in Germany, where he was trained as an economist, E. F. Schumacher migrated to Britain in 1937. After being interned during World War II, he worked in a number of public service agencies, and was employed for 20 years at the British National Coal Board. Schumacher is renowned as the author of the highly influential *Small Is Beautiful.* He was also the founder, in 1966, of the Intermediate Technology Development Group, which had as its principal focus the development of technologies that were appropriate to the needs of less developed countries.

SIERRA CLUB. Founded in May 1892 by **John Muir** and his associates, the Sierra Club aimed to protect and preserve the natural environment, notably the Sierra Nevada, and encourage people to appreciate the region. From its inception the Sierra Club campaigned and lobbied the highest levels of government to protect nature.

Its first success was in checking proposals to reduce Yosemite Park in size. In 1910 it contributed to the successful campaign to establish Glacier National Park. In collaboration with other organizations it applied pressure for the formation of a National Park Service (which was achieved in 1916) and protection of redwood forests (in 1919). The Sierra Club contributed to or led campaigns for the expansion of Sequoia National Park (1926), Grand Canyon National Park (1975), and Redwood National Park (1978) and the creation of numerous parks and reserves: Admiralty Island (1932), Kings Canyon (1940), Point Reyes National Seashore, California (1962), Parade Island National Seashore, Texas (1962), Big Thicket Preserve, Texas (1974),

Big Cypress Reserve, Florida (1974), and Hells Canyon Recreation Area (1975).

Over time the Sierra Club broadened its focus from supporting legislation that protected forests and wilderness, like the 1964 Wilderness Act, which created a National Wilderness Preservation System, to lobbying for the enactment of the National Environmental Protection Act and foundation of the Environmental Protection Agency (1970) and the reinforcement of the Clean Air Act (in 1977, 1987, and 1990). Other major campaigns include the protection of about 0.8 million acres of land managed by the Forest Service (Colorado Wilderness Act, 1993), reversal of a decision by the World Bank to loan U.S.$500 million to Brazil for the construction of 147 new dams in the Amazon region, enactment of legislation to designate 6.8 million acres of wilderness in 18 states (1984), the successful prosecution of a suit against plans to remove 1.5 million acres of land from the Bureau of Land Management inventory of wilderness areas, and the enactment of the Alaska National Interest Lands Conservation Act (1980), which assigned 375 million acres as national parks refuges and wilderness areas.

The Sierra Club's success in these campaigns corresponds to a steady increase in membership. In 1897 the club had 350 members. In the first half of the century there was a steady rise to 7,000 in 1952 and 10,000 in 1956. In 1950 the club formed a chapter outside California for the first time. Between 1952 and 1969, under the proactive leadership of **David Brower** and in the context of a growing awareness of environmental problems (triggered by popular works like *Silent Spring* and reaction to the economic development that followed the post-World War II reconstruction), membership of the club increased tenfold, to 70,000. This trend continued and corresponded to the upsurge of new environmental groups and political organizations. In 1970 the club had 100,000 members; in 1976, 165,000; in 1985, 348,000; and in 1986, 400,000. By 1993–94 the club had 550,000 members, in 63 chapters and 396 groups. It had published around 600 titles and sold over 12 million books and calendars.

Although the Sierra Club has continued to concentrate its campaigns on the preservation of lands and ancient forests, it has broadened its agenda to include issues like the protection of endangered species, **population growth**, free trade agreements and their impact on the environment, policies by international agencies like the World Bank, energy policy (and its impact on global warming or the **greenhouse effect**), pollution of air and water, and waste management and recycling.

Though independent of any political organization, the Sierra Club has on two occasions endorsed a presidential candidate, one being Bill Clinton in 1992, and has signified its approval of congressional candidates. This is not necessarily inconsistent with its mission statement: "To explore, enjoy and protect the wild places of the earth; to practice and promote the responsible use of the earth's ecosystems and resources; to educate and enlist humanity to protect and restore the quality of the natural and human environment; and to use all lawful means to carry out these objectives."

SILENT SPRING. It takes much more than a scientific discovery to bring about a shift in perceptions about environmental protection and create mass political support for it. One of the most important breakthroughs was the articulation of the discovery that the quality of human life could be seriously threatened by certain types of economic growth and forms of industrial development. *Silent Spring*, by **Rachel Carson,** provides a striking illustration of how such a discovery can be effectively disseminated. The publication of the book in 1962 has widely been credited with setting in motion the mass environmental movements in the latter half of the twentieth century.

Although the book was a landmark scientific study, its impact is not solely attributable to its scientific character. Carson had for many years been disturbed by the impact of chemical pesticides like dichloro-diphenyl-trichloroethane (DDT) on wildlife, its habitat, and human life. In sharing her findings with others, she went much further than presenting scientific evidence. She challenged the entire approach of the chemical and other industries, their "arrogance" in assuming that "nature exists for the convenience of man," and their failure to appreciate that "The history of life on earth has been a history of interaction between living things and their surroundings."

The book elicited an immediate response from the chemical industry. It spent hundreds of thousands of dollars to prevent the widespread dissemination of the work and in trying to discredit it. However, sales of hardback copies alone amounted to 500,000, and in 1963 it was published in 15 countries. Throughout the United States people were concerned that the use of DDT would lead to the extinction of treasured symbols like the bald eagle. Publicity surrounding the book led to the establishment of a special panel of the Science Advisory Committee by President Kennedy, which supported the arguments presented by Carson about the hazards of pesticides.

The impact of the book went far beyond the chemical industry and the government. *Silent Spring* provided a major impetus to the environmental movement, serving for many as a manifesto for questioning the prevailing approaches to progress and the **quality of life.** There had already been warnings about the dangers of DDT to the environment. One important difference between prior accounts and *Silent Spring* lay in Carson's ability to place scientific discoveries in the context of a fundamental questioning of how people thought about the environment. The timing of the work may also have been an important factor; there was a more receptive audience in the 1960s than in the past.

SLOVAKIA. *See* **CZECHOSLOVAKIA.**

SMALL IS BEAUTIFUL. The widespread use of the expression "small is beautiful" originates from the best-selling book of that title by British economist **E. F. Schumacher.** Schumacher argued not so much against all large-scale endeavors as about their suitability. For some undertakings it may well be necessary to advocate a vast structure, for example, developing certain institutions and agencies in a city may require a substantial amount of money.

Apart from his focus on the suitability or appropriateness of the size of cities, technology, and institutions and agencies, Schumacher was concerned about the tendency to assume that immensity corresponds to efficient and effective structures. He provided many illustrations of how small-scale structures (nation-states, cities, government and nongovernmental organizations, and technologies) may often be much more effective in achieving objectives like prosperity and environmental protection than large-scale ones. Schumacher, rather than advocating an "idolatry of smallness," argues that we have simply gone too far, both in our beliefs and practices, in the opposite direction. His book also targets the values that arise from a preoccupation with materialism (*see* **POSTMATERIALISM**), and he links his thesis to debates about the plundering of the environment, thereby evoking some of the issues suggested in discussions of *The Limits to Growth.*

SOCIAL ECOLOGY. The term "ecology" has been adapted in a variety of ways to characterize different modes of organizing or thinking about the green movement. Social ecology represents, in certain respects, a contrast to **deep ecology.** Whereas deep ecology is concerned about the exploitation of the environment, social ecology, as understood by anarchist-writer Murray Bookchin, represents the view that the endeavor of human beings to dominate nature has its origins in their attempt to dominate each other. Bookchin differentiates social ecology from efforts to deal with environmental concerns by adopting new technologies (like solar or wind power). He uses social ecology to promote new social structures that include dismantling the power of centralized bureaucracies and hierarchies and focusing instead on the practice of **direct democracy**. There are strong parallels between arguments for social ecology and those proposed by **fundamentalists** in the green movement.

SOCIALIZATION. The term "socialization" has been used in arguments by the political scientist Ronald Inglehart about a shift from material to postmaterial values. Inglehart's central argument is that postmaterialists are more likely than materialists to take economic security for granted and place more emphasis on aesthetic and intellectual development than on the pursuit of material goals. These postmaterialist values are said to underpin the rise of the green movement (see **POSTMATERIALISM**). Socialization is based on the understanding that the nature of people's upbringing, or socialization, prior to adulthood will have a lasting impact and be relatively independent of changes in economic fortunes and political upheavals. Inglehart has postulated two hypotheses: the scarcity hypothesis and the socialization hypothesis. The first is based on the assumption that people in affluent societies are more likely than those in societies experiencing relatively high levels of material deprivation to be able to pursue intellectual, aesthetic, and social goals—postmaterialist goals. The second is that the decline in these values is not inevitable during an economic recession. The effect of poverty on values can be held in check by the socialization of individuals into certain values during particular phases of the life cycle.

People who are socialized in different historical eras, which may be characterized either by affluence or deprivation, will later in life react differently to the economic, social, and political environment. Studies of political behavior have shown, for example, that many people have continued to identify with the same political party from their youngest years to old age. Several studies have shown significant differences in value priorities between people who grew up during the Great Depression and those who were raised during the affluent postwar years. Those who experienced the Great Depression were more likely to have materialist values, even following improvements in socioeconomic conditions and radical changes in the political system.

One difficulty with the argument about the rise of postmaterialism has been Inglehart's apparent failure to specify the precise relationship between socialization and scarcity of material goods (which is said to be pivotal in influencing whether or not someone develops postmaterialist values). There is an apparent contradiction between the two notions; at the very least, they cannot be applied at the same time since socialization implies that values are constant or stable, whereas scarcity is based on the idea of a change in values under certain social and economic circumstances. Inglehart may have been too selective in applying these notions, overemphasizing socialization in relation to adult values and applying the scarcity argument to the formative years of a person's life. He may have failed to apply scarcity to adulthood and thereby neglected the analysis of change within a particular generation as a consequence of social and economic transformations.

SOCIETY FOR THE PRESERVATION OF WILD FAUNA OF THE EMPIRE. Founded in 1903, the Society for the Preservation of Wild Fauna of the Empire (later renamed the Flora and Fauna Preservation Society) was the first international environmental association. The society initially focused on protecting fauna in colonized territories. It was backed both by naturalists and hunters who regretted the consequences of their past practices. The association was the first of many endeavors to achieve cooperation in protecting wildlife in Africa. *See also* **AFRICAN SPECIAL PROJECT; AFRICAN WILDLIFE.**

SPACESHIP EARTH. Our planet has often been compared with a spaceship in order to emphasize how reliant we are on our natural surroundings and that we should be aware of the consequences of disregarding our need for resources like air and water in order to survive. The term "spaceship earth" was used in July 1965 in a famous address by Adlai Stevenson, the U.S. ambassador to the United Nations.

The idea was given an added environmental twist in 1966 in an essay on "The Economics of Coming Spaceship Earth" by Kenneth Boulding, an economist from the University of Michigan. Boulding drew a sharp contrast between a "cowboy" economy based on production, consumption, and the careless exploitation of natural resources and a "spaceman" economy, which attached value to maintaining the quality and complexity of the total capital stock.

SPIRITUALITY. The notion of spirituality has been promoted by some sections of the green movement to refer to the spiritual qualities of nature. In the nineteenth century the spiritual qualities of nature were highlighted by pioneers of the movement for preservation of wilderness areas like **John Muir.** Interest in them can be linked to ideas about a shift in values from materialism to **postmaterialism** and the notion of **deep ecology.** There is a parallel between the regard for the spiritual features of and holistic approaches to nature, the latter arguing that the whole is more than the sum of the parts. In *Breaking Through* Walter and Dorothy Schwarz draw a distinction between **industrial society,** in which life is fragmented and materialistic, and an approach to life that is far more complete because it includes spirituality.

Spirituality is said to include the aesthetic, caring and loving aspects of existence. The fact that it cannot be measured and categorized the way one can classify and gauge levels of pollution, votes for a green party, or the implementation of a waste management policy has meant that it has not generally been overtly used in promoting the green movement. When it has been advanced, as in the work by **Rudolf Bahro** on *Building the Green Movement*, it has been derided, often by supporters of the green movement.

STEADY-STATE ECONOMY. The term "steady-state economy" was used by American economist Herman Daly to outline a possibility for dealing with some of the problems identified in 1970s debates about **the limits to growth.** The argument for a steady-state economy is a plea for either a sustainable economy or **sustainable development.** There are two main aspects to Daly's argument for a sustainable economy. The predominant suggestion is that our economy is ultimately governed by the laws of thermodynamics. The other aspect is a principle-centered approach to human existence, derived from certain "moral first principles." The first law of thermodynamics is that in a closed system no energy is produced or consumed, only modified. The second law declares that heat may not of itself pass from a cooler to a hotter substance. Daly refers to this as the law of entropy, which entails the gradual decrease in the amount of usable energy as a result of the process of modification of matter.

The only addition to the power supply comes from solar energy. However, in our society the rate of modification of existing matter surpasses the rate of replacement by solar energy. Daly concludes that we are the only species living beyond our "solar budget" and are moving toward the irreparable destruction of the biosphere. To deal with these problems, Daly advocates a steady-state economy, which would be based on a specified size of population (*see* **POPULATION GROWTH**) and wealth. There would be flexibility for changing these sizes according to the availability of technologies and changes in values. However, a pivotal concept underlying any specification in size of population and wealth would be the "throughput of resources." Throughput, he emphasizes, "begins with depletion (followed by production and consumption) and ends with an equal amount of waste effluent or pollution."

The specification of throughput of resources implies that human beings, through moral principles and technology, would determine the rate of economic growth to a much greater extent than a system in which the growth of population and capital tends to shape technological and moral development. Daly stresses the importance of ethical first principles like knowledge, self-discipline, and restraint on the accumulation of desires. He joins other critics of modern **industrial society** in questioning preoccupation with the power of scientific knowledge and necessity for economic growth. Instead, he proposes a greater emphasis on sharing scarce resources and controlling population growth. Other first principles promoted by Daly include the notion of holism (*see* **SPIRITUALITY; STEWARDSHIP**). Whatever the objections raised to his ideas, Daly has brought about a notable shift in perceptions about the limits to and possibilities for reshaping the economy and linking it to concern about the environment.

STEWARDSHIP. The notion of the stewardship of nature is derived from the Judeo-Christian tradition. Although this tradition has often been linked to the secular belief in progress, it includes not only the notion of human dominion over nature, but of responsibility for it. A similar custodial view toward nature can be found in Aboriginal culture. Philosophers like Robin Attfield, author of *The Ethics of Environmental Concern*, have drawn attention to examples in the teachings of the Eastern Church of a compassionate view toward animals, justified in terms of the common origins of humans and animals as "creatures of God." The most well-known Western examples of this compassionate view can be found in the work of St. Francis of Assisi. Recognition of moral obligations to nature and future generations is present in the Christian tradition.

Stewardship has been adopted both by new political movements and established organizations. Despite the diversity of green parties and their focus on local concerns, some agreement on basic principles like stewardship and the needs of future generations has emerged. In his influential work on a **steady-state economy** American economist Herman Daly evokes as his first principles the notions of holism and stewardship as counters to the preoccupation with the power of scientific knowledge and necessity for economic growth. At the national government level there has been an acknowledgement in the 1990s of the notion of stewardship, for instance in documents like the White Paper prepared by the British government entitled *This Common Inheritance* (*see* **UNITED KINGDOM**).

SUSTAINABLE DEVELOPMENT. The term "sustainable development" has been used by international agencies ever since the 1972 **UN Conference on the Human Environment** that was held in Stockholm. It became an integral part of the vocabulary of public policy in Western democracies by the end of the 1980s. Prior to that, national governments had considered the development of national strategies for conservation, with the aim of integrating conservation and development. Arguments for sustainable development are major efforts by governments and other established organizations to provide an alternative to favoring development over environmental protection. Sustainable development was defined by the **World Commission on Environment and Development,** which was formed in 1983 by the United Nations, as meeting "the needs of the present without compromising the ability of future generations to meet their own needs." The commission provided a comprehensive statement on how to address both environmental and economic concerns and to recommend that all organizations strive to incorporate ecological wisdom into their economic and social decisions. The commission attempted to demonstrate that emphasis on materialism (*see* **POSTMATERIALISM**) and economic growth will not necessarily damage the environment if it is guided by principles of **ecology** and preoccupied with the renewability of resources. Economic growth was, however, "absolutely essential in order to relieve the great poverty that is deepening in much of the developing world."

In their attempts to influence the agenda for change that was being shaped by an increasingly powerful green movement, governments have exploited sustainable development much more fully than in the past. They have begun to formulate long-term plans for the integration and interdependence of conservation and development, retention of options for the future use of resources, and a focus on the underlying causes as well as the symptoms of environmental damage. Interest in these principles was rekindled by the reformulation of sustainable development by the World Commission on Environment and Development and growing awareness about environmental problems like the **greenhouse effect** and the depletion of the **ozone layer.**

Concern about these kinds of issues (especially among advanced industrialized nations) and the enduring questions about social justice and economic development that are repeatedly raised in discussions about the future direction of less developed countries have prompted intense efforts to define a new agenda based on the concept of sustainable development. There has consequently been an increase in awareness of the possibilities for promoting development without harming the environment or maintaining a balance between development and the environment.

The idea of sustainable development has been used to forge close links between economic and environmental concerns by governments, business organizations, and environmental groups. For some critics, however, sustainable development is a new form of managerialism, an attempt to quantify, according to economic criteria, the costs and benefits of environmental damage. This is seen in some quarters as a retrograde step. Others regard the debate over sustainable development as creating the possibility for resolving the tension between environmental protection and economic development. They argue that we need to pursue development within a framework that recognizes the basis of prosperity, both now and for future generations, as the proper maintenance of community resources.

Though sustainable development has been tailored by different social actors to suit their particular circumstances, the debate over this issue has created an opportunity for governments to move from a defensive posture (toward the green movement) to one that enables them to influence arguments about the environment and economy. Governments have adopted the role of arbiter between competing interests, calling for a "balance" between economic and environmental perspectives.

Government agencies have, in some countries, extended the definition of standard of living from pure economic and material measures like income levels and consumption of goods to include the idea of **quality of life** (which may cover the environment, social justice, and personal freedoms) and embrace a variety of values including ecological, aesthetic, and ethical considerations. Governments, like environmental and business groups, have discovered opportunities for developing new markets, products, and technologies in response to these public concerns (*see* **GREEN CONSUMERISM**).

The adoption of concepts like sustainable development is also linked to the attempt by governments to control or influence debates about the environment. Ideas like sustainable development are open to a wide variety of interpretations. If these frameworks are too precise (or insufficiently vague), the potential for conflict might be increased. Although governments have placed more emphasis than ever before on environmental protection, they have not downplayed economic objectives. Rather, they have attempted to incorporate the environment into decision-making and production processes and services. For some environmentalists support for sustainable development represents a fraudulent attempt to divert efforts from the fundamental problems that affect our planet. Others, however, are prepared to consider the possibilities for overcoming the tension between development and environmental protection.

The strategies pursued by government agencies for implementing sustainable development may include legislation that ensures that environmental concerns form part of planning at all levels of government activity; rewards for government and private organizations that reduce levels of pollution and penalties for those who do not; and the promotion of initiatives to develop industries in the field of environmental protection.

In the 1990s green organizations and political movements have also put forward numerous proposals for combining with environmental protection issues like employment. Trade unions, business organizations, and industrial groups have become more aware of the importance of the burgeoning environmental protection industry and market for treating and recycling waste, reducing air pollution, and cleaning water.

Although many of these initiatives are significant changes in political, social, and economic life, it is worth noting that human societies have been engaged in forms of sustainable development for centuries. The practice of Aboriginals of setting fire to the bush served at least two purposes: to force out animals that could then be hunted and bring about the renewal of vegetation and plant life that would in turn attract animals. Another example is the opposition by foresters in Australia at the turn of the century to the exploitation of forests on the grounds of preserving timber for future generations. The foresters were criticized for obstructing the tide of progress, namely, land settlement. There is a parallel between this position and the support for sustainable development by the World Commission for Environment and Development.

SWEDEN. Regarded for many decades as the archetype of a social democratic and corporatist state, Sweden has nonetheless experienced difficulties in accommodating the demands of the green movement. Although the Swedish government was primarily interested in production and economic development, in the 1960s it developed structures to address some environmental concerns like the pollution of the air and water and mercury poisoning of fish and birds. A major legislative initiative, the Environment Protection Act, 1969, targeted, among other things, the problem of water pollution. There were also parallel efforts to coordinate the activities of diffuse government bodies by forming a National Environment Protection Board. Among the successes of these initiatives is the improvement in the quality of water through the treatment of effluents from sewage. This has been the result of massive expenditure by the state on sewage treatment plants.

Concern about other environmental issues can be traced to the 1940s, when the government, concerned about damage to its lakes and rivers by **acid rain,** created a network of observers across Europe to record levels of acid pollution. The Swedes were at the forefront of international efforts in the 1970s to convene the **UN Conference on the Human Environment** held in Stockholm in 1972.

The most divisive environmental issue of the 1970s, and the one that exposed the weakness of the dominant corporatist regime in Sweden, was nuclear power. The Swedish government has widely been regarded as one of the most open and responsive to environmental concerns. Anxiety about the development of nuclear power posed a dual threat to the government. First, Sweden relied more than most advanced industrial countries on very high levels of energy consumption for its economic development. Second, the major partners in the Swedish success story, the government, big business and the trade unions, appeared unable to include the new social movements, notably those concerned about nuclear power, in the corporatist system.

The issue of nuclear power was first taken up by a major political party, the Center Party (formerly, the Agrarian Party), during the 1976 elections. The opposition of the Center Party to nuclear power proved decisive insofar as it led to the Social Democratic Party's loss of power for the first time in 44 years and to formation of a coalition government between the Center Party, the Moderate Party, and the People's Party. The failure of all the major parties to come to address the issue of nuclear power and the defeat of a referendum advocated by the Center Party to end the expansion of nuclear power projects were crucial in the formation of Miljöpartiet de Gröna (*see* **GREEN PARTIES, SWEDEN**).

The catastrophes at **Three Mile Island** in 1979 and, even more significantly, **Chernobyl** in 1986 played a crucial role in shifting public opinion on environmental issues. The Chernobyl accident had a greater direct impact on Sweden than on any other country outside the Soviet Union, and many restrictions had to be introduced on the consumption of fresh fruit and vegetables as well as on both livestock imported into Sweden and that produced by Swedes. At the 1988 elections environmental issues were prominent on the political agenda and included debates on how to bring about the closure of all nuclear power plants, legislation and taxation to combat all forms of pollution, investment in alternatives to coal and oil for producing energy (including greater use of natural gases, solar energy and wind power), restrictions on the use of chemicals in agriculture, new automobile speed limits, reductions in chlorine emissions from pulp mills, and much stricter regulation of the use of chlorofluorocarbons.

As in other countries, the major parties in Sweden have adopted many of the policies advocated by new social movements and green political organizations. Noting the significant changes in public opinion, they have responded to the continuing success of green parties, particularly at the local and regional levels. Tension still remains in Sweden between the growing awareness of dangers to the environment and the imperative to remain competitive in economic growth and development.

T

TASMANIA. An island that is part of the Australian federation and, in 1979, became the center of international attention as a result of the dispute over the proposed construction of the **Franklin Dam.** A strong green movement had been established during the campaign to save Lake Pedder and by the formation of the **United Tasmania Group,** which contested state elections from 1972. This group gave rise to the Tasmanian Wilderness Society in 1976 (renamed the **Wilderness Society**) and played a central role in the campaign against the Franklin Dam and a nationwide protest movement for the protection of forests and wilderness areas.

Opposition over several decades to industrial projects, especially to attempts by the Hydroelectric Commission to determine energy policy, produced a strong commitment, exemplified by activists like Bob Brown, and a variety of organizational structures. In 1989 green groups also campaigned successfully against the construction of a large pulp mill at Wesley Vale in northern Tasmania. These factors, along with an electoral system that made it possible for small parties to gain representation in parliament, led to the May 1989 election of five green independent candidates, who polled 17 percent of the vote across the state, to the House of Assembly, which is made up of 36 members (*see* **GREEN PARTIES, AUSTRALIA**).

After the failure of a historic "accord" between the greens and the ALP, the vote for the ALP dropped to its lowest ever in the 1992 elections. The green independents retained their seats, though their share of the vote declined to 13.4 percent. The success of the new Liberal government represented the triumph of groups that were fundamentally opposed to many aspects of the green agenda for reform. Yet, Tasmania remains one of the strongholds of the green movement.

THINK GLOBALLY, ACT LOCALLY. This concept has been attributed to environmentalist René Dubos and used as a slogan by the green movement in its endeavors to establish alternative ways of social action at the local level and demonstrate both in symbolic and practical terms the possibility for transforming the world. The focus on acting locally corresponds to the focus on decentralization in influential works like *A Blueprint for Survival* and in writings on **bioregionalism,** as well as in the orientation of many green political organizations and social movements. The slogan has been used to great effect in mobilizing people to take action in their local communities with respect to environmental protection; the creation of alternative lifestyles, including the provision of social and other services; and campaigns directed against specific industries, notably the weapons industry, and enterprises that have a deleterious impact on the environment.

THREE MILE ISLAND. The site of a nuclear power plant in Harrisburg, Pennsylvania, and of a near-catastrophe in March 1979. Radioactive gases were emitted from the plant and pregnant women and young children in the surrounding district were evacuated. The accident was caused by defects in machinery and negligence on the part of those responsible for the efficient supervision of the equipment, particularly in dealing with the emergency situation. The publicity surrounding this incident helped to mobilize further **antinuclear protests** in the United States and other countries. An additional stimulus to these protests was provided by a popular film based on similar events, entitled *The China Syndrome.*

TORREY CANYON. In the 1960s a number of catastrophes served to draw attention to the need for both a more powerful green movement and improved action by governments dealing with environmental problems. The collision of the oil tanker *Torrey Canyon* in March 1967 with rocks off the southwestern coast of England led to the spill of 875,000 barrels of oil. Much of it ended up on the shores of Cornwall and Brittany. Attempts to deal with the catastrophe were slow and very costly. Although governments have responded, to some degree, to the concerns brought up by the green movement, there is still considerable room for improvement, as demonstrated by the more recent and disastrous spill from the oil tanker *Exxon Valdez.*

TRAGEDY OF THE COMMONS. In a paper first published in 1968, biologist Garrett Hardin coined this term to describe the transition from a period when it was possible, without any deleterious consequences, to allow people to use common land to feed their cattle to one in which such action leads to catastrophe. In the first stage population levels are low. It is therefore plausible to imagine unhindered access to common land. In the second stage, with an increase in population and animals, the attempt to maximize use of common land, while yielding some benefit to each individual, ultimately has devastating consequences on the community as a whole. Hardin argued that the principle of freedom in the use of the commons needed to be set aside in favor of coercion for the good of the entire community. He proposed a variety of mechanisms, including restrictions on access to the commons, the introduction of taxes and charges to reduce pollution and control waste disposal, and a highly controversial proposal to impose constraints on the right to bear children (*see* **POPULATION GROWTH**).

TRAINER, TED. *See* **DEINDUSTRIALIZATION.**

U

UNITED KINGDOM. One of the most striking features about the green movement in the United Kingdom is the inverse relationship between the strength of green political organizations (*see* **GREEN PARTIES, UNITED KINGDOM**) and the degree of access afforded by the bureaucracy to environmental groups. The failure of the Green Party has often been attributed to the restrictive electoral system. At the same time, the administration has been open to ideas of environmental groups ever since the 1960s, and especially following the debate about *The Limits to Growth*, about the threats posed to the environment by pollution, and the expansion of the nuclear power industry.

The development of environmental policies can be viewed from at least three perspectives. The first has already been discussed, the access by environmental groups to the administration. The second involves attempts by the major political parties to adopt important elements of the concerns articulated most forcefully by the green movement. The third relates to specific policy initiatives.

Although British politics were dominated from 1979 onwards by Conservative governments, there have been some significant changes in their approaches to the environment as well as in the policies of their opponents. The preoccupation of the Conservative government with reducing the role of the state meant that there was initially little concentration on addressing environmental problems. Rather, the focus was on removing impediments to the operation of a free market. This resulted in a partial reduction in influence and access by environmental groups to government agencies. Although environmental groups did not sever their links with established institutions, they were, to an extent, forced to adopt a more militant approach and began to appeal directly to the public for support. They were able to exert influence, especially in public inquiries, in the system of parliamentary select committees (established in 1979) and through local authorities.

In 1979 the Liberal Party appeared to be the only one of the major parties to take environmental issues seriously and was certainly the only one to express strong doubts about the desirability of economic growth. By the mid-1980s, the United Kingdom, under the Conservative government led by Margaret Thatcher, had been labeled by many commentators as the "dirty man of Europe," partly because of its reluctance to implement directives by the European Union on environmental protection and partly because of the resolution shown by the government to promote economic development regardless of the social and environmental costs. The government came under pressure from its own ranks on issues like the protection of rural land (the Green Belt), implementation of the Wildlife and Countryside Act, and **acid rain** and from a Royal Commission on Environmental Pollution for being unresponsive to urgent problems and not coordinating work by different government agencies.

Additionally, the government was becoming aware of the drift of public concern about the environment and in 1984 introduced reforms in a number of areas, including greater coordination of the activities of government agencies to combat pollution and statutory intervention to discourage certain farming practices and encourage preservation of the rural landscape. In 1985 the government came under further pressure, on this occasion from the Labour and Social Democratic Parties, which produced detailed policy statements on environmental protection. However, it was only after their third successive electoral victory, in 1987, that the Conservatives began to consider the environment a key issue on the political agenda. On 27 September 1988, in a speech delivered to the Royal Society, Margaret Thatcher used the growing concern about problems like **greenhouse** gas emissions, the depletion of the **ozone layer**, and **acid rain** to place the environment high on the national political agenda for the first time.

Within the Conservative Party the tide was also turning against certain aspects of its pro-development policies, particularly facilitating the decline of the influence of local authorities over planning and the aggressive approach to the development of land for housing. The minister for the environment, Nicholas Ridley, came under intense pressure for promoting free market policies in this area. Rather than concede to the environmentalists, he espoused the importance of market mechanisms in addressing environmental problems, notably the **polluter pays principle** and the need for **sustainable development**. Nonetheless, he was replaced by Chris Patten, who was far more interested in the preservation of the landscape, enforcing government controls over planning of the landscape, and engaging in dialogue with environmental groups.

Although there was a strong reaction among some Conservatives against softening the government's approach to economic development, in 1990 Patten directed the production of a White Paper entitled

This Common Inheritance. Though it contained few specific policy commitments, the document attempted to reinforce the new prominence given to environmental protection and outline principles for action including the **precautionary principle**, the notion of **stewardship**, sustainable development, and the value of both statutory intervention and market mechanisms.

Although the environment still did not feature as a key issue in electoral politics, at the level of government administration the influence of environmental groups and of scientific experts was on the rise. Among the major reforms was the creation in 1987 of Her Majesty's Inspectorate of Pollution to coordinate the inspection of pollution. At first the inspectorate had few effective powers. However, the introduction of the Environmental Protection Act in 1990 provided the inspectorate with the necessary legal basis for fulfilling some of its potential as a pivotal agency in regulating industry. Although the inspectorate has had to address many difficulties in actually implementing the legislation for controlling pollution, its creation is a significant innovation.

The attempt of legislators to coordinate the activities of government agencies and achieve an improved level of integration in institutional structures for addressing pollution problems reflects the success environmental groups have had in bringing pressure to bear on the authorities. Other important reforms included the creation of a National Rivers Authority. All these agencies have been successful in court cases against numerous polluters. Directives issued by the European Union have also played a crucial role in challenging established practices and in introducing reforms.

Typical of the successful pragmatic approach adopted by some environmental groups is that taken by **Friends of the Earth**, which in 1989 published *The Environmental Charter for Local Government.* The environmentalists were responding to requests by local government officials for advice on "best practices." The adoption by a large number of local authorities of all or some elements of the charter reflects both the broad influence of ideas about environmental protection and success of environmental groups, at least at the local level, in changing policies and behavior. The issues addressed by local authorities include strategies for recycling resources and promoting fuel efficiency, conducting audits of performance in environmental protection, and implementing specific policies within a certain period of time.

In sum, the green movement in the United Kingdom, which has largely taken the shape of environmental groups lobbying for change through established structures at local and national levels, has brought about significant shifts in policy and begun to reshape some of the established institutions.

UNITED NATIONS CONFERENCE ON THE ENVIRONMENT AND DEVELOPMENT (UNCED). The UN Conference on the Environment and Development was held in Rio de Janeiro in June 1992. Often referred to as the Earth Summit, it was the largest international gathering of this kind, with delegates from 178 countries. It was also seen as the sequel to the **UN Conference on the Human Environment,** which had been held in Stockholm in 1972 and brought together governments, government agencies, and environmental groups to debate environmental questions.

The decision to hold another conference was made following a December 1989 resolution by the UN General Assembly. The choice of Rio de Janeiro as the venue for the conference was also important as it gave due recognition to the significance of less developed countries in efforts to address environmental issues. The meeting, with its focus on environment and development, was also a response to the efforts of agencies like the **World Commission on Environment and Development** to bring about a new understanding of the relationship between these issues. The report by the World Commission on Environment and Development had already become, for many governments and some nongovernmental agencies, the basis for developing a dialogue between environmentalists and developers. There was considerable skepticism among the media and environmentalists about the possibility of effective action emerging from the Rio conference. Reports on the conference reflected the central role of the media in spreading awareness of environmental problems and expressing the impatience with the delays in the implementation of new policies.

A major difficulty for the conference was to reconcile the divergent perspectives of developed and developing countries. The economic implications of environmental protection are particularly acute for the latter. The agenda in this sphere has been dominated by arguments over who should pay for environmental protection and over the "hypocrisy" of developed nations that consume a disproportionate share of resources and expect developing countries to take drastic measures to save the environment. There has also been tension between environmentalism in the developed world and the needs for survival and improvement of material conditions in developing nations. The goals of environmentalists in the West may also clash with the policies of particular regimes. For example, environmentalists and trade unionists in Western countries have attempted to prevent trade with countries like Malaysia in rainforest timbers.

Another dimension of international conflict lies in the different positions adopted by major powers or trading blocs on environmental issues, illustrated by the divergent positions of the United States and the European Union over the signing of international treaties on the emission of carbon dioxide, aid programs to developing countries, and regulating species protection or **biodiversity**. Conferences like the one held in Rio de Janeiro have contributed to the growing realization that national governments are having great difficulty in dealing with international economic problems as well as with environmental ones. Still, with the endorsement of several agreements at the conference, governments representing over 150 countries signaled at least a commitment to combat global problems.

Among the major agreements emerging from the conference was the plan to implement **sustainable development**, outlined in a document entitled *Agenda 21*. This document covered a vast range of topics including international cooperation, combating poverty, consumption patterns, population, the atmosphere, the oceans, indigenous peoples, women, nongovernmental organizations, technology transfer, education, public awareness, and training, as well as integrated decision making and international institutional arrangements. In an effort to ensure that member states devised national plans of action to implement *Agenda 21*, the United Nations established a Commission on Sustainable Development in December 1992. Every year all member states are to report to this commission on measures they have adopted to implement *Agenda 21*.

Another key initiative of the 1992 conference was the Framework Convention on Climate Change, which outlined principles that would underlie efforts to deal with problems like global warming, particularly the **greenhouse effect**. The convention was endorsed by 154 countries and the European Union. One of the most significant recommendations contained in this convention was that developed countries should, by the year 2000, reduce their greenhouse gas emissions to 1990 levels. However, governments were able to evade this requirement if they could prove that this would cause them economic difficulties.

Other important agreements to emerge from the conference were the Convention on Biological Diversity, Declaration on Environment and Development, and enactment of Forest Principles. As with the agreement on Climate Change, the Convention on Biological Diversity included many escape clauses for nations that were unwilling to implement aspects of it. The United States refused to sign it on the grounds that it would undermine its biotechnology industry, though 155 nations as well as the European Union did sign the agreement. Despite the understandable and justifiable criticisms both of the conference and kinds of agreements that resulted from it, UNCED remains a significant advance in getting the environment onto the political agenda of nation-states and the international community.

UNITED NATIONS CONFERENCE ON THE HUMAN ENVIRONMENT (UNCHE). Held between 5 and 16 June 1972 in Stockholm, Sweden, UNCHE signaled a significant breakthrough in getting governments, governmental agencies, and environmental groups together to discuss and recognize the importance of environmental problems. Official delegates from 113 countries took part in the conference. Among the principal themes was how to address problems of pollution. On some issues, like testing nuclear weapons and monitoring the use of toxic chemicals, there was disagreement between major powers like the United States and other countries. A more popular measure, suggested by the United States, was a moratorium, lasting ten years, on trading in whales.

One significant outcome of the conference was the focus by less developed countries on the connection between environmental protection and economic development (and their concern about any attempt by industrialized developed countries to slow the pace of development in poorer countries). This concern contributed to discussion about the possibility of **sustainable development** and a shift in perceptions among many environmental groups in more developed countries toward a more global view of environmental issues and problems. Another long-term outcome was the emergence, following the conference, of many more grassroots nongovernmental environmental groups in less developed nations. This can partly be attributed to the enthusiasm generated by the conference for further action pertaining to the environment and economic development.

The conference also led to further cooperation between nation-states. As regards the establishment of institutional mechanisms and structures to facilitate this cooperation, the formation of **UNEP** was one of the most visible outcomes of the 1972 conference.

UNITED NATIONS CONFERENCE ON THE LAW OF THE SEA (UNCLOS). The United Nations has supported three conferences on marine law. The first two were in 1958 and 1960. The third lasted from 1973 to 1982, and took up issues like the depletion of fish stocks, marine pollution and the creation of exclusive economic zones for sovereign nations. Although the Convention of the Law of the Sea was signed by 189 countries in 1982, this did not include major industrialized powers (like the United States, Japan, Germany, the United Kingdom and France). The latter objected to a clause that attempted to turn into common ownership the mineral wealth deposited on the ocean beds. UNCLOS only came into force in 1994 and entailed the creation of exclusive economic zones stretching out 200 nautical miles from a nation's coastline. However, the effort to declare the oceans a common heritage remains a source of tension between nations.

UNITED NATIONS ENVIRONMENT PROGRAMME (UNEP). This program was established in 1972 following the **UN Conference on the Human Environment** (UNCHE). In order to develop further the cooperation that had been achieved between government and nongovernmental organizations by the conference, the UN General Assembly supported the creation of a Governing Council of UNEP. The council would include representatives from 58 countries. They would be elected by the General Assembly for a period of three years at a time. The primary roles of UNEP were to coordinate and stimulate activities across all agencies of the United Nations.

In 1973 the Governing Council proposed three core objectives for the organization. The first was to increase knowledge, through the interdisciplinary study of ecological systems, "for an integrated and rational management of the resources of the biosphere, and for safeguarding human well-being as well as ecosystems." The second was to "support an integrated approach to the planning and management of development, including that of natural resources," with an awareness of the effects on the environment and social and economic considerations. The third was to provide assistance, particularly to developing countries, "to help mobilize additional financial resources for the purpose of providing the required technical assistance, education, training and free flow of information and exchange of experience, with a view to promoting the full participation of developing countries in the national and international efforts for the preservation and enhancement of the environment" (*UNEP: Two Decades of Achievement and Challenge*). In response to the 1972 UNCHE recommendations, UNEP developed three approaches, which they labeled environmental assessment, environmental management, and supporting measures.

UNEP also established mechanisms for the collection and exchange of information. The system came to be known as Earthwatch. An important element in this arrangement is the International Referral System, known as INFOTERRA. INFOTERRA has become the most extensive mechanism for the exchange of information on environmental issues in the world. Around 150 countries and 6,500 institutions participate in the system. INFOTERRA has also created additional networks for research and information, including the Global Environment Monitoring System (GEMS), International Register of Potentially Toxic Chemicals (IRPTC), and Global Resource Information Database (GRID).

Promoting environmental management, UNEP has contributed to the drafting of numerous international treaties like the 1973 **Convention on International Trade in Endangered Species**, the 1979 Bonn Convention on the Conservation of Migratory Species of Wild Animals, the 1985 Vienna Convention for the Protection of the Ozone Layer, the 1987 Montreal Protocol on Substances that Deplete the Ozone Layer, the 1992 Framework Convention on Climate Change, and the 1992 Convention on Biological Diversity. In order to assist with the management of water resources it initiated a scheme for the Environmentally Sound Management of Inland Waters, which led to an agreement between eight African countries to monitor the use of the Zambezi River Basin. Another important initiative by UNEP was its Regional Seas Program, which, beginning in the mid-1970s, brought together countries to protect the coastline and oceans around the world.

The success or failure of UNEP's initiatives depends to a large degree on financial support from national governments and the latter's willingness to implement agreements. A large proportion of the objectives that UNEP has set for itself remain to be realized. However, it has raised awareness about environmental issues among political elites; coordinated action by numerous agencies at the local, national, and international levels; and successfully implemented some of its plans.

UNITED TASMANIA GROUP (UTG). The United Tasmania Group was formed in March 1972 as a direct response to the failure by traditional political parties to consider the full implications of the destruction of Tasmania's Lake Pedder in order to promote a hydroelectric system. The UTG was formed by the Lake Pedder Action Committee and was the first political organization in Australian history to adopt a **new politics** platform. In the 1972 state elections it came close to winning a seat in the Tasmanian parliament after contesting four seats and polling about 7 percent of the vote for them. Both the UTG and the **Values Party** (formed in 1972 in New Zealand) are regarded by some commentators as the first green parties. The UTG (and the Values Party) combined opposition to industrial development with some of the preoccupations of social movements from the 1960s like the need for political reform and social change.

The manifesto of the UTG represented some of the central tenets of the alternative environmental paradigm described by Stephen Cotgrove in *Catastrophe or Cornucopia* and the postmaterialist values (*see* **POSTMATERIALISM**) identified by Ronald Inglehart in *The*

Silent Revolution. The UTG espoused a "new ethic" that condemned "the misuse of power for individual or group prominence based on aggression against man or nature." It advocated an aesthetic and harmonious relationship between human beings and nature and undertook to create new institutions that were based on participatory democracy (*see* **DIRECT DEMOCRACY**), justice, and equal opportunity.

Although the UTG participated in nine electoral contests between 1972 and 1976, it failed to gain any seats and by 1977 began to decline as a political organization. In its place emerged a new organization, the Tasmanian Wilderness Society (*see* **WILDERNESS SOCIETY**), which provided a structure for mobilizing protestors, especially against development projects like the **Franklin Dam**. The UTG had served as a vehicle for training a new generation of political activists who were to wage highly successful campaigns and influence environmental policy making and new political organizations in **Tasmania** and in **Australia**.

V

VALUES PARTY. The Values Party, formed in May 1972 in Wellington, New Zealand, was the first party to be established at the national level and champion both environmental protection and participatory democracy (*see* **DIRECT DEMOCRACY**). At the November 1972 elections it competed in 43 of the 87 electorates. It polled 3.9 percent of the vote in these electorates and 2.7 percent of the vote across the nation. In 1975 the party improved its performance, obtaining 5.2 percent of the total vote and attracting many former Labour Party supporters. The pinnacle for the Values Party, in electoral terms, was a 9 percent vote in the January 1976 Nelson by-election. Thereafter, the party went into decline, receiving 2.8 percent of the vote in 1978 and only 0.2 percent in 1981. By then many of its members had questioned the worth of contesting elections, especially in a simple plurality electoral system which discriminated heavily against minor parties.

However, the Values Party had played a crucial part in directing attention away from the preoccupation with material prosperity and economic growth. The person primarily responsible for the formation of the party was Tony Brunt, a former journalist who, like many other young people, felt that traditional political organizations were failing to articulate the important issues of the day. Support for the party came from young people with high levels of formal education and upper middle classes. It also came from former adherents of all the major parties, as well as from activists in radical left-wing political groups. Later, the adherents of the latter, especially in the city of Christchurch, began to exert a great deal of influence over the party.

In the early stages of its development, the party was influenced by ideas like those propounded by the **Club of Rome**, the study *The Limits to Growth*, and the British publication *A Blueprint for Survival*. The 1972 party manifesto, *Blueprint for New Zealand*, adapted these ideas and focused on a wide range of **quality of life** issues, notably the depletion of nonrenewable resources, **population growth** and the dangers associated with industrialization and technological change.

On a more positive note, the party focused on the need for a change in values with less emphasis on affluence and more on the fulfillment of spiritual needs (*see* **SPIRITUALITY**). The party denounced the old political system for its short-term approach to policymaking, resorting to expediency, and excessive focus on electoral contests. As regards environmental issues, during the 1972 election campaign the Values Party mobilized opposition to the proposed development of a hydroelectric system that threatened Lake Manapouri on the South Island.

While this campaign helped to unify supporters of the party, the attempt to develop organizational structures presented a number of difficulties. Concern about participatory democracy and decentralization led to the party's almost ceasing to exist as a national organization until a new constitution was formulated and implemented at the 1974 party conference. By 1978 there was concern among many members that the party, particularly the groups based in Christchurch, had moved too far toward bureaucratization and conventional organizational practices.

In parallel with these tensions over organizational structures were divisions over policy. The Values Party had begun with a strong focus on quality of life issues. This approach had been partly undermined by the economic considerations that came to dominate the national and international political agenda following the oil crisis of 1973. The group in Christchurch, which had always been interested in economic issues from a socialist point of view, attempted to focus on developing a party program covering a wide range of economic and social questions. The kinds of issues addressed by social movements, such as campaigns against the introduction of nuclear power and restrictive laws on abortion, continued to play an important role.

The party was not very successful either in forming alliances with social movements or in retaining the allegiance of key groups within its own ranks. In 1979 the group from Christchurch, led by Toni Kunowski, having failed to force the majority into adopting a more professional approach to the organization of the party and having been defeated in a contest for the leadership of the party, formed a separate political organization called Socialist Network. The party never recovered from these divisions, even after it adopted the name Values: The Green Party of Aotearoa. Finally, in March 1990 members of the party participated in the creation of a new political organization, the Greens. In 1996 the Greens contested the elections as part of a coalition of parties called the Alliance. This association secured 10 percent of the vote and a total of 13 out of 120 seats in the parliament.

Apart from its own internal conflicts and difficulties, the Values Party was negatively affected by the ability of the Labour Party to adapt to issues like the widespread opposition to nuclear power. However, the possibility remained for the revival of a green political organization. In the 1987 elections the antinuclear stand of the Labour Party ensured its success in attracting environmentalists. However, in 1990 neither this issue nor the reform of environmental legislation could prevent the Greens from running in the elections. Although it had virtually no policies and refused to appoint leaders in the conventional sense, the new party polled 6.6 percent of the national vote, thus demonstrating the enduring strength of the green political movement. The Greens had also polled almost 20 percent of the vote in some electorates. The constant problem, however, was the electoral system, which made it very difficult for them to gain any formal representation.

VALUING THE ENVIRONMENT. Discussions about **sustainable development** have, in recent times, led to numerous efforts to place a value on the environment, through the introduction of measures like **pollution charges** and **carbon taxes**, and reconceptualize or challenge economic beliefs in the power of the **gross national product.**

One of the most concerted efforts to bring about a change in perceptions and policies came, perhaps surprisingly, under Chris Patten, the British minister for the environment in the 1989 Conservative government led by Margaret Thatcher. Patten appointed as his advisers a team led by Professor David Pearce. Their *Blueprint for a Green Economy* outlined a range of specific measures for achieving sustainable development by placing values on the environment. Their work also drew together suggestions made by many other economists about how to deal with the problems of "goods" like water and the atmosphere that have no price attached to them and have therefore been overexploited (*see also TRAGEDY OF THE COMMONS*).

Pearce and his collaborators pointed to the inefficiency of a market system that did place a value on certain resources. Among their proposed reforms was the introduction of market-based incentives, like pollution charges and carbon taxes, for changing behavior toward the environment.

VEREINTE GRÜNE ÖSTERREICHS. *See* **GREEN PARTIES, AUSTRIA.**

W

WARD, BARBARA. (1914–1982). Well known as the author of several works on environmental protection, Barbara Ward coauthored, with **René Dubos**, the highly influential book *Only One Earth*. This publication contained a powerful critique of advanced industralized market economies and influenced the environmental policy agenda of the United Nations, which had commissioned the work. In 1968 Ward was appointed to the position of Schweitzer Professor of International Economic Development at Columbia University and, in 1973, to the presidency of the International Institute for Environment and Development.

WILDERNESS SOCIETY. The power of social movements like those concerned about the environment lies partly in their ability to mobilize people. By organizing popular protests, environmental groups have influenced political processes and parliamentary politics. Campaigns like the one by the Tasmanian Wilderness Society against the flooding of the Franklin and lower Gordon Rivers (*see* **FRANKLIN DAM**) contributed to a rapid rise in the membership of this organization. By 1983 the society had 7,332 members and, reflecting its national appeal, changed its name to the Wilderness Society. Branches had been formed in all states and campaigns for the preservation of forests were being conducted across Australia.

The radicalism of the Wilderness Society signaled the entry of a new generation of environmentalists on the political scene. Apart from mobilizing large numbers of people, new environmental groups raised substantial financial support. In 1982 the estimated annual budget for the Wilderness Society was around A\$1 million. Of that, A\$130,000 was spent on a campaign for a referendum on the proposed Franklin Dam. The Wilderness Society was able to sustain and develop its financial and popular base during the 1980s, bolstered by the entrepreneurial activities of Wilderness Shops, which took in several million dollars. After declining to 5,171 in 1985, membership of the Wilderness Society rose from 5,930 to 7,002 between 1987 and 1988 and up to 10,819 in 1989 and 16,377 in 1991. Since then, environmental groups have become aware of the limits to their growth and competition among them for supporters—as the rise in numbers of one group may be at the expense of another.

The Wilderness Society was one among several environmental groups invited by the government in **Australia** to participate in discussion groups on ecologically **sustainable development**. However, the association has always expressed concern about the predominance of economic interests in these gatherings. The Wilderness Society has been sharp in its criticism of any attempt by government to initiate development projects in forests. The rise in support during the 1980s for groups like the Wilderness Society has contributed to a stronger focus by traditional political organizations on environmental issues. The Wilderness Society has also played an important part in endorsing candidates for parties like the **Australian Democrats** and green parties in Australia.

WORLD COMMISSION ON ENVIRONMENT AND DEVELOPMENT. For some time people have questioned the capacity of national governments to address the consequences of the economic interdependence between nations. More recently, this skepticism has been extended to their capacity to focus on environmental problems. One of the most significant initiatives for achieving cooperation between nation-states that has emerged is the work by the World Commission on Environment and Development. The commission was formed following a September 1983 resolution by the UN General Assembly to explore further the connection between environmental protection and economic development.

The inaugural meeting of the World Commission on Environment and Development was held in October 1984 in Geneva. The chair of the commission was **Gro Harlem Brundtland**, who had previously served as prime minister of Norway. The 23-member commission included twelve representatives from less developed nations, seven from Western, developed countries, and four from communist countries. Work by the commission focused on the following topics: **population growth** and human resources, food security, **biodiversity**, energy and industry, urbanization, the international economy, peace and security, and, above all, forms of cooperation between national governments for addressing these issues. It then provided backing for a large number of studies on these topics and arranged meetings in ten countries to elicit the views of a wide range of individuals and organizations.

The outcome of these extensive deliberations was the 1987 publication of a report entitled *Our Common Future*. Not surprisingly, the report pointed out that prevailing institutional mechanisms centered around local, regional, and national governments were inadequate to deal with the serious problems confronting people. In other words, it was difficult to imagine a solution to problems like **acid rain**, the **greenhouse effect**, and depletion of the **ozone layer** without cooperation between different governments. Moreover, the commission felt that environmental protection and economic development had to be viewed as interdependent rather than conflicting principles. To convey this point of view it used the term "**sustainable development.**"

Our Common Future became a key source for deliberations by established organizations that were under pressure to adapt to new challenges from the rising green movement. Arguments for sustainable development in the 1990s were major efforts by governments and other established organizations to provide alternatives to the idea of development *versus* environmental protection. The commission defined sustainable development as meeting "the needs of the present without compromising the ability of future generations to meet their own needs." However, the notion and practice of sustainable development were not entirely novel. Conservationists, including foresters, have for many decades argued against the outright exploitation of forests on the grounds of preserving timber for future generations. *Our Common Future* ensured that the idea of sustainable development became more widely known and was applied to all economic activities.

In many countries this report was also taken as a useful basis for developing a dialogue between environmentalists and developers. The commission had provided a comprehensive statement on how to address both environmental and economic concerns and how all organizations should strive to incorporate ecological wisdom into their economic and social decisions. The report attempted to demonstrate that emphasis on materialism and economic growth (*see* **THE LIMITS TO GROWTH**) will not necessarily damage the environment if it is guided by principles of **ecology** and preoccupied with the renewability of resources. Economic growth was seen as "absolutely essential in order to relieve the great poverty that is deepening in much of the developing world."

The final chapter of the report made a number of proposals for "institutional and legal change." They included the incorporation of sustainable development as a term of reference for the principal agencies of national governments; the creation, where they were lacking, of national environmental protection and natural resources management agencies; the strengthening, through increased funding, of **UNEP**; a greater focus on global environmental assessment and reporting; strengthening international cooperation on this matter; broadening and intensifying the contribution to sustainable development by the scientific community and nongovernmental organizations; greater cooperation with industry groups; strengthening and extending existing international conventions and agreements; and drafting and implementing a universal declaration and a convention on environmental protection and sustainable development.

WORLD CONSERVATION STRATEGY. The World Conservation Strategy was initiated by the **International Union for the Conservation of Nature and Natural Resources (IUCN)**. The strategy focused on how to identify and deal with threats to species and ecosystems and the preservation of genetic diversity for the purposes of agricultural development. The project was formulated in conjunction with the **UN Environment Programme** and the **World Wildlife Fund**. Its announcement in March 1980 in about 40 countries received considerable attention. In their attempts to set the agenda for change, some governments more fully exploited notions such as **sustainable development**, which had been promoted by organizations like the IUCN. Sustainable development has been used by international agencies ever since the **UN Conference on the Human Environment** (Stockholm, 1972). The publication of the *World Conservation Strategy: Living Resource for Sustainable Development* in 1980 provided a major impetus to arguments about sustainable development. The report recommended the development of national strategies for conservation with the aim of integrating conservation and development.

Some governments implemented the recommendations of the World Conservation Strategy and developed national conservation strategies. The Australian government noted that the successful implementation of its national strategy presupposed widespread acceptance of the following principles: the integration and interdependence of conservation and development, the retention of options for future use, a focus on the underlying causes and symptoms of environmental damage, the accumulation of knowledge for the future, and education of the community about the integration of sustainable development and conservation. Although this initiative was largely forgotten for several years, like the World Conservation Strategy it later formed an important part of the process of reconciling environment and development.

WORLD WIDE FUND FOR NATURE (also known as WORLD WILDLIFE FUND) (WWF). The stimulus to the formation of the WWF, which is now one of the largest conservation organizations in the world, was provided by eminent British ornithologist Julian Huxley after a visit he made to East Africa in 1960. Huxley wrote three articles in *The Observer* weekly magazine in which he disclosed his concerns about the destruction of wildlife caused by agricultural practices and poaching. In collaboration with Max Nicholson, the director general of the Nature Conservancy Council in Britain, Huxley brought together a group of well-known scientists (including ornithologist Peter Scott, who was vice president of the IUCN) to establish an international fundraising organization for nature conservation. To emphasize the independence of the new organization its headquarters were established in Switzerland, which enjoyed the reputation of a neutral country in international affairs.

Officially founded on 11 September 1961, the WWF aimed to establish offices in as many countries as possible to facilitate the process of fundraising and oversee various projects. The objective was to cooperate with nongovernmental organizations like the IUCN, the International Council for Bird Preservation (later named Birdlife International), the International Waterfowl Research Bureau, and International Youth Federation for the Study and Conservation of Nature.

Assisted by dignitaries like the Duke of Edinburgh, the WWF rapidly succeeded in raising large sums of money: within three years it had secured about U.S.$1.9 million to support conservation projects all over the world, including India, Kenya, and the Galapagos Islands. The WWF also excelled in promoting itself, notably through the use of its black and white panda logo. Thirty years later, in 1995, the WWF had well over five million supporters, 23 national organization offices, and 22 program offices. It had by this time allocated over U.S.$525 million in 11,000 projects spread across 130 countries.

The WWF has continuously lobbied governments on conservation issues and often been granted access to the policy-making process and been successful in bringing about significant changes in policy and its successful implementation. From its inception the WWF has influenced governments to establish and protect national parks and conservation areas. In the 1970s it was instrumental in assisting the Indian government to establish reserves for tigers. It launched campaigns to protect tropical rainforests and create sanctuaries for whales, dolphins, and seals. It also contributed to the effective operation of the Trade Records Analysis of Fauna and Flora in Commerce, an organization that drew attention to the trade in wildlife and wildlife products, notably ivory and rhino horn, which might lead to the extinction of certain species. The WWF has also cooperated in initiatives like the **World Conservation Strategy**, launched by the IUCN and **UNEP.**

Throughout its existence, the WWF has been highly innovative in raising funds. In 1970 the president of WWF International, Prince Bernhard of the Netherlands, initiated the 1001 fund, which in effect asked 1,001 individuals to contribute U.S.$10,000 each and thereby raise U.S.$10 million. In 1979 a "Save the Rhino" campaign raised

U.S.$1 million. In 1983 the WWF came up with the idea of persuading postal organizations in over 130 countries to depict threatened species on postage stamps, an initiative that by the early 1990s had raised another U.S.$10 million. The WWF also organized agreements between less developed and wealthy nations so that instead of repaying part of their national debt to the developed nations the emerging nations spent an agreed sum on conservation measures.

In order to make known its commitment to addressing a wide range of environmental issues, the organization changed its name to the World Wide Fund for Nature in 1986, though in Canada and the United States it kept the original name.

In its mission statement for the 1990s the WWF set three goals: preservation of biological diversity (*see* **BIODIVERSITY**), particularly the preservation of tropical forests, wetlands, coasts, and coral reefs; sustainable use of natural resources, with a view both to improving the **quality of life** for human beings and preserving the foundations for the regeneration of resources; and reducing pollution and waste. To achieve these objectives the WWF has adopted five mechanisms: sponsoring field projects; conducting publicity campaigns including the mobilization of its supporters to apply pressure on government; conducting educational campaigns, especially among young people in schools; distributing information through its own publications and other media in order to attract further funding and support for its activities; and cooperating with other nature conservation organizations and providing them with both expertise and financial support.

WORLD WILDLIFE FUND. *See* **WORLD WIDE FUND FOR NATURE.**

WYHL. The proposal by politicians and planners to build a nuclear power plant near the village of Wyhl in Baden-Württemberg, Federal Republic of Germany, in the early 1970s was perceived as a major threat to the livelihood of winegrowers in that region. The discovery by the local population that the minister president of that state was also the chair of the supervisory board of the company whose subsidiary was awarded the contract to build the power plant provoked further opposition to the project.

In 1975 local protestors against the project were joined by students and other young people from the city of Freiburg. The campaign also drew people from the Alsace region. Like the campaign against the proposed nuclear power plant in **Brokdorf** in north Germany, the campaign at Wyhl drew together people from the countryside and the cities in what were later to become wide-ranging **antinuclear pro-**

tests and set in motion the emergence of green political organizations and parties.

Y

YELLOWSTONE NATIONAL PARK. Following an act of Congress, endorsed in 1872, Yellowstone National Park was created in Wyoming. The park covered an area of 800,000 hectares and was the first national park to be formally created by a government.

Bibliography

The influence of the green movement has not only been enhanced by but has also stimulated writings on the reshaping of the economy, relationships between human beings and nature, ways of reforming the political system, and introduction of new policies to deal with a wide range of issues, including damage to the environment and the emergence of new social structures.

While there are many books on the development of the green movement, a considerable portion of the available information appears in a more ephemeral form, articles and monographs. The regular publications that have emerged in the wake of the green movement contain many useful articles on the concepts and issues that occupy scholars, for example, journals like *Environmental Politics* and *Environmental Values*. There are numerous magazines and journals that have contributed to the articulation of green issues, not least *The Ecologist*.

Interest in environmental issues among policymakers has been stimulated by highly influential works that have attempted to reconcile development with the environment. The section of this bibliography that focuses on the economy includes the report by the World Commission on Environment and Development, *Our Common Future*, which has become a standard point of reference for policymakers. There are many other important works that offer ideas on how to reshape the economy. David Pearce and his collaborators have produced several influential books, including *Blueprint for a Green Economy*. Stephan Schmidheiny, in *Changing Course: A Global Business Perspective on Development and the Environment*, and Ernst Ulrich von Weiszäcker, in *Earth Politics*, present a wide range of ideas on how business and government can work toward addressing many of the key concerns of the green movement. Also included are pivotal works on economics like those by Herman Daly on *Steady-State Economics*, Arthur Cecil Pigou on *The Economics of Welfare*, and E. J. Mishan on *The Costs of Economic Growth*.

The section on green concepts includes works by writers who have made accessible to a mass public critiques of prevailing approaches to dealing with the environment. Among these works are *Silent Spring* by Rachel Carson, *The Population Bomb* by Paul Ehrlich, *A Sand County*

Almanac by Aldo Leopold, *The Limits to Growth* by Dennis Meadows and his collaborators, and *Small Is Beautiful* by E. F. Schumacher. The influence of the green movement on modern societies has been given a powerful impetus by these writers. Extracts from influential works are contained in several valuable collections of essays, for instance, in *The Green Reader*, edited by Andrew Dobson, and in *The Politics of the Environment*, edited by Robert Goodin. This section on green concepts also includes critiques and alternatives to some of the ideas of proponents of the green movement, for example, *The Green Crusade: Rethinking the Roots of Environmentalism* by Charles T. Rubin, *Green Political Theory* by Robert Goodin, and *The Post-Industrial Utopians* by Boris Frankel.

The section on green issues is inevitably representative, given the wide range of topics that have been covered by scholars of the green movement. Similarly, there is a vast array of green groups that deserve attention. While some of the works mentioned above provide a useful overview, there are valuable studies on particular themes like *A New World Order: Grassroots Movements for Global Change* by Paul Ekins and *The Case for Animal Rights* by Tom Regan.

The section on the green movement is divided into three parts. The first "general" section includes mainly sociological accounts of how the green movement can be regarded a social movement that redefines the boundaries of political action. A special issue of the journal *Social Research*, edited by Jean Cohen and published in 1985, includes valuable essays by writers like Klaus Eder, Claus Offe, and Jean Cohen. Other sociological approaches to the green movement can be found in works like Alberto Melucci's *Nomads of the Present* and Alain Touraine's *Anti-Nuclear Protest*. An accessible analysis of sociological approaches can be found in Alan Scott, *Ideology and the New Social Movements*. The next section focuses on green groups, including environmental organizations. One of the most useful studies mentioned here is *The Global Environmental Movement* by John McCormick. This section, entitled "New Politics," includes works that attempt to understand the green movement as a novel political phenomenon or the articulation of concerns that had until recently received limited attention on the political agenda. A useful collection of analytical studies in this field can be found in *New Politics*, edited by Ferdinand Müller-Rommel and Thomas Poguntke.

The section on green parties is divided into books and articles covering different countries. Among the works that bring together accounts of the development of green parties in various countries are *Green Parties: An International Guide*, by Sara Parkin; *New Politics in Western Europe: The Rise and Success of Green Parties and Alternative Lists*, edited by Ferdinand Müller-Rommel; and *The Green Challenge: The*

Development of Green Parties in Europe, edited by Dick Richardson and Chris Rootes. The next section, on green policies, is again divided into works on different countries. There are many perceptive studies that examine one or two countries and are useful for the analysis of environmental policy in different settings, for example David Vogel's *National Styles of Regulation: Environmental Policy in Great Britain and the United States,* Daniel Fiorino's *Making Environmental Policy,* Martin Jänicke's *State Failure,* and Albert Weale's *The New Politics of Pollution.* Other valuable studies include Martin Jänicke and Helmut Weidner's *National Environmental Politics: A Comparative Study of Capacity-Building* and James Lester's *Environmental Politics and Policy—Theories and Evidence.*

The section on green politics offers accounts of developments in various countries. There are significant studies, like Herbert Kitschelt's *The Logics of Party Formation,* which compares developments in Belgium and West Germany, as well as a series of monographs on *Green Politics* edited by Wolfgang Rüdig, which are an important source of information and investigation of green political organizations around the world. The final section, on international relations, contains works that focus largely on specific issues or on the global aspects of environmental diplomacy. These include *Ozone Diplomacy* by Richard Benedick, *Environmental Diplomacy* by Lawrence Susskind, *Global Environmental Politics* by Gareth Porter and Janet Welsh Brown, and *The Global Politics of the Environment* by Lorraine Elliott.

Contents

Bulgaria
Central Europe
Eastern Europe
France
Germany
Ireland
Italy
Latin America
New Zealand
United Kingdom
United States

9. INTERNATIONAL RELATIONS

10. INTERNET SITES

1. Biography

Parkin, Sara. *The Life and Death of Petra Kelly*. London: Pandora Press, 1994.
Pearce, Fred. *Green Warriors*. London: Bodley Head, 1991.

2. Economy

Anderson, Kym, and Richard Blackhurst. *The Greening of World Trade Issues*. New York: Harvester Wheatsheaf, 1992.
Anderson, Terry L., and Donald R. Leal. *Free Market Environmentalism*. San Francisco: Pacific Research Institute for Public Policy, 1991.
Baumol, W. J., and W. E. Oates. *The Theory of Environmental Policy*. 2nd ed. Cambridge: Cambridge University Press, 1988.
Boulding, Kenneth E. "The Economics of Coming Spaceship Earth." In *Environmental Quality in a Growing Economy*, edited by Henry Jarrett,. 3–14. Baltimore: Johns Hopkins University Press, 1966.
Business Council of Australia. *Achieving Sustainable Development. A Discussion Paper by the Business Council of Australia*. Melbourne: Business Council of Australia, 1990.
———. *Development and the Environment. A Policy Statement of the Business Council of Australia*. Melbourne: Business Council of Australia, 1990.
Cairncross, Frances. *Costing the Earth: What Governments Must Do; What Consumers Need to Know; How Business Can Profit*. London: The Economist, 1991.

Cline, William R. *Global Warning: The Benefits of Emission Abatement.* Paris: OECD, 1992.

Daly, Herman. "Steady-state Economics vs. Growthmania: A Critique of the Orthodox Conceptions of Growth, Wants, Scarcity and Efficiency." *Policy Sciences* 5 (1974): 149–67.

———. *Steady-State Economics.* San Francisco: Freeman, 1977.

———. "The Steady-State Economy: What, Why and How?" In *The Sustainable Society,* edited by Dennis Pirages. New York: Praeger, 1977.

Daly, Herman, and John B. Cobb. *For the Common Good: Redirecting the Economy Toward Community, the Environment and a Sustainable Future.* Boston: Beacon Press, 1989.

Daly, Herman E., and Kenneth N. Townsend. *Valuing the Earth: Economics, Ecology, Ethics.* Cambridge, Mass.: MIT Press, 1993.

Eckersley, Robyn. "Free Market Environmentalism: Friend or Foe?" *Environmental Politics* 2, no. 1 (1993): 1–19.

Ekins, Paul, ed. *The Living Economy.* London: Routledge, 1986.

Elkington, John, and Julia Hailes. The *Green Consumer Guide.* London: Gollancz, 1988.

Elkington, John, and Tom Burke. *The Green Capitalists: Industry's Search for Environmental Excellence.* London: Gollancz, 1987.

Fisher, Anthony C. *Resource and Environmental Economics.* Cambridge: Cambridge University Press, 1981.

Freeman, A. Myrick III, Robert H. Haveman, and Allen V. Kneese. *The Economics of Environmental Policy.* New York: Wiley, 1973.

Helm, Dieter. *Economic Policy towards the Environment.* Oxford: Blackwell, 1991.

Kneese, Allen V., and Charles L. Schultze. *Pollution, Prices and Public Policy.* Washington, D.C.: Brookings Institution, 1975.

MacNeill, Jim, et al. *Beyond Interdependence: The Meshing of the World's Economy and the Earth's Ecology.* Oxford and New York: Oxford University Press, 1991.

Martinez-Alier, Juan. *Ecological Economics.* Oxford: Blackwell, 1990.

Mishan, E. J. *The Costs of Economic Growth.* Harmondsworth, U.K.: Penguin, 1967–1969.

Moran, Alan, Andrew Chisholm, and Michael Porter, eds. *Markets, Resources and the Environment.* Sydney: Allen and Unwin, 1991.

Oates, Wallace E. *The Economics of the Environment.* Aldershot: Edward Elgar, 1992.

Opschoor, Johannes B., and Hans Vos. *The Application of Economic Instruments for Environmental Protection in OECD Member Countries.* Paris: OECD, 1989.

Pearce, David. *Blueprint 2: Greening the World Economy.* London:

Earthscan in association with the London Environmental Economics Centre, 1991.

———. *Economic Values and the Natural World*. London: Earthscan, 1993.

Pearce, David, April Markandya, and Edward B. Barbier. *Blueprint for a Green Economy*. London: Earthscan, 1989.

Pearce, David, and R. Kerry Turner. *Economics of Natural Resources and the Environment*. Hemel Hempstead: Harvester Wheatsheaf, 1990.

Pearce, David, and Jeremy Warford. *World Without End: Economics, Environment and Sustainable Development*. Oxford: Oxford University Press, World Bank, 1993.

Pigou, Arthur Cecil. *The Economics of Welfare*. London: Macmillan, 1920.

Redclift, Michael. *Sustainable Development*. London: Methuen, 1987.

Renner, Michael. *Jobs in a Sustainable Economy*. Washington, D.C.: Worldwatch Institute, 1991.

Repetto, Robert, et al. *Green Fees: How a Tax Shift Can Work for the Environment and the Economy*. Washington, D.C.: World Resources Institute.

Rich, Bruce. *Mortgaging the Earth: The World Bank, Environmental Impoverishment, and the Crisis of Development*. Boston: Beacon Press, 1994.

Schmidheiny, Stephan, with the Business Council for Sustainable Development. *Changing Course: A Global Business Perspective on Development and the Environment*. Cambridge, Mass.: MIT Press, 1992.

Schmidt-Bleek, Friedrich, and Heinrich Wohlmeyer, eds. *Trade and the Environment*. Laxenburg, Austria: IIASA, 1992.

Schwarz, Walter, and Dorothy Schwarz. *Breaking Through*. Bideford, England: Green Books, 1987.

Smart, Bruce, ed. *Beyond Compliance: A New Industry View of the Environment*. Washington, D.C.: World Resources Institute, 1992.

Starke, Linda. *Signs of Hope: Working towards Our Common Future*. Oxford and New York: Oxford University Press, 1990.

Swanson, Timothy M., and Edward B. Barbier, eds. *Economics for the Wilds*. London: Earthscan, 1992.

Tisdell, Clement A. *Economics of Environmental Conservation: Economics for Environmental and Ecological Management*. Amsterdam: Elsevier, 1991.

———. *Environmental Economics: Policies for Environmental Management and Sustainable Development*. Aldershot: Edward Elgar, 1993.

Turner, R. Kerry. *Sustainable Environmental Economics and Management: Principles and Practice*. London: Belhaven Press, 1993.

UNCED. *Report of the UN Conference on Environment and Development.* A/CONF/151/26. 5 vols. New York: UN, 1992.

von Weizsäcker, Ernst U. *Not a Miracle Solution, but Steps Towards an Ecological Reform of the Common Agricultural Policy.* Bonn: Institute for European Environmental Policy, 1987.

————. *Earth Politics.* London: Zed Books, 1994.

von Weizsäcker, Ernst U., and Jochen Jessinghaus. *Ecological Tax Reform: A Policy Proposal for Sustainable Development.* A study prepared for Stephan Schmidheiny. London and Atlantic Highlands, N.J.: Zed Books, 1992.

Wicke, Lutz. *Umweltökonomie.* 3rd ed. Munich: Vahlen, 1991.

Winter, Georg. *Business and the Environment.* New York: McGraw-Hill, 1989.

World Commission on Environment and Development. *Our Common Future.* Melbourne: Oxford University Press, 1990.

3. Green Concepts

Attfield, Robin. *The Ethics of Environmental Concern.* Oxford: Blackwell, 1983.

Bahro, Rudolf. *Socialism and Survival.* London: Heretic Books, 1982.

————. *Building the Green Movement.* London: Heretic Books, 1986.

Beck, Ulrich. *Risk Society.* Newbury Park, Calif.: Sage, 1992.

Benton, Ted. *Natural Relations: Animal Rights and Social Justice.* London: Verso, 1993.

Boggs, Carl. "The Green Alternative and the Struggle for a Post-Marxist Discourse." *Theory and Society* 15 (1986): 869–99.

Bookchin, Murray. *Post-Scarcity Anarchism.* Berkeley, Calif.: Ramparts Press, 1971.

————. *Toward an Ecological Society.* Montreal: Black Rose Books, 1980.

Bramwell, Anna. *Ecology in the 20th Century: A History.* London and New Haven: Yale University Press, 1989.

Capra, Fritjof. *The Turning Point.* London: Fontana, 1983.

Carson, Rachel. *Silent Spring.* Boston: Houghton Mifflin, 1962.

Commoner, Barry. *The Closing Circle: Nature, Man, and Technology.* New York: Knopf, 1971.

Cotgrove, Stephen. *Catastrophe or Cornucopia.* Chichester: Wiley, 1982.

Council on Environmental Quality. *The Global 2000 Report to the President.* Harmondsworth, U.K.: Penguin, 1982.

Dobson, Andrew, ed. *The Green Reader.* London: André Deutsch, 1991.

Dobson, Andrew, and Paul Lucardie, eds. *The Politics of Nature: Ex-*

plorations in Green Political Theory. London and New York: Routledge, 1993.

Dryzek, John. *Rational Ecology: Environment and Political Economy.* Oxford: Blackwell, 1987.

———. *The Politics of the Earth: Environmental Discourses.* Oxford: Oxford University Press.

Dubos, René. *The Wooing of Earth: New Perspectives on Man's Use of Nature.* New York: Scribner's, 1980.

———. *Celebrations of Life.* New York: McGraw-Hill, 1981.

Dunlap, Riley, and Karl van Liere. The "New Environmental Paradigm." *Journal of Environmental Education* 9 (1978): 10–19.

Eckersley, Robyn. *Environmentalism and Political Theory.* London: UCL Press, 1992.

Ehrlich, Paul R. *The Population Bomb.* New York: Ballantine, 1968.

Ehrlich, Paul R., and Anne Ehrlich. *The Population Explosion.* New York: Simon and Schuster, 1990.

Elliot, Robert. "Faking Nature." *Inquiry* 25, no. 1 (1982): 81–93.

Feinberg, Joel. "The Rights of Animals and Unborn Generations." In *Philosophy and Environmental Crisis,* edited by William T. Blackstone, 43–68. Athens: University of Georgia Press, 1974.

Fox, Warwick. *Toward a Transpersonal Ecology.* Boston: Shambhala, 1990.

Frankel, Boris. *The Post-Industrial Utopians.* Cambridge: Polity Press, 1987.

Goldsmith, Edward. *The Great U-Turn: De-Industrializing Society.* Bideford, England: Green Books, 1988.

Goldsmith, Edward, Robert Allen, Michael Allaby, John Davoll, and Sam Lawrence. "A Blueprint for Survival." *The Ecologist* 2, no. 1 (1972): 8–22.

Goodin, Robert E. *Green Political Theory.* Cambridge: Polity Press, 1992.

———. "The High Ground Is Green." *Environmental Politics* 1, no. 1 (1992): 1–8.

Goodin, Robert E., ed. *The Politics of the Environment.* Aldershot, U.K.: Edward Elgar, 1994.

Gorz, André. *Capitalism, Socialism, Ecology.* London: Verso, 1994.

Hardin, Garrett. "The Tragedy of the Commons." *Science* 162, no. 3859 (13 December 1968): 1243–48.

Hardin, Garrett, and J. Baden. *Managing the Commons.* San Francisco: Freeman, 1980.

Huber, Josef. *Die verlorene Unschuld der Ökologie.* Frankfurt: Fischer, 1982.

Jonas, Hans. *The Imperative of Responsibility: In Search of an Ethics for the Technological Age.* Chicago: University of Chicago Press, 1985.

Kelly, Petra. *Fighting for Hope.* London: Chatto and Windus, The Hogarth Press, 1984.

Leopold, Aldo. *A Sand County Almanac.* 1949. Reprint, Oxford: Oxford University Press, 1977.

Lovelock, J. *Gaia: A New Look at Life on Earth.* Oxford: Oxford University Press, 1979.

————. *Healing of Gaia: Practical Medicine for the Planet.* New York: Harmony Books, 1991.

Lovins, Amory B. *Soft Energy Paths: Towards a Durable Peace.* London: Penguin, 1977.

Maddox, John. *The Doomsday Syndrome.* London: Macmillan, 1972.

Malthus, Thomas. *An Essay on the Principle of Population.* 1798. Reprint edited by Philip Appleman. New York: W.W. Norton, 1976.

Marsh, George Perkins. *Man and Nature.* 1864. Reprint, Cambridge, Mass.: Harvard University Press, 1965.

Meadows, Donella H., Dennis L. Meadows, Jorgen Randers, and William W. Behrens III. *The Limits to Growth.* New York: New American Library, 1972.

Mellor, Mary. "Green Politics: Ecofeminist, Ecofeminine or Ecomasculine?" *Environmental Politics* 1, no. 1 (1992): 229–51.

Merchant, Carolyn. *The Death of Nature.* New York: Harper and Row, 1980.

————. *Radical Ecology: The Search for a Livable World.* London and New York: Routledge, 1992.

Morrison, Denton E., and Riley E. Dunlap. "Environmentalism and Elitism: A Conceptual and Empirical Analysis." *Environmental Management* 10 (1986): 581–89.

Müller-Rommel, Ferdinand. "Die Posmaterialismusdiskussion in der empirischen Sozialforschung: Politisch und wissenschaftlich überlebt oder noch immer zukunftsweisend?" *Politische Vierteljahresschrift* 24 (1983): 218–28.

Myers, Norman. *The Sinking Ark: A New Look at the Problem of Disappearing Species.* Oxford: Pergamon Press, 1979.

Naess, Arne. "The Shallow and the Deep, Long-Range Ecology Movement: A Summary." *Inquiry* 16, no. 1 (1973): 95–100.

————. *Ecology, Community and Lifestyle.* Cambridge: Cambridge University Press, 1989.

Nash, Roderick. "The American Invention of National Parks." *American Quarterly* 22, no. 3 (1970): 726–35.

————. *Wilderness and the American Mind.* New Haven, Conn.: Yale University Press, 1973.

Nicholson, Max. *The New Environmental Age*. Cambridge: Cambridge University Press, 1987.

Ophuls, William. "The Politics of the Sustainable Society." In *The Sustainable Society*, edited by Dennis Pirages. New York: Praeger, 1977.

O'Riordan, Tim. *Environmentalism*. London: Pion, 1981.

Owen, Denis. *What Is Ecology?* 2nd ed. Oxford: Oxford University Press, 1980.

Paehlke, Robert. *Environmentalism and the Future of Progressive Politics*. New Haven, Conn.: Yale University Press, 1989.

Passmore, John. "Attitudes to Nature." In *Nature and Conduct*, edited by R. S. Peters. 251–64. London: Macmillan, 1975.

———. *Man's Responsibility for Nature*. 2nd ed. London: Duckworth, 1980.

Pepper, David. *The Roots of Modern Environmentalism*. London: Routledge, 1986.

———. *Eco-Socialism: From Deep Ecology to Social Justice*. London: Routledge, 1993.

Ponting, Clive. *A Green History of the World*. Harmondsworth, U.K.: Penguin, 1991.

Porritt, Jonathan. *Seeing Green: The Politics of Ecology Explained*. London: Blackwell, 1984.

———. *The Coming of the Greens*. London: Fontana, 1988.

Redclift, Michael, and Ted Benton, eds. *Social Theory and the Environment*. London: Routledge, 1994.

Richardson, Dick. "The Green Challenge: Philosophical, Programmatic and Electoral Considerations." In *The Green Challenge: The Development of Green Parties in Europe*, edited by Dick Richardson and Chris Rootes, 4–22. London and New York: Routledge, 1995.

Rubin, Charles T. *The Green Crusade: Rethinking the Roots of Environmentalism*. New York: Free Press, 1994.

Sagoff, Mark. "On Preserving the Natural Environment." *Yale Law Journal* 84, no. 2 (1974): 205–67.

Sale, Kirkpatrick. *The Schumacher Lectures Vol. 2*. London: Random Century Limited, 1974.

———. *Dwellers in the Land: The Bioregional Vision*. Philadelphia: New Society Publishers, 1991.

Sandbach, Francis. *Environment: Ideology and Policy*. Oxford: Blackwell, 1980.

Schumacher, E. F. *Small Is Beautiful: Economics as If People Mattered*. New York: Harper and Row, 1973.

Simonis, Udo, E. "Ecological Modernization of Industrial Society: Three Strategic Elements." *International Social Science Journal* 121 (1989): 347–61.

Sylvan, Richard, and David Bennett. *The Greening of Ethics*. Cambridge: White Horse Press, 1994.

Trainer, Ted. *Abandon Affluence!* London: Zed Books, 1985.

Ward, Barbara, and René Dubos. *Only One Earth*. Harmondsworth, U.K.: Penguin, 1972.

World Commission on Environment and Development. *Our Common Future*. Melbourne: Oxford University Press, 1990.

Yearley, Steven. *The Green Case: A Sociology of Environmental Issues, Arguments and Politics*. London: Harper Collins, 1991.

Young, Stephen C. "The Different Dimensions of Green Politics." *Environmental Politics* 1, no. 1 (1992): 9–44.

4. Green Issues

Bandyopadhyay, Jayanta, and Vandana Shiva. "Chipko: Rekindling India's Forest Culture." *Ecologist* 17 (1987): 26–34.

Barnaby, Frank. "The Environmental Impact of the Gulf War." *Ecologist* 21 (1991): 166–72.

Benton, Ted. *Natural Relations: Ecology, Animal Rights and Social Justice*. London: Verso, 1993.

Blowers, Andrew, David Lowry, and Barry D. Solomon. *The International Politics of Nuclear Waste*. Basingstoke, U.K.: Macmillan, 1991.

Bolton, Geoffrey. *Spoils and Spoilers: Australians Make Their Environment, 1780–1980*. Sydney: Allen and Unwin, 1981.

Boyle, Stewart, and John Ardill. *The Greenhouse Effect: A Practical Guide to the World's Changing Climate*. London: Hodder and Stoughton, 1989.

Buttel, Fred. "Environmentalization: Origins, Processes, and Implications for Rural Social Change." *Rural Sociology* 57 (1992): 1–27.

Cole, H. S. D., Christopher Freeman, Marie Hohoda, and K. L. R. Pavitt. *Thinking about the Future: A Critique of "The Limits to Growth."* London: Chatto & Windus, 1973.

De Onis, Juan. *The Green Cathedral: Sustainable Development of Amazonia*. New York: Oxford University Press, 1992.

Ehrlich, Paul R., and Anne H. Ehrlich. *Population, Resources, Environment*. San Francisco: Freeman, 1970.

Ekins, Paul. *A New World Order: Grassroots Movements for Global Change*. London and New York: Routledge, 1992.

International Union for Conservation of Nature and Natural Resources. *World Conservation Strategy*. Switzerland: International Union for Conservation of Nature and Natural Resources, the United Nations Environment Programme, and the World Wildlife Fund, 1980.

Irvine, Sandy. *Beyond Green Consumerism*. London: Friends of the Earth, 1987.

Kemp, Ray. *The Politics of Radioactive Waste Disposal*. Manchester: Manchester University Press, 1992.

Leggett, Jeremy. "The Environmental Impact of War: A Scientific Analysis and Greenpeace's Reaction." In *Environmental Protection and the Law of War*, edited by Glen Plant, 75–81. London: Belhaven Press, 1992.

Lerner, Steve. *Beyond the Earth Summit: Conversations with Advocates of Sustainable Development*. Bolinas, Calif.: Common Knowledge Press Commonweal, 1991.

Marshall, A. J. *The Great Extermination: A Guide to Anglo-Australian Cupidity, Wickedness and Waste*. London and Melbourne: Heinemann, 1966.

Meadows, Donella H., Dennis L. Meadows and Jorgen Randers. *Beyond the Limits*. London: Earthscan Publications, 1992.

Mesarovic, Mihailo D., and Eduard Pestel. *Mankind at the Turning Point: The Second Report to the Club of Rome*. London: Hutchinson, 1975.

Mintzer, Irving M., ed. *Confronting Climate Change: Risks, Implications and Responses*. Cambridge: Cambridge University Press, 1992.

Mounfield, Peter. *World Nuclear Power*. London and New York: Routledge, 1991.

Nelkin, Dorothy, and Michael Pollack. "Political Parties and the Nuclear Debate in France and Germany." *Comparative Politics* 2 (1980): 127–42.

———. *The Atom Besieged*. Cambridge Mass.: MIT Press, 1981.

Pearce, Fred. *Turning Up the Heat*. London: Bodley Head, 1989.

Peters, Rob, and Thomas Lovejoy, eds. *Global Warming and Biodiversity*. New Haven, Conn.: Yale University Press, 1992.

Pickering, Kevin T., and Lewis A. Owen. *An Introduction to Global Environmental Issues*. London and New York: Routledge, 1994.

Plumwood, Val. "Nature, Self, and Gender: Feminism, Environmental Philosophy, and the Critique of Rationalism." *Hypatia* 6, no. 1 (1991): 3–27.

Prins, Gwyn, ed. *Defended to Death: A Study of the Nuclear Arms Race*. Harmondsworth, U.K.: Penguin, 1983.

Regan, Tom. *The Case for Animal Rights*. London: Routledge, 1988.

Roddewig, Richard. *Green Bans. The Birth of Australian Environmental Politics*. Sydney: Hale and Ironmonger, 1978.

Schneider, Stephen. *Global Warming: Are We Entering the Greenhouse Century?* San Francisco: Sierra Club Books, 1989.

Shrivastava, Paul. *Bhopal: Anatomy of a Crisis*. London: Paul Chapman, 1992.

Simon, Julian L. *Population Matters: People, Resources, Environment, and Immigration.* New Brunswick, N.J.: Transaction Publications, 1989.

Taylor, Richard. *Against the Bomb.* Oxford: Clarendon Press, 1988.

United Nations Environment Programme. *Convention on Biological Diversity.* 5 June 1992. Na. 92–7807. Nairobi: UNEP, 1992.

———. *UNEP: Two Decades of Achievement and Challenge.* Nairobi: UNEP, 1992.

Yaroshinskaya, Alla. *Chernobyl: The Forbidden Truth.* Oxford: John Carpenter, 1994.

5. Green Movement

General

Boggs, Carl. *Social Movements and Political Power.* Philadelphia: Temple University Press, 1986.

Bramwell, Anna. *Blood and Soil: Walther Darré and Hitler's Green Party.* Bourne End, England: The Kensal Press, 1985.

Brand, Karl-Werner. "Cyclical Aspects of New Social Movements: Waves of Cultural Criticism and Mobilization Cycles of New Middle-Class Radicalism." In *Challenging the Political Order,* edited by Russell Dalton and Manfred Kuechler, 23–42. Cambridge: Polity Press, 1990.

———. *Neue Soziale Bewegungen: Entstehung, Funktion und Perspektive neuer Protestpotentiale.* Opladen, Germany: Westdeutscher Verlag, 1982.

Brand, Karl-Werner, Detlef Büsser, and Dieter Rucht. *Aufbruch in eine neue Gesellschaft: Neue soziale Bewegungen in der Bundesrepublik Deutschland.* Frankfurt/New York: Campus, 1986.

Capra, Fritjof, and Charlene Spretnak. *Green Politics: The Global Promise.* London: Hutchinson, 1984.

Cohen, Jean L. "Strategy or Identity: New Theoretical Paradigms and Contemporary Social Movements." *Social Research* 52, no. 4 (1985): 663–716.

Dalton, Russell. "Alliance Patterns of the European Environmental Movement." In *Green Politics Two,* edited by Wolfgang Rüdig, 59–85. Edinburgh: Edinburgh University Press, 1992.

Eder, Klaus. "The 'New Social Movements': Moral Crusades, Political Pressure Groups, or Social Movements." *Social Research* 52, no. 4 (1985): 869–90.

Fox, Stephen. *John Muir and His Legacy: The American Conservation Movement.* Boston: Little, Brown, 1981.

Guggenberger, Bernd. *Bürgerinitiativen in der Parteiendemokratie.* Stuttgart: Kohlhammer, 1980.

Guggenberger, Bernd, and Udo Kempf, eds. *Bürgerinitiativen und Repräsentatives System.* 2nd ed. Opladen, Germany: Westdeutscher Verlag, 1984.

Jamison, Andrew, Ron Eyerman, and Jacqueline Cramer. *The Making of the New Environmental Consciousness: A Comparative Study of the Environmental Movements in Sweden, Denmark and the Netherlands.* Edinburgh: Edinburgh University Press, 1991.

Melucci, Alberto. *Nomads of the Present: Social Movements and Individual Needs in Contemporary Society.* London: Century Hutchison, 1989.

Offe, Claus. "New Social Movements: Challenging the Boundaries of Institutional Politics." *Social Research* 52, no. 4 (1985): 817–68.

Pakulski, Jan. *Social Movements: The Politics of Moral Protest.* Melbourne: Cheshire, 1991.

Scott, Alan. *Ideology and the New Social Movements.* London: Unwin Hyman, 1990.

Touraine, Alain. *Anti-Nuclear Protest.* Cambridge: Cambridge University Press, 1983.

Green Groups

Banuri, Tariq, and Frédérique Apffel Marglin, eds. *Who Will Save the Forests? Knowledge, Power and Environmental Destruction.* London: Zed Books, 1993.

Bramble, Barbara, and Gareth Porter. "Non-Governmental Organisations and the Making of U.S. International Environmental Policy." In *The International Politics of the Environment: Actors, Interests and Institutions,* edited by Andrew Hurrell and Benedict Kingsley, 313–53. Oxford: Clarendon Press, 1992.

Byrne, Paul. *The Campaign for Nuclear Disarmament.* London: Croom Helm, 1988.

Colchester, Marcus, and Larry Lohmann, eds. *The Struggle for the Land and the Fate of the Forests.* Penang: World Rainforest Movement; London: Zed Books, 1993.

Dalton, Russell J. *The Green Rainbow: Environmental Groups in Western Europe.* New Haven, Conn.: Yale University Press, 1994.

Diani, Mario. *Green Networks: A Structural Analysis of the Italian Environmental Movement.* Edinburgh: Edinburgh University Press, 1995.

Dunlap, Riley E., and Angelo G. Mertig, eds. *American Environmentalism: The U.S. Environmental Movement 1970–1990.* New York: Taylor and Francis, 1992.

Edwards, Michael, and David Hulme. *Making a Difference: NGOs and*

Development in a Changing World. London: Earthscan Publications, 1992.

Ekins, Paul. *A New World Order: Grassroots Movements for Global Change*. London and New York: Routledge, 1992.

Fisher, Julie. *The Road from Rio: Sustainable Development and the Nongovernmental Movement in the Third World*. Westport, Conn.: Praeger, 1993.

Foreman, David, and Bill Haywood, eds. *Ecodefense: A Field Guide to Monkeywrenching*. Tucson, Ariz.: Ned Ludd Books, 1985.

Fox, Stephen. *John Muir and His Legacy: The American Conservation Movement*. Boston: Little, Brown, 1981.

Ghai, Dharam, and Jessica M. Vivian, eds. *Grassroots Environmental Action: People's Participation in Sustainable Development*. London: Routledge, 1992.

Gottlieb, Robert. *Forcing the Spring: The Transformation of the American Environmental Movement*. Washington, D.C.: Island Press, 1993.

Jancar, Barbara. "Chaos as an Explanation of the Role of Environmental Groups in East European Politics." In *Green Politics Two*, edited by Wolfgang Rüdig, 156–84. Edinburgh: Edinburgh University Press, 1992.

Kitschelt, Herbert. "Political Opportunity Structures and Political Protest: Anti-nuclear Movements in Four Democracies." *British Journal of Political Science* 16 (1986): 57–85.

Lowe, Philip, and Jane Goyder. *Environmental Groups in Politics*. London: Allen & Unwin, 1983.

McCormick, John. "International Nongovernmental Organizations: Prospects for a Global Environmental Movement." In *Environmental Politics and the International Arena: Movements, Parties, Organizations and Policy*, edited by Sheldon Kamieniecki, 131–43. Albany: State University of New York Press, 1993.

———. *The Global Environmental Movement*. 2nd ed. London: Wiley, 1995.

Milbrath, Lester. *Environmentalists: Vanguard for a New Society*. Albany: State University of New York Press, 1984.

Minnion, John, and Philip Bolsover, eds. *The CND Story*. London: Allison and Busby, 1983.

Predelli, Line Nyhagen. "Ideological Conflict in the Radical Environmental Group Earth First!" *Environmental Politics* 4, no. 1 (1995): 123–29.

Princen, Thomas, and Matthias Finger, with contributions by Jack P. Manno and Margaret L. Clark. *Environmental NGOs in World Politics: Linking the Local and the Global*. London, New York: Routledge, 1994.

Rochon, Thomas. *Mobilizing for Peace: Antinuclear Movements in Western Europe*. Princeton, N.J.: Princeton University Press, 1988.

Rucht, Dieter. "Environmental Movement Organizations in West Germany and France." In *Organizing for Change: International Social Movement Research Series*, edited by Bert Klandermans, vol. 2, 61–94. Greenwich, Conn.: JAI Press, 1989.

———. "Ecological Protest as Calculated Law-breaking: Greenpeace and Earth First! in Comparative Perspective." In *Green Politics Three*, edited by Wolfgang Rüdig, 66–89. Edinburgh: Edinburgh University Press, 1995.

Rüdig, Wolfgang. *Anti-Nuclear Movements*. London: Longman, 1990.

Sale, Kirkpatrick. *The Green Revolution: The American Environmental Movement 1962–1992*. New York: Hill and Wang, 1993.

Shabecoff, Philip. *A Fierce Green Fire: The American Environmental Movement*. New York: Hill and Wang, 1993.

Shiva, Vandana. *Staying Alive: Women, Ecology and Development*. London: Zed Books, 1989.

———. *Monocultures of the Mind: Perspectives on Biodiversity and Biotechnology*. London: Zed Books, 1993.

Taylor, Richard, and Colin Pritchard. *The Protest Makers: The British Nuclear Disarmament Movement of 1958–1965 Twenty Years On*. Oxford: Pergamon, 1980.

Warhurst, John. "The Australian Conservation Foundation: The Development of a Modern Environmental Interest Group." *Environmental Politics* 3, no. 1 (1994): 68–90.

Wells, Edward R. and Alan M. Schwartz. *Historical Dictionary of North American Environmentalism*. Lanham, Md.: Scarecrow Press, 1997.

New Politics

Barnes, Samuel H., and Max Kaase et al. *Political Action*. Beverly Hills, Calif.: Sage, 1979.

Dalton, Russell. "Cognitive Mobilization and Partisan Dealignment in Advanced Industrial Democracies." *Journal of Politics* 46 (1984): 264–84.

———. *Citizen Politics: Public Opinion and Political Parties in Advanced Industrial Democracies*. 2nd ed. Chatham, N.J.: Chatham House, 1996.

Dalton, Russell, and Manfred Kuechler, eds. *Challenging the Political Order: New Social Movements in Western Democracies*. Cambridge: Polity Press, 1990.

Inglehart, Ronald. "The Silent Revolution in Europe: Intergenerational Change in Post-Industrial Societies." *American Political Science Review* 65, no. 4 (1971): 991–1017.

————. *The Silent Revolution*. Princeton, N.J.: Princeton University Press, 1977.

————. "Value Change in Industrial Societies." *American Political Science Review* 81, no. 4 (1987): 1289–1303.

————. *Culture Shift in Advanced Industrial Society*. Princeton, N.J.: Princeton University Press, 1990.

Jahn, Detlef. "The Rise and Decline of New Politics and the Greens in Sweden and Germany." *European Journal of Political Research* 24, no. 2 (1993): 177–94.

Lafferty, William. "Basic Needs and Political Values: Some Perspectives from Norway on Europe's Silent Revolution." *Acta Sociologica* 19 (1976): 117–36.

Marsh, Alan. "The Silent Revolution, Value Priorities, and the Quality of Life in Britain." *American Political Science Review* 32, no. 1 (1975): 1–30.

————. *Protest and Political Consciousness*. Beverly Hills, Calif., and London: Sage, 1977.

Müller-Rommel, Ferdinand, and Thomas Poguntke, eds. *New Politics*. Aldershot, U.K.: Dartmouth Publishing, 1995.

Poguntke, Thomas. "New Politics and Party Systems." *West European Politics* 10, no. 1 (1987): 76–88.

6. Green Parties

Australia

Bean, Clive, and Elim Papadakis. "Minor Parties and Independents: Electoral Bases and Future Prospects." In *Party Systems, Representation and Policy Making: Australian Trends in Comparative Perspective*, edited by Ian Marsh and John Uhr, 111–26. *Australian Journal of Political Science*, special issue 30, 1995.

Commonwealth of Australia. *Our Country: Our Future*. Canberra: Australian Government Publishing Service, 1989.

Hay, P. R. "Vandals at the Gate: The Tasmanian Greens and the Perils of Sharing Power." In *Green Politics Two*, edited by Wolfgang Rüdig, 86–110. Edinburgh: Edinburgh University Press, 1992.

Hutton, Drew, ed. *Green Politics in Australia*. Sydney: Angus and Robertson, 1987.

Papadakis, Elim. *Politics and the Environment: The Australian Experience*. Sydney: Allen and Unwin, 1993.

————. *Environmental Politics and Institutional Change*. Cambridge: Cambridge University Press, 1996.

Papadakis, Elim, and Clive Bean. "Minor Parties and Independents: The

Electoral System." In *Party Systems, Representation and Policy Making: Australian Trends in Comparative Perspective*, edited by Ian Marsh and John Uhr, 97–110. *Australian Journal of Political Science*, special issue 30, 1995.

Austria

Frankland, E. Gene. "The Austrian Greens: From Electoral Alliance to Political Party." In *Green Politics Three*, edited by Wolfgang Rüdig, 192–216. Edinburgh: Edinburgh University Press, 1995.

Haerpfer, Christian. "Austria: The 'United Greens' and the 'Alternative List/Green Alternative'." In *New Politics in Western Europe: The Rise and Success of Green Parties and Alternative Lists*, edited by Ferdinand Müller-Rommel, 23–38. Boulder, Colo.: Westview Press, 1989.

Lauber, Volkmar. "The Austrian Greens." *Environmental Politics* 3, no. 1 (1995): 313–19.

Waller, Michael. "The Dams on the Danube." *Environmental Politics* 1, no. 1 (1992): 121–27.

Belgium

Deschouwer, Kris. "Belgium: The 'Ecologists' and 'AGALEV'." In *New Politics in Western Europe: The Rise and Success of Green Parties and Alternative Lists*, edited by Ferdinand Müller-Rommel, 39–54. Boulder, Colo.: Westview Press, 1989.

Hooghe, Marc. "The Green Parties in the Belgian General Elections of 24 November 1991: Mixed Blessings." *Environmental Politics* 1, no. 1 (1992): 287–91.

———. "The Greens in the Belgian Elections of 21 May 1995: Growing Doubts." *Environmental Politics* 4, no. 4 (1995): 253–57.

Kitschelt, Herbert. "The Medium Is the Message: Democracy and Oligarchy in Belgian Ecology Parties." In *Green Politics One*, edited by Wolfgang Rüdig, 82–114. Edinburgh: Edinburgh University Press, 1990.

Rihoux, Benoît. "Belgium: Greens in a Divided Society." In *The Green Challenge: The Development of Green Parties in Europe*, edited by Dick Richardson and Chris Rootes, 91–108. London and New York: Routledge, 1995.

Comparative

Alber, Jens. "Modernization, Cleavage Structures, and the Rise of Green Parties and Lists in Europe." In *New Politics in Western Eu-*

rope: The Rise and Success of Green Parties and Alternative Lists, edited by Ferdinand Müller-Rommel, 195–210. Boulder, Colo.: Westview Press, 1989.

Doherty, Brian. "The Fundi-Realo Controversy: An Analysis of Four European Green Parties." *Environmental Politics* 1, no. 1 (1992): 95–120.

Kitschelt, Herbert. "Left-Libertarian Parties: Explaining Innovation in Competitive Systems." *World Politics* 15 (1988): 194–234.

———. "Organizational Strategy of Belgian and German Ecology Parties." *Comparative Politics* 20, no. 2 (1988): 127–54.

Kitschelt, Herbert, and Staf Hellemans. *Beyond the European Left*. Durham, N.C.: Duke University Press, 1990.

Kreuzer, Markus. "New Politics: Just Post Materialist? The Case of the Austrian and Swiss Greens." *West European Politics* 13, no. 1 (1990): 12–30.

Müller-Rommel, Ferdinand. "Social Movements and the Greens." *European Journal of Political Research* 13, no. 1 (1985): 53–67.

———. "Green Parties and Alternative Lists Under Cross-National Perspective." In *New Politics in Western Europe: The Rise and Success of Green Parties and Alternative Lists*, edited by Ferdinand Müller-Rommel, 5–22. Boulder, Colo.: Westview Press, 1989.

———. "New Political Movements and 'New Politics' Parties in Western Europe." In *Challenging the Political Order*, edited by Russell Dalton and Manfred Kuechler, 209–31. Cambridge: Polity Press, 1990.

———. *Grüne Parteien in Westeuropa: Entwicklungsphasen und Erfolgsbedingungen*. Opladen, Germany: Westdeutscher Verlag, 1993.

Müller-Rommel, Ferdinand, ed. *New Politics in Western Europe: The Rise and Success of Green Parties and Alternative Lists*. Boulder, Colo.: Westview Press, 1989.

Parkin, Sara. *Green Parties: An International Guide*. London: Heretic Books, 1989.

Poguntke, Thomas. "The 'New Politics Dimension' in European Green Parties." In *New Politics in Western Europe: The Rise and Success of Green Parties and Alternative Lists*, edited by Ferdinand Müller-Rommel, 175–94. Boulder, Colo.: Westview Press, 1989.

Rootes, Chris. "Environmental Consciousness, Institutional Structures and Political Competition in the Formation and Development of Green Parties." In *The Green Challenge: The Development of Green Parties in Europe*, edited by Dick Richardson and Chris Rootes, 232–52. London and New York: Routledge, 1995.

Rüdig, Wolfgang, and Mark Franklin. "Green Prospects: The Future of Green Parties in Britain, France and Germany." In *Green Politics*

Two, edited by Wolfgang Rüdig, 37–58. Edinburgh: Edinburgh University Press, 1992.

Czechoslovakia

Jelicka, Petr, and Tomas Kostelecky. "The Development of the Czechoslovak Green Party since the 1990 Election." *Environmental Politics* 1, no. 1 (1992): 72–94.

———. "Czechoslovakia: Greens in a Post-Communist Society." In *The Green Challenge: The Development of Green Parties in Europe*, edited by Dick Richardson and Chris Rootes, 208–31. London and New York: Routledge, 1995.

Denmark

Schüttemeyer, Suzanne S. "Denmark: 'De Grønne'." In *New Politics in Western Europe: The Rise and Success of Green Parties and Alternative Lists*, edited by Ferdinand Müller-Rommel, 55–60. Boulder, Colo.: Westview Press, 1989.

Europe

Bowler, Shaun, and David M. Farrell. "The Greens at the European Level." *Environmental Politics* 1, no. 1 (1992): 132–36.

Buck, Karl H. "Europe: The 'Greens' and the 'Rainbow Group' in the European Parliament." In *New Politics in Western Europe: The Rise and Success of Green Parties and Alternative Lists*, edited by Ferdinand Müller-Rommel, 176–74. Boulder, Colo.: Westview Press, 1989.

Carter, Neil. "The Greens in the 1994 European Parliamentary Elections." *Environmental Politics* 3, no. 1 (1994): 495–502.

Curtice, John. "The 1989 European Election: Protest or Green Tide?" *Electoral Studies* 8 (1989): 217–30.

Harrison, Lisa. "Green Parties in Europe—Evidence from Sub-National Elections." *Environmental Politics* 3, no. 1 (1995): 295–304.

Richardson, Dick, and Chris Rootes, eds. *The Green Challenge. The Development of Green Parties in Europe*. London: Routledge, 1995.

Rihoux, Benoît. "Belgium: Greens in a Divided Society." In *The Green Challenge: The Development of Green Parties in Europe*, edited by Dick Richardson and Chris Rootes, 91–108. London and New York: Routledge, 1995.

Rüdig, Wolfgang. "The Greens in Europe: Ecological Parties and the European Elections of 1984." *Parliamentary Affairs* 38 (1985): 56–72.

Finland

Paastela, Jukka. "Finland: The 'Vihreät'." In *New Politics in Western Europe: The Rise and Success of Green Parties and Alternative Lists*, edited by Ferdinand Müller-Rommel, 81–86. Boulder, Colo.: Westview Press, 1989.

France

Cole, Alistair, and Brian Doherty, "France: *Pas commes les autres*—the French Greens at the crossroads." In *The Green Challenge: The Development of Green Parties in Europe*, edited by Dick Richardson and Chris Rootes, 45–65. London and New York: Routledge, 1995.

Hainsworth, Paul. "Breaking the Mould: the Greens in the French Party System." In *French Political Parties in Transition*, edited by Alistair Cole, 91–105 Aldershot, U.K.: Dartmouth, 1990.

Holliday, Ian. "Dealing in Green Votes: France, 1993." *Government and Opposition* 29, no. 1 (1994): 64–79.

Kitschelt, Herbert. "La Gauche libertaire et les écologistes." *Revue Française de Science Politique* 40, no. 3 (1990): 339–65.

Prendiville, Brendan. "France: 'Les Verts'." In *New Politics in Western Europe: The Rise and Success of Green Parties and Alternative Lists*, edited by Ferdinand Müller-Rommel, 87–100. Boulder, Colo.: Westview Press, 1989.

———. "French Ecologists at the Crossroads: The Regional and Cantonal Elections of March 1992 in France." *Environmental Politics* 1, no. 3 (1992): 448–57.

———. "The French Greens, Inside Out." *Environmental Politics* 1, no. 1 (1992): 283–87.

Germany

Alber, Jens. "Modernisierung, neue Spannungslinien und die politischen Chancen der Grünen." *Politische Vierteljahresschrift* 26, no. 3 (1985): 211–26.

Bürklin, Wilhelm. "Governing Left Parties Frustrating the Radical Non-Established Left: The Rise and Inevitable Decline of the Greens." *European Sociological Review* 3, no. 2 (1987): 109–26.

Chandler, William, and Alan Siaroff. "Postindustrial Politics in Germany and the Origins of the Greens." *Comparative Politics* 18 (1986): 303–25.

Dicke, Klaus, and Tobias Stoll. "Freies Mandat, Mandatsverzicht des Abgeordneten und das Rotationsprinzip der GRÜNEN." *Zeitschrift für Parlamentsfragen* 16, no. 4 (1985): 451–65.

Fogt, Helmut. "Basisdemokratie oder Herrschaft der Aktivisten? Zum Politikverstandnis der Grünen." *Politische Vierteljahresschrift* 25, no. 1 (1984): 97–114.

Frankland, E. Gene. "Federal Republic of Germany: 'Die Grünen'." In *New Politics in Western Europe: The Rise and Success of Green Parties and Alternative Lists*, edited by Ferdinand Müller-Rommel, 61–80. Boulder, Colo.: Westview Press, 1989.

————. "Germany: The Rise, Fall and Recovery of Die Grünen." In *The Green Challenge: The Development of Green Parties in Europe*, edited by Dick Richardson and Chris Rootes, 23–44. London and New York: Routledge, 1995.

Frankland, E. Gene, and Donald Schoonmaker, eds. *Between Protest and Power: The Green Party in Germany*. Boulder, Colo.: Westview Press, 1992.

Hülsberg, Werner. "After the West German Elections." *New Left Review* 152 (1987): 85–99.

————. *The German Greens*. London: Verso Press, 1988.

Ismayr, Wolfgang. "Die Grünen im Bundestag: Parlamentarisierung und Basisanbindung." *Zeitschrift für Parlamentsfragen* 16, no. 3 (1985): 299–321.

Jesinghausen, Martin. "General Election to the German Bundestag on 16 October 1994: Green Pragmatists in Conservative Embrace or a New Era for German Parliamentary Democracy?" *Environmental Politics* 3, no. 1 (1995): 108–13.

Kolinsky, Eva. "The Greens in Germany: Prospects of a Small Party." *Parliamentary Affairs* 37, no. 4 (1984): 434–47.

————. "The West-German Greens—A Women's Party?" *Parliamentary Affairs* 41, no. 1 (1988): 129–49.

Mewes, Horst. "The West German Green Party." *New German Critique* 28 (1983): 51–85.

Müller-Rommel, Ferdinand. "The German Greens in the 1980s: Short-term Cyclical Protest or Indicator of Transformation?" *Political Studies* 37, no. 1 (1989): 114–22.

Papadakis, Elim. *The Green Movement in West Germany*. London: Croom Helm, 1984.

————. "Social Movements, Self-limiting Radicalism and the Green Party in West Germany." *Sociology* 22, no. 3 (1988): 433–54.

Poguntke, Thomas. "The Organization of a Participatory Party—the German Greens." *European Journal of Political Research* 15 (1987): 609–33.

————. "Party Activists versus Voters: Are the German Greens Losing Touch with the Electorate?" In *Green Politics One*, edited by Wolfgang Rüdig, 29–46. Edinburgh: Edinburgh University Press, 1990.

————. *Alternative Politics. The German Green Party*. Edinburgh: Edinburgh University Press, 1993.

————. "Goodbye to Movement Politics? Organisational Adaptation of the German Green Party." *Environmental Politics* 2, no. 1 (1993): 379–404.

Raschke, Joachim. *Die Grünen: Wie sie wurden, was sie sind*. Cologne: Bund Verlag, 1993.

Rebe, Bernd. "Die erlaubte verfassungwidrige Rotation." *Zeitschrift für Parlamentsfragen* 16, no. 4 (1985): 468–74.

Roberts, Geoffrey K. "The Green Party in Germany: 1990–1991." *Environmental Politics* 1, no. 1 (1992): 128–31.

Scharf, Thomas. *The German Greens: Challenging the Consensus*. Oxford and Providence, R.I.: Berg, 1994.

Greece

Demertzis, Nicolas. "Greece: Greens at the Periphery." In *The Green Challenge: The Development of Green Parties in Europe*, edited by Dick Richardson and Chris Rootes, 193–207. London and New York: Routledge, 1995.

Ireland

Farrell, David M. "Ireland: The 'Green Alliance'." In *New Politics in Western Europe: The Rise and Success of Green Parties and Alternative Lists*, edited by Ferdinand Müller-Rommel, 123–30. Boulder, Colo.: Westview Press, 1989.

Italy

Diani, Mario. "Italy: The 'Liste Verdi'." In *New Politics in Western Europe: The Rise and Success of Green Parties and Alternative Lists*, edited by Ferdinand Müller-Rommel, 113–22. Boulder, Colo.: Westview Press, 1989.

Pridham, Geoffrey. "Italian Small Parties in Comparative Perspective." In *Small Parties in Western Europe: Comparative and National Perspectives*, edited by Ferdinand Müller-Rommel and Geoffrey Pridham, 71–94. London: Sage, 1991.

Rhodes, Martin. "*Piazza* or *Palazzo?* The Italian Greens and the 1992 Elections." *Environmental Politics* 1 (1992): 437–42.

————. "The Italian Greens: Struggling for Survival." *Environmental Politics* 3, no. 1 (1995): 305–12.

————. "Italy: Greens in an Overcrowded Political System." In *The Green Challenge: The Development of Green Parties in Europe*, edited by Dick Richardson and Chris Rootes, 168–92. London and New York: Routledge, 1995.

Luxembourg

Hirsch, Mario. "The 1984 Luxembourg Election." *West European Politics* 8, no. 1 (1985): 116–18.

Koelble, Thomas. "Luxembourg: The 'Greng Alternative'." In *New Politics in Western Europe: The Rise and Success of Green Parties and Alternative Lists*, edited by Ferdinand Müller-Rommel, 131–38. Boulder, Colo.: Westview Press, 1989.

Netherlands

Lucardie, Paul. "General Elections in the Netherlands, May 1994: The Triumph of Grey Liberalism." *Environmental Politics* 3, no. 1 (1995): 119–22.

Lucardie, Paul, Jelle van der Knoop, Wijbrandt van Schuur, and Gerrit Voerman. "Greening the Reds or Reddening the Greens? The Case of the Green Left in the Netherlands." In *Green Politics Three*, edited by Wolfgang Rüdig, 90–111. Edinburgh: Edinburgh University Press, 1995.

Lucardie, Paul, Gerrit Voerman, and Wijbrandt van Schuur. "Different Shades of Green: A Comparison between Members of *Groen Links* and *De Groenen*." *Environmental Politics* 2, no. 1 (1993): 40–62.

Voerman, Gerrit. "The Netherlands: Losing Colours, Turning Green." In *The Green Challenge: The Development of Green Parties in Europe*, edited by Dick Richardson and Chris Rootes, 109–27. London and New York: Routledge, 1995.

New Zealand

Rainbow, Stephen L. "The New Zealand Values Party: Challenging the Poverty of Progress 1972–1989." In *Green Politics Two*, edited by Wolfgang Rüdig, 111–33. Edinburgh: Edinburgh University Press, 1992.

———. "Why Did New Zealand and Tasmania Spawn the World's First Green Parties?" *Environmental Politics* 1, no. 1 (1992): 321–46.

Spain

Aguilar-Fernández, Susana. "The Greens in the 1993 Spanish General Election: A Chronicle of a Defeat Foretold." *Environmental Politics* 3, no. 1 (1994): 153–58.

Sweden

Affigne, Anthony. "Environmental Crisis, Green Party Power: Chernobyl and the Swedish Greens." In *Green Politics One*, edited by Wolfgang Rüdig, 115–52. Edinburgh: Edinburgh University Press, 1990.

Bennulf, Martin. "Sweden: The Rise and Fall of *Miljöpartiet de gröna.*" In *The Green Challenge: The Development of Green Parties in Europe*, edited by Dick Richardson and Chris Rootes, 128–45. London and New York: Routledge, 1995.

———. "The 1994 Election in Sweden: Green or Grey?" *Environmental Politics* 3, no. 1 (1995): 114–18.

Bennulf, Martin, and Sören Holmberg. "The Green Breakthrough in Sweden." *Scandinavian Political Studies* 13 (1990): 165–84.

Vedung, Evert. "The Environmentalist Party and the Swedish Five Party Syndrome." In *When Parties Fail*, edited by Kay Lawson and Peter Merkl, 76–109. Princeton, N.J.: Princeton University Press, 1988.

———. "Sweden: The *Miljöpartiet de Gröna.*" In *New Politics in Western Europe: The Rise and Success of Green Parties and Alternative Lists*, edited by Ferdinand Müller-Rommel, 139–54. Boulder, Colo.: Westview Press, 1989.

Switzerland

Church, Clive. H. "The Development of the Swiss Green Party." *Environmental Politics* 1, no. 1 (1992): 252–82.

———. "Switzerland: Greens in a Confederal Polity." In *The Green Challenge: The Development of Green Parties in Europe*, edited by Dick Richardson and Chris Rootes, 146–67. London and New York: Routledge, 1995.

Finger, Matthias, and Simon Hug. "Green Politics in Switzerland." *European Journal of Political Research* 21, no. 3 (1992): 289–306.

Hug, Simon. "The Emergence of the Swiss Ecological Party: A Dynamic Model." *European Journal of Political Research* 18, no. 6 (1990): 645–70.

Ladner, Andreas. "Switzerland: The 'Green' and 'Alternative Parties'." In *New Politics in Western Europe: The Rise and Success of Green Parties and Alternative Lists*, edited by Ferdinand Müller-Rommel, 155–75. Boulder, Colo.: Westview Press, 1989.

United Kingdom

Bennie, Lynne, Mark Franklin, and Wolfgang Rüdig. "Green Dimensions: The Ideology of the British Greens." In *Green Politics Three*, edited by Wolfgang Rüdig, 217–39. Edinburgh: Edinburgh University Press, 1995.

Byrne, Paul. "Great Britain: The 'Green Party'." In *New Politics in Western Europe: The Rise and Success of Green Parties and Alternative Lists*, edited by Ferdinand Müller-Rommel, 101–12. Boulder, Colo.: Westview Press, 1989.

Frankland, E. Gene. "Does Green Politics have a Future in Britain? An American Perspective." In *Green Politics One*, edited by Wolfgang Rüdig, 7–28. Edinburgh: Edinburgh University Press, 1990.

McCulloch, Alistair. "The Green Party in England and Wales: Structure and Development, The Early Years." *Environmental Politics* 1, no. 1 (1992): 418–36.

———. "The Ecology Party in England and Wales: Branch Organisation and Activity." *Environmental Politics* 2, no. 1 (1993): 20–39.

Rootes, Chris. "The New Politics and the New Social Movements: Accounting for British Exceptionalism." *European Journal of Political Research* 22 (1992): 171–91.

———. "Britain: Greens in a Cold Climate." In *The Green Challenge: The Development of Green Parties in Europe*, edited by Dick Richardson and Chris Rootes, 66–90. London and New York: Routledge, 1995.

Rüdig, Wolfgang, and Philip Lowe. "The Withered 'Greening' of British Politics: A Study of the Ecology Party." *Political Studies* 34 (1986): 262–84.

United States

Lowe, Philip. "Red-Green U.S. Style: The Rise and Demise of the Citizens Party, 1979–1984." In *Green Politics Three*, edited by Wolfgang Rüdig, 112–53. Edinburgh: Edinburgh University Press, 1995.

Rensenbrink, John. *The Greens and the Politics of Transformation*. San Pedro, Calif.: R. & E. Miles, 1992.

7. Green Policies

Australia

Galligan, Brian, and Georgina Lynch. *Integrating Conservation and Development: Australia's Resource Assessment Commission and the Testing Case of Coronation Hill*. Canberra: Federalism Research Centre Discussion Paper No. 14, 1992.

Hay, Peter R., Robyn Eckersley, and Geoff Holloway, eds. *Environmental Politics in Australia and New Zealand*. Hobart: Centre for Environmental Studies, 1989.

Papadakis, Elim. "Environmental Policy." In *Consensus and Restructuring: Hawke and Australian Public Policy*, edited by Christine Jennett and Randal Stewart, 339–55. Melbourne: Macmillan, 1990.

Pybus, Cassandra, and Richard Flanagan, eds. *The Rest of the World Is Watching*. Sydney: Pan Macmillan, 1990.

Toyne, Philip. *The Reluctant Nation*. Sydney: ABC Books, 1994.

Walker, Ken. *Australian Environmental Policy*. Sydney: University of New South Wales Press, 1992.

Baltic States

Eckerberg, Katarina. "Environmental Problems and Policy Options in the Baltic States: Learning from the West?" *Environmental Politics* 3, no. 1 (1994): 445–78.

Canada

Boardman, Robert, ed. *Canadian Environmental Policy: Ecosystems, Politics, and Process*. Toronto: Oxford University Press, 1992.

Doern, G. Bruce, ed. *Getting It Green: Case Studies in Canadian Environmental Regulation*. Toronto: C.D. Howe Institute, 1990.

Hoberg, George. "Sleeping with an Elephant: The American Influence on Canadian Environmental Regulation." *Journal of Public Policy* 11, no. 1 (1991): 107–32.

Skogstad, Grace, and Paul Kopas. "Environmental Policy in a Federal System: Ottawa and the Provinces." In *Canadian Environmental Policy*, edited by Robert Boardman, 43–59. Toronto: Oxford University Press, 1992.

Toner, Glen, and Bruce Doern. "Five Political and Policy Imperatives in Green Plan Formation: The Canadian Case." *Environmental Politics* 3, no. 1 (1994): 395–420.

Comparative

Boehmer-Christiansen, Sonja A. "Anglo-German Contrasts in Environmental Policy-making." *International Environmental Affairs* 4, no. 4 (1992): 140–59.

Boehmer-Christiansen, Sonja A., and Jim Skea. *Acid Politics: Environmental and Energy Policies in Britain and Germany*. London and New York: Belhaven Press, 1991.

Brown, Lester R., et al. *State of the World 1994*. London: Earthscan, 1994.

Caldwell, Lynton D. *International Environmental Policy: Emergence and Dimensions*. 2nd ed. Duke Press Policy Studies. Durham, N.C., and London: Duke University Press, 1990.

Chertow, Marian R., and Daniel C. Esty. *Thinking Ecologically: The Next Generation of Environmental Policy*. New Haven: Yale University Press, 1997.

Dasgupta, Partha, and Karl-Goran Maler, eds. *The Environment and Emerging Development Issues*. New York: Clarendon Press, 1997.

Dietz, Frank J., Udo E. Simonis, and Jan van der Straaten, eds. *Sustainability and Environmental Policy—Restraints and Advances*. Berlin: Edition Sigma, 1992.

Eckersley, Robyn, ed. *Markets, the State and the Environment: Towards Integration*. Melbourne: Macmillan, 1995.

Fiorino, Daniel J. *Making Environmental Policy*. Los Angeles: University of California Press, 1995.

————. "Environmental Policy and the Participation Gap." In *Democracy and the Environment*, edited by William M. Lafferty and James Meadowcroft, 194–212. Cheltenham, U.K.: Edward Elgar, 1996.

Fischer, Frank, and Michael Black, eds. *Green Environmental Policy: The Politics of a Sustainable Future*. New York: St. Martin's Press, 1995.

Gonzalez, George, G., Sheldon Kamieniecki, and Robert O. Vos. *Flashpoints in Environmental Policy Making*. Albany: State University of New York Press, 1997.

Jänicke, Martin. *State Failure. The Impotence of Politics in Industrial Society*. Cambridge, U.K.: Polity Press, 1990.

————. "Conditions for Environmental Policy Success: An International Comparison." *The Environmentalist* 12, no. 1 (1992): 47–58.

Jänicke, Martin, et al. "Structural Change and Environmental Impact: Empirical Evidence on 31 Countries in East and West." *Intereconomics* 24 (1989): 24–34.

Jänicke, Martin, and Helmut Weidner. *Successful Environmental Policy. A Critical Evaluation of 24 Cases*. Berlin: Edition Sigma, 1995.

Jänicke, Martin, and Helmut Weidner, eds. *National Environmental Politics. A Comparative Study of Capacity-Building*. Berlin: Springer, 1997.

Lester, James P., ed. *Environmental Politics and Policy — Theories and Evidence*. 2nd ed. Durham, N.C.: Duke University Press, 1995.

Lipschutz, Ronnie D., and Ken Conca, eds. *The State and Social Power in Global Environmental Politics*. New York: Columbia University Press, 1993.

Reich, Michael R. "Mobilizing for Environmental Policy in Italy and Japan." *Comparative Politics* 16 (1984): 379–402.

Scheberle, Denise. *Federalism and Environmental Policy: Trust and the*

Politics of Implementation. Washington, D.C.: Georgetown University Press.

Smith, Zachary A. *The Environmental Policy Paradox.* Englewood Cliffs, N.J.: Prentice-Hall, 1992.

Vogel, David. *National Styles of Regulation: Environmental Policy in Great Britain and the United States.* Ithaca, N.Y.: Cornell University Press, 1986.

von Weizsäcker, Ernst Ulrich. *Earth Politics.* London: Zed Books, 1994.

Weale, Albert. "The Greening of the European Polity." *West European Politics* 14, no. 4 (1991): 193–98.

————. *The New Politics of Pollution.* Manchester: Manchester University Press, 1992.

Weale, Albert, Timothy O'Riordan, and L. Kramme. *Controlling Pollution in the Round: Change and Choice in Environmental Regulation in Britain and Germany.* London: Anglo-German Foundation for the Study of Industrial Society, 1991.

Czechoslovakia

Fagin, Adam. "Environment and Transition in the Czech Republic." *Environmental Politics* 3, no. 1 (1994): 479–94.

Eastern Europe

Carter, Francis W., and David Turnock. *Environmental Problems in Eastern Europe.* London: Routledge, 1993.

Fisher, Duncan. *Paradise Deferred: Environmental Policymaking in Central and Eastern Europe.* London: Royal Institute of International Affairs/Ecological Studies Institute, 1992.

Jancar-Webster, Barbara. "Eastern Europe and the Former Soviet Union." In *Environmental Politics in the International Arena: Movements, Parties, Organisations, and Policy,* edited by Sheldon Kamieniecki. New York: State University of New York Press, 1993.

Jancar-Webster, Barbara, ed. *Environmental Action in Eastern Europe: Responses to Crises.* New York and London: M. E. Sharpe, 1993.

Russell, Jeremy. *Energy and Environmental Conflicts in East/Central Europe: The Case of Power Generation.* London: Royal Institute of International Affairs/World Conservation Union, 1991.

European Union

Baker, Susan. "Environmental Policy in the European Union: Institutional Dilemmas and Democratic Practice." In *Democracy and the*

Environment, edited by William M. Lafferty and James Meadow-croft, 213–33. Cheltenham, U.K.: Edward Elgar, 1996.

———. "Punctured Sovereignty, Border Regions and the Environment within the European Union." In *Nations and States: Borders, Frontiers of Sovereignty in the New Europe*, edited by Liam O'Dowd and Tom Wilson, 19–50. Aldershot, U.K.: Avebury, 1996.

Baldock, David, and Tony Long. *The Mediterranean Environment under Pressure: The Influence of the CAP on Spain and Portugal and the "IMPs" in France, Greece and Italy*. London: Institute for European Environmental Policy, 1987.

Collins, Ken, and David Earnshaw. "The Implementation and Enforcement of European Community Environmental Legislation." *Environmental Politics* 1, no. 4 (1992): 213–49.

Commission of the European Communities. *The State of the Environment in the European Community*. Brussels: ECommission, 1992.

———. *Towards Sustainability: A European Community Programme of Policy and Action in Relation to the Environment and Sustainable Development*. Brussels: EC Commission, 1992.

———. *Administrative Structures for Environmental Management in the European Community*. Luxembourg: Office for Official Publications of the European Communities, 1993.

Faure, John, John Vervaele, and Albert Weale, eds. *Environmental Standards in the European Union in an Interdisciplinary Framework*. Antwerp: Maklu, 1994.

Haigh, Nigel. *EEC Environmental Policy and Britain*. London: Longman, 1989.

———. *The EC and Integrated Environmental Policy*. London: IEEP, 1992.

———. *Manual of EC Environmental Policy*. London: Institute for European Environmental Policy, 1992.

Johnson, Stanley P., and Guy Corcell. *The Environmental Policy of the European Communities*. International Environmental Law and Policy Series. London: Graham and Trotman, 1989.

Judge, David, ed. *A Green Dimension for the European Community*. London: Frank Cass, 1993.

Lodge, Juliet. "Environment: Towards a Clean Blue-Green EC." In *The European Community and the Challenge of the Future*, edited by Juliet Lodge, 319–26. London: Pinter, 1989.

Sands, Philippe. "European Community Environmental Law: Legislation, the ECJ and Common Interest Groups." *Modern Law Review* 53, no. 5 (1990): 685–98.

Skou Andersen, Mikael, and Duncan Liefferink, eds. *European Environmental Policy: The Pioneers*. Manchester: Manchester University Press, 1997.

Van Der Straaten, Jan. "A Sound European Environmental Policy: Challenges, Possibilities and Barriers." In *A Green Dimension for the European Community*, edited by David Judge, 65–83. London: Frank Cass, 1993.

Vandermeersch, Dirk. "The Single European Act and the Environmental Policy of the European Economic Community." *European Law Review* 12, no. 6 (1987): 407–29.

Verhoeve, Barbara, et al. *Maastricht and the Environment: The Implications for the EC's Environmental Policy of the Treaty on European Union Signed at Maastricht on 7 February 1992*. London: Institute for European Environmental Policy, 1992.

Wilkinson, D. *Maastricht and the Environment*. London: Institute for European Environmental Policy, 1992.

Wurzel, Rüdiger. "Environmental Policy." In *The European Community and the Challenge of the Future*, 2nd ed., edited by Juliet Lodge, 178–99. London: Pinter, 1993.

Finland

Storsved, Ann-Sofie. "The Debate on Establishing the Ministry of the Environment in Finland in the Light of Environmental Ideologies." *Environmental Politics* 2, no. 1 (1993): 304–26.

Germany

Aguilar, Susana. "Corporatist and Statist Designs in Environmental Policy: The Contrasting Roles of Germany and Spain in the European Community Scenario." *Environmental Politics* 2, no. 1 (1993): 223–47.

Boehmer-Christiansen, Sonja. A. "Taken to the Cleaners: The Fate of the East German Energy Sector since 1990." *Environmental Politics* 1, no. 1 (1992): 196–228.

Federal Ministry for the Environment, ed. *Environmental Protection in Germany*. Bonn: Economica Verlag, 1992.

Papadakis, Elim. "Green Issues and Other Parties: *Themenklau* or New Flexibility?" In *Policy Making in the West German Green Party*, edited by Eva Kolinsky, 61–85. Oxford: Berg Publishers, 1989.

Rehbinder, Eckhard. "Rethinking Environmental Policy." In *Developments in German Politics*, edited by Gordon Smith, William Paterson and Stephen Padgett, 227–46. London: Macmillan, 1992.

Weidner, Helmut. *25 Years of Modern Environmental Policy in Germany. Treading a Well-worn Path to the Top of the International Field*. WZB-Discussion papers FS II 95–301. Berlin: Wissenschaftszentrum Berlin, 1995.

Greece

Koufakis, Ioanna. "Country Reports: Greece." *European Environmental Law Review* (Oct. 1994): 244–45.

Pridham, Geoffrey, Susannah Verney, and Dimitrios Konstadakopulos. "Environmental Policy in Greece: Evolution, Structures and Process." *Environmental Politics* 4, no. 2 (1995): 244–70.

Japan

Weidner, Helmut. *Basiselemente einer erfolgreichen Umweltpolitik: Eine Analyse und Evaluation der Instrumente der japanischen Umweltpolitik.* Berlin: edition sigma, 1996.

Netherlands

Van der Straaten, Jan. "The Dutch National Environmental Policy Plan: To Choose or To Lose." *Environmental Politics* 1, no. 1 (1992): 45–71.

Soviet Union

Feshbach, Murray, and Alfred Friendly, Jr. *Ecocide in the USSR: Health and Nature under Siege.* London: Aurum Press, 1992.

Jancar, Barbara. *Environmental Management in the Soviet Union and Yugoslavia.* Durham, N.C.: Duke Press Policy Studies, 1987.

Mnatsakanian, Ruben A. *Environmental Legacy of the Former Soviet Republics.* Edinburgh, Centre for Human Ecology: University of Edinburgh, 1992.

Pryde, Philip R. *Environmental Management in the Soviet Union.* Cambridge: Cambridge University Press, 1991.

Stewart, John Massey, ed. *The Soviet Environment: Problems, Policies and Politics.* Cambridge: Cambridge University Press, 1992.

Ziegler, Charles E. *Environmental Policy in the USSR.* London: Frances Pinter, 1987.

Spain

Aguilar, Susana. "Corporatist and Statist Designs in Environmental Policy: The Contrasting Roles of Germany and Spain in the European Community Scenario." *Environmental Politics* 2, no. 1 (1993): 223–47.

United Kingdom

Jordan, Andrew. "Integrated Pollution Control and the Evolving Style and Structure of Environmental Regulation in the UK." *Environmental Politics* 2, no. 1 (1993): 405–27.

Rose, Chris. *The Dirty Man of Europe: The Great British Pollution Scandal.* London: Simon & Schuster, 1990.

United States

Gore, Albert. *Earth in the Balance: Ecology and the Human Spirit.* Boston: Houghton Mifflin, 1992.

Portney, Kent E. *Controversial Issues in Environmental Policy.* Newbury Park, Calif.: Sage, 1992.

Ringquist, Evan J. *Environmental Protection at the State Level: Policies and Progress in Controlling Pollution.* New York: M.E. Sharpe, 1993.

Vittes, Elliot. "After the 1992 US Elections: Clinton and Environmental Policy." *Environmental Politics* 3, no. 1 (1994): 146–52.

8. Green Politics

General

Downs, Anthony. "Up and Down with Ecology—The Issue-Attention Cycle." *The Public Interest* 28 (1972): 38–50.

Garner, Robert. *Environmental Politics.* New York: Prentice-Hall, 1995.

Gorz, André. *Ecology as Politics.* London: Pluto, 1980,

Irvine, Sandy, and Alec Ponton. *A Green Manifesto.* London: Macdonald, 1988.

Joppke, Christian. "Social Movements during Cycles of Issue Attention: The Decline of the Antinuclear Energy Movements in West Germany and the USA." *British Journal of Sociology* 42, no. 1 (1991): 43–60.

Klandermans, Bert, Hanspeter Kriesi, and Sidney Tarrow, eds. *From Structure to Action: Comparing Movement Research Across Cultures.* Greenwich, Conn.: JAI Press, 1988.

Lowe, Philip, and Wolfgang Rüdig. "Political Ecology and the Social Sciences." *British Journal of Political Science* 16, no. 4 (1986): 513–50.

Rohrschneider, Robert. "Citizens' Attitudes Towards Environmental Issues: Selfish or Selfless?" *Comparative Political Studies* 21, no. 3 (1988): 347–67.

———. "The Roots of Public Opinion toward New Social Movements: An Empirical Test of Competing Explanations." *American Journal of Political Science* 34, no. 1 (1990): 1–30.

————. "Public Opinion toward Environmental Groups in Western Europe: One Movement or Two?" *Social Science Quarterly* 72, no. 2 (1991): 251–66.

Rüdig, Wolfgang, ed. *Green Politics One.* Edinburgh: Edinburgh University Press, 1990.

————. *Green Politics Two.* Edinburgh: Edinburgh University Press, 1992.

————. *Green Politics Three.* Edinburgh: Edinburgh University Press, 1995.

Ryle, Martin. *Ecology and Socialism.* London: Random Century, 1988.

Comparative

Kitschelt, Herbert. *The Logics of Party Formation: Ecological Politics in Belgium and West Germany.* Ithaca, N.Y. and London: Cornell University Press, 1989.

Rootes, Chris. "Environmental Consciousness, Institutional Structures and Political Competition in the Formation and Development of Green Parties." In *The Green Challenge: The Development of Green Parties in Europe,* edited by Dick Richardson and Chris Rootes, 232–52. London and New York: Routledge, 1995.

Young, Stephen C. *The Politics of the Environment.* Manchester: Baseline Books, 1993.

Social Bases

Cotgrove, Stephen, and Andrew Duff. "Environmentalism, Middle-Class Radicalism and Politics." *Sociological Review* 28, no. 2 (1980): 333–51.

————. "Environmentalism, Values and Social Change." *British Journal of Sociology* 32, no. 1 (1981): 92–110.

Eckersley, Robyn. "Green Politics and the New Class: Selfishness or Virtue?" *Political Studies* 37, no. 2 (1989): 205–23.

Galtung, Johan. "The Green Movement: A Socio-Historical Explanation." *International Sociology* 1, no. 1 (1986): 75–90.

Jones, Robert, and Riley Dunlap. "The Social Bases of Environmental Concern." *Rural Sociology* 57, no. 1 (1992): 28–47.

Kriesi, Hanspeter. "New Social Movements and the New Class in the Netherlands." *American Journal of Sociology* 94, no. 5 (1989): 1078–116.

Parkin, Frank. *Middle Class Radicalism: The Social Bases of the Campaign for Nuclear Disarmament.* Manchester: Manchester University Press, 1968.

Van Liere, Kent, and Riley E. Dunlap. "The Social Bases of Environmental Concern: A Review of Hypotheses, Explanations and Empirical Evidence." *Public Opinion Quarterly* 44, no. 2 (1980): 181–98.

Australia

Bean, Clive, Ian McAllister, and John Warhurst, eds. *The Greening of Australian Politics: The 1990 Federal Election.* Melbourne: Longman Cheshire, 1990.

Economou, Nicholas M. "Accordism and the Environment: The Resource Assessment Commission and National Environmental Policy-Making." *Australian Journal of Political Science* 28, no. 3 (1993): 399–412.

Hay, P. R., and M. G. Haward. "Comparative Green Politics: Beyond the European Context." *Political Studies* 36, no. 4 (1988): 433–48.

McAllister, Ian. "Dimensions of Environmentalism: Public Opinion, Political Activism and Party Support in Australia." *Environmental Politics* 3, no. 1 (1994): 22–42.

McAllister, Ian, and Donley Studlar. "Trends in Public Opinion on the Environment in Australia." *International Journal of Public Opinion Research* 5, no. 4 (1993): 353–61.

Papadakis, Elim. "Minor Parties, the Environment and the New Politics." In *The Greening of Australian Politics*, edited by Clive Bean, Ian McAllister, and John Warhurst, 33–53. Melbourne: Longman Cheshire, 1990.

———. "Does the New Politics Have a Future?" In *Australia Compared*, edited by Francis G. Castles, 239–57. Sydney: Allen and Unwin, 1991.

———. "New Aspirations, Changing Patterns of Representation and Electoral Behaviour." In *Governing in the 90s*, edited by Ian Marsh, 3–29. Melbourne: Longman Cheshire, 1992.

———. "Development and the Environment." In *The 1993 Federal Election*, edited by Clive Bean, 66–80. *Australian Journal of Political Science,* special issue 29, 1994.

Austria

Pelinka, Anton. "The Nuclear Power Referendum in Austria." *Electoral Studies* 2, no. 3 (1983): 253–61.

Brazil

Pádua, Jose. "The Birth of Green Politics in Brazil: Exogenous and Endogenous Factors." In *Green Politics Two*, edited by Wolfgang Rüdig, 134–55. Edinburgh: Edinburgh University Press, 1992.

Bulgaria

Baumgartl, Bernd. "Green Mobilization against Red Politics: Environmentalists' Contribution to Bulgaria's Transition." In *Green Politics Three*, edited by Wolfgang Rüdig, 154–91. Edinburgh: Edinburgh University Press, 1995.

Central Europe

Kára, Jan. "Geopolitics and the Environment: The Case of Central Europe." *Environmental Politics* 1, no. 1 (1992): 186–95.

Eastern Europe

Waller, Michael, and Frances Millard. "Environmental Politics in Eastern Europe." *Environmental Politics* 1, no. 1 (1992): 159–85.

France

Bridgford, Jeff. "The Ecologist Movement and the French General Election 1978." *Parliamentary Affairs* 31, no. 3 (1978): 314–23.

Cerney, Philip G., ed. *Social Movements and Protest in France*. London: St. Martin's Press, 1982.

Müller-Rommel, Ferdinand, and Helmut Wilke. "Sozialstruktur und 'Postmaterialistische' Werteorientierungen von Ökologisten: Eine empirische Analyse am Beispiel Frankreichs." *Politische Vierteljahresschrift* 22, no. 3 (1981): 383–97.

Prendiville, Brendan, and Tony Chafer. "Activists and Ideas in the Green Movement in France." In *Green Politics One*, edited by Wolfgang Rüdig, 177–209. Edinburgh: Edinburgh University Press, 1990.

Germany

Bürklin, Wilhelm P. "The Split between the Established and the Non-Established Left in Germany." *European Journal of Political Research* 13 (1985): 283–93.

Markovits, Andrei, and Philip S. Gorski. *The German Left: Red, Green and Beyond*. Cambridge, U.K.: Polity Press, 1993.

Ireland

Baker, Susan. "The Evolution of the Irish Ecology Movement." In *Green Politics One*, edited by Wolfgang Rüdig, 47–81. Edinburgh: Edinburgh University Press, 1990.

Italy

Diani, Mario. "The Italian Ecology Movement: From Radicalism to Moderation." In *Green Politics One*, edited by Wolfgang Rüdig, 153–76. Edinburgh: Edinburgh University Press, 1990.

Latin America

Goodman, David, and Michael Redclift, eds. *Environment and Development in Latin America: The Politics of Sustainability*. Manchester: Manchester University Press, 1991.

New Zealand

Rainbow, Stephen L. *Green Politics*. Auckland and Oxford: Oxford University Press, 1994.

United Kingdom

Flynn, Andrew, and Philip Lowe. "The Greening of the Tories: The Conservative Party and the Environment." In *Green Politics Two*, edited by Wolfgang Rüdig, 9–36. Edinburgh: Edinburgh University Press, 1992.

McCormick, John. *British Politics and the Environment*. London: Earthscan, 1991.

Robinson, Mike. *The Greening of British Party Politics*. Manchester: Manchester University Press, 1992.

Rootes, Christopher A. "The Greening of British Politics." *International Journal of Urban and Regional Research* 15, no. 2 (1991): 287–97.

United States

Dunlap, Riley E. "Public Opinion and Environmental Policy." In *Environmental Politics and Policy*, edited by J. P. Lester, 87–134. Durham, N.C.: Duke University Press, 1989.

9. International Relations

Benedick, Richard Eliot. *Ozone Diplomacy. New Directions in Safeguarding the Planet*. Cambridge, Mass.: Harvard University Press, 1991.

Brenton, Tony. *The Greening of Machiavelli: The Evolution of Interna-*

tional Environmental Politics. London: Earthscan/Royal Institute of International Affairs, 1994.

Carroll, John E., ed. *International Environmental Diplomacy: The Management and Resolution of Transfrontier Environmental Problems*. Cambridge: Cambridge University Press, 1990.

Elliott, Lorraine. *The Global Politics of the Environment*. London: Macmillan, 1998.

Hurrell, Andrew, and Benedict Kingsbury, eds. *The International Politics of the Environment: Actors, Interests, and Institutions*. Oxford: Clarendon Press, 1992.

————. "A Crisis of Ecological Viability? Global Environmental Change and the Nation State." *Political Studies* 43, no. 1 (1994): 146–65.

Imber, Mark. "Too Many Cooks? The Post-Rio Reform of the UN." *International Affairs* 69, no. 1 (1993): 55–70.

Johnson, Stanley. *The Earth Summit: The United Nations Conference on Environment and Development*. London: Graham and Trotman/Martinus Nijhoff, 1993.

Käkönen, Jyrki, ed. *Perspectives on Environmental Conflict and International Politics*. London and New York: Pinter, 1992.

Lafferty, William M. "The Politics of Sustainable Development: Global Norms for National Implementation." *Environmental Politics* 5, no. 2 (1996): 53–75.

Lipschutz, Ronnie D., and Ken Conca, eds. *The State and Social Power in Global Environmental Politics*. New York: Columbia University Press, 1993.

Miller, Marian. *The Third World in Global Environmental Politics*. Boulder, Colo.: Lynne Rienner, 1995.

Miller, Morris. *Debt and Environment, Converging Crises*. New York: United Nations, 1990.

Porter, Gareth, and Janet Welsh Brown. *Global Environmental Politics*. 2nd ed. Boulder, Colo.: Westview Press, 1996.

Rowlands, Ian H., and Malory Greene, eds. *Global Environmental Change and International Relations*. Basingstoke: Macmillan, with *Millennium: Journal of International Studies*, 1992.

Sand, Peter. *Lessons Learned in Global Environmental Governance*. New York: World Resources Institute, 1990.

————. *The Effectiveness of International Environmental Agreements: Survey of Existing Legal Instruments*. Cambridge: Grotius Publications, 1992.

Sands, Philippe. "Enforcing Environmental Security: The Challenges of Compliance with International Obligations." *Journal of International Affairs* 46, no. 2 (1993): 367–90.

————. *Greening International Law*. International Law and Sustainable Development Series. London: Earthscan, 1993.

Stoett, Peter. "International Politics and the Protection of Great Whales." *Environmental Politics* 2, no. 1 (1993): 277–303.

Susskind, Lawrence. *Environmental Diplomacy: Negotiating More Effective Global Agreements*. New York: Oxford University Press, 1994.

Susskind, Lawrence, and Connie Ozawa. "Negotiating More Effective International Environmental Agreements." In *The International Politics of the Environment: Actors, Interests and Institutions*, edited by Andrew Hurrell and Benedict Kingsley, 142–79. Oxford: Clarendon Press, 1992.

Thomas, Caroline. *The Environment in International Relations*. London: Royal Institute of International Affairs, 1992.

Vogler, John. *The Global Commons. A Regime Analysis*. Chichester, U.K.: Wiley, 1995.

Vogler, John, and Mark Imber, eds. *The Environment and International Relations*. London: Routledge, 1996.

Young, Oran. *International Cooperation: Building Regimes for Natural Resources and the Environment*. Ithaca, N.Y.: Cornell University Press, 1989.

————. "Global Environmental Change and International Governance." *Millennium: Journal of International Studies* 19, no. 3 (1990): 337–46.

————. *International Governance: Protecting the Environment in a Stateless Society*. Ithaca, N.Y.: Cornell University Press, 1994.

10. Internet Sites

http://merlin.alleg.edu/maniate/GepEd/geped.html. This is a project on teaching global environmental politics.

http://utopia.knoware.nl/users/oterhaar/greens/intlhome.htm.

About the Author

ELIM PAPADAKIS (B.A. Hons. University of Kent at Canterbury; Ph.D. London University) is professor of Modern European Studies at the Australian National University. His principal areas of expertise are environmental politics and policy, public opinion, and the development of the welfare state. Apart from serving as a member of the Australian Research Council, Humanities and Social Sciences Panel, and as vice president of the Australian Sociological Association, he has held positions on the editorial boards of the *Australian Journal of Political Science* and the *Australian and New Zealand Journal of Sociology*. In addition to numerous articles in professional journals, his publications include *Environmental Politics and Institutional Change* (1996), *Politics and the Environment: The Australian Experience* (1993), and *The Green Movement in West Germany* (1984).